Contexts 2

The Rape of the Lock

CONTEXTS: SELECTED LITERARY WORKS IN THEIR HISTORICAL SETTINGS

Maynard Mack, General Editor

Contexts 2

The Rape of the Lock

William Kinsley

Archon Books

Hamden, Connecticut

1979

Library of Congress Cataloging in Publication Data

Kinsley, William 1934-
   The rape of the lock.

   (Contexts, selected literary works in their
historical settings ; 2)
   Bibliography: p.

   1. Pope, Alexander, 1688-1744. Rape of the
lock — Sources. I. Pope, Alexander, 1688-1744.
Rape of the lock. II. Title.
PR3629.K5   821'.5   79-20161
ISBN 0-208-01633-3

© 1979 by The Shoe String Press, Inc.
First published 1979 as an Archon Book,
an imprint of The Shoe String Press, Inc.,
Hamden, Connecticut 06514

Printed in the United States of America

To The Ladies
In My Life:

A. M. K.

P. A. P.

T. H. K.

T. F. H.

A.-M. K.

C. P. K.

E. M. K.

CONTENTS

VI. Periodical Essays 248

VII. Key 286

Acknowledgments

I should like to thank Maynard Mack for his encouragement of this and other projects. My colleagues Patrick Mahony, Eugene Vance, and Richard Robillard offered timely suggestions, as did James King of McMaster University, Frank Ellis of Smith College, and especially Helen Williams of the University of Edinburgh. My old friend J. G. Keogh has contributed more than he knows and than I can specify. For the knowledge of books so indispensable to the understanding of *The Rape of the Lock*, my chief debt is to the late Geoffrey Tillotson, who annotated it for the Twickenham Edition. For the equally indispensable knowledge of womankind, I must thank especially those to whom this anthology is dedicated.

The Mills Memorial Library of McMaster University, Hamilton, Ontario provided the facsimiles of the *Iliad*, the *Aeneid*, *The Dispensary*, and the *Spectator*. The Beinecke Rare Book and Manuscript Library, Yale University, provided the facsimiles of Boileau, *Le Comte de Gabalis*, *Gondibert*, the *Tatler*, and the *Guardian*. I gratefully acknowledge the help of these institutions and their staffs, especially Mrs. Charlotte Stewart, Director of McMaster's Archives and Research Collections.

I am grateful for permission to reproduce the following copyrighted material:

A selection from Livy, *The Early History of Rome*, translated by Aubrey de Sélincourt (Penguin Classics, 1971), pp. 50-51. Copyright © the Estate of Aubrey de Sélincourt, 1960.

Selections from *The Poems of John Dryden*, edited by James Kinsley, © Oxford University Press 1958, by permission of the Oxford University Press.

Selections from *Six Restoration Plays*, edited with an introduction and notes by John Harold Wilson. Riverside Editions B 38; reprinted by permission of Houghton Mifflin Company; copyright © 1959 by John Harold Wilson.

Selections from John Milton, *Paradise Lost*, ed. Merritt Y. Hughes, copyright © 1962 by the Odyssey Press, Inc.; reprinted by permission of the Bobbs-Merrill Company, Inc.

xi

INTRODUCTION

I

Some time in 1711, probably in late summer, two Roman Catholic families living near London became embroiled in a quarrel touched off by a trivial enough incident that does not seem untypical of upper-class young men: Robert, Lord Petre, had mischievously snipped a lock of hair from the fair head of Miss Arabella Fermor. As a means of persuading the two families to place this incident in its proper perspective, John Caryll, a leader of the Catholic community and a friend and benefactor of Pope, asked the young poet to write a poem that would "laugh them together again." Pope complied willingly; the original two-canto version of *The Rape of the Lock* was probably completed before the end of September, and seems to have produced the desired effect. Its success led its admirers to multiply copies of it, which soon began to circulate outside the families concerned. Partly out of fear that an imperfect version might appear in print in a pirated edition, Pope authorized its publication in Bernard Lintot's *Miscellaneous Poems and Translations* (May 1712).

During the next year Pope occupied himself intermittently with the addition of the "machinery" which would transform a delightful piece of *vers de société* into the even more delightful mock-epic masterpiece we now have. He also had to contrive a means of shielding Arabella from the rumors and insinuations that had followed the poem's first publication and that might be revived by this elaborate new version. These literary and social tasks were largely completed by the end of the year, and the poem appeared on 2 March 1714. Its success was extraordinary: it sold three thousand copies in four days, and a fourth edition appeared in 1715. If we can trust John Gay's poetic description of the bookseller's district in 1716, its appeal had spread far beyond the elegant circles to which it had originally been addressed:

> Pleas'd sempstresses the *Lock's* fam'd *Rape* unfold,
> And *Squirts* read *Garth*, till apozems grow cold.

> (*Trivia*, 2: 563-64)

II

This social context provided one kind of inspiration for the poem; that the poem still lives, and to some degree keeps alive the memory of the society that produced it, is due in no small measure to the many literary contexts to which it alludes. Since *The Rape of the Lock* is a mock-epic or "heroi-comical poem," the most important of these literary contexts is what can be called the "epic tradition." This tradition was an intricately interwoven cultural complex; by Pope's time, it included the following elements, among others: the texts of the *Iliad*, the *Odyssey*, and the *Aeneid*; the traditions of commentary and exegesis that had grown up around these texts; translations of them into European vernaculars; critical theorizing, beginning in the Renaissance, about the nature of the epic and what the modern writer should do to produce his own epic poem; modern works such as Vida's *Christiad* and Milton's *Paradise Lost* that were inspired by the ancient epics and the modern theories; certain conventional episodes — funeral games, descents to the underworld, elaborate descriptions of the hero's armor, and many others — thought to be characteristic of the epic or even indispensable to it; classical stylistic conventions and their vernacular counterparts, which constituted an elevated style commensurate with the importance of the epic subject; and perhaps most important, the ethical values affirmed, explicitly or implicitly, by the poems.

In Pope's time, the term "heroic" was more common in these contexts than "epic." The terms were often used interchangably, but "heroic" could also embrace a broader tradition including the chivalric romances of the middle ages, narrative poems like Ariosto's *Orlando Furioso* and Spenser's *Faerie Queene* that mingled the chivalric and the classical, and the heroic drama of the Restoration. To distill for the sake of simplicity, we may say that the epic presents a hero who embodies in a preeminent way the values of his civilization and who engages in an action which enables him to reveal these values and on the outcome of which the fate of his civilization depends. The whole complex enjoyed great cultural prestige; many of Dryden's cultivated contemporaries would have seconded his affirmation that "a heroick Poem, truly such, is undoubtedly the greatest Work which the Soul of Man is capable to perform."

Also stated simply, the mock-epic is the result of separating the epic style and conventions from their normal epic subjects and attaching them to trivial situations like the prank described above.

2

Pope's infinite ingenuity has compressed into his seven-hundred-odd lines miniaturized versions of virtually every conventional situation that the epic tradition offered him: for the epic games — boxing, chariot racing, javelin throwing — we have cards; for Milton's titanic angels and the Greek and Roman gods we have the diaphanous sylphs; for the shield of Achilles we have the petticoat of Belinda. There is a kind of pedantry at work here, as in Joyce and all writers who depend heavily on earlier literature, but the pedantry is transformed by a comic spirit and by a poet's love for the devices of his predecessors. And the mock-epic is not unique in its exploitation of earlier literature; nearly all Western artists — including television writers, film makers, and singers — consciously work within a tradition, exploiting or ridiculing conventions which they expect their audiences to recognize to some degree. The mock-epic merely concentrates and intensifies this tendency.

The mock-epic separation of a style from its natural subject immediately calls attention to the style and brings to the foreground questions about its meaning that remain implicit or taken for granted when it is performing its natural function. Boxing gloves on a prizefighter arouse no comment; on the present editor they would provoke many questions indeed. Mock-epic questions usually lead to two sorts of answers, though it must be emphasized that it is up to the reader to formulate them. Like much modern poetry, the mock-epic operates by juxtaposition; the reader has to articulate the relationships between the images juxtaposed. The immediate effect of the disparity between style and subject is to emphasize the triviality of the latter, to diminish it; in the present case, Pope is suggesting to the Fermor and Petre families that a lock of hair is not worth a prolonged estrangement. At the same time, the epic style and the many heroic episodes that it recalls can confer new kinds of significance on the trivial subject. The seriousness with which the otherwise sensible families took the affair of the lock might imply an inversion of values much graver than the incident that revealed the inversion. Thomas Shadwell, as presented in Dryden's *Mac Flecknoe*, is mean and ridiculous enough, but it is no laughing matter when such a writer sets the artistic tone for a whole culture. The mock-epic invites us to see infinity in a lock of hair as well as in a grain of sand.

This kind of mock-epic allusion relies on the traditions and conventions of the epic, on features shared by many epic poems. Pope complements it by another kind of allusion that relies primarily on the power of particular expressions, on what is unique or memorable in previous works. For a simple example, consider this description of the sylphs taking their stations: "Some, Orb in Orb, around the Nymph extend" (2:138). A reader familiar with *Paradise Lost* would recall a similar phrase used of the angels and would remember that it appeared in a partly similar situation:

> Thus when in Orbs
> Of circuit inexpressible they stood,
> Orb within Orb, the Father infinite,
> ... thus spake.

(5:594-99)

The verbal echo operates like the use of conventions noted above, juxtaposing Milton's angels to Pope's sylphs and God the Father to Belinda and posing a similar set of questions: Does Belinda play a role in Pope's poem analogous to that of God in *Paradise Lost*? Does she aspire to such a role? Does the parallel emphasize the difference in importance between her and Milton's God? Do her aspirations therefore reduce her stature even farther? Or is she a fitting divinity for the world of the poem? If so, are those who worship her perhaps no more substantial than the sylphs?

The Rape of the Lock of course alludes to many literary contexts besides the epic tradition: Ovid, the mock-epic tradition, the *Spectator*, and a number of others. Many of them interact in the famous description of Belinda's dressing table:

> And now, unveil'd, the *Toilet* stands display'd,
> Each Silver Vase in mystic Order laid.
> First, rob'd in White, the Nymph intent adores
> With Head uncover'd, the *Cosmetic* Pow'rs.
> A heav'nly Image in the Glass appears,   125
> To that she bends, to that her Eyes she rears;
> Th'inferior Priestess, at her Altar's side,
> Trembling, begins the sacred Rites of Pride.
> Unnumber'd Treasures ope at once, and here
> The various Off'rings of the World appear;   130
> From each she nicely culls with curious Toil,
> And decks the Goddess with the glitt'ring Spoil.
> This Casket *India*'s glowing Gems unlocks,
> And all *Arabia* breathes from yonder Box.
> The Tortoise here and Elephant unite,   135
> Transform'd to *Combs*, the speckled and the white.
> Here Files of Pins extend their shining Rows,
> Puffs, Powders, Patches, Bibles, Billet-doux.
> Now awful Beauty puts on all its Arms;
> The Fair each moment rises in her Charms,   140
> Repairs her Smiles, awakens ev'ry Grace,
> And calls forth all the Wonders of her Face;
> Sees by Degrees a purer Blush arise,
> And keener Lightnings quicken in her Eyes.
> The busy *Sylphs* surround their darling Care;   145

These set the Head, and those divide the Hair,
Some fold the Sleeve, whilst others plait the Gown;
And *Betty's* prais'd for Labours not her own.

The table is presented first as an altar, with the silver vases as signs of the opulence that is normal both in Belinda's world and in ecclesiastical furnishings. Behind the "cosmetic powers" that the nymph adores we may hear "cosmic" as a ground swell, especially in the context of the rest of the passage. "Heav'nly" (line 125) unites two of the poem's worlds: like "divine" it is both a religious term and a cliché of empty flattery, and as it might apply to herself Belinda would presumably be willing to take it in either sense. The real goddess here is not Belinda herself, however, but her image in the mirror, something as unsubstantial as the sylphs and the playing cards; all the operations of the toilette are judged according to their effect on that image. In a sense it is appropriate that Belinda should worship this image of herself; she is a devotee of Beauty, after all, and within this poem who is more beautiful than she? But we may begin to think in other directions if we recall how Eve was infatuated with her own image in a pool of water on first waking after her creation, an episode which in turn recalls Ovid's Narcissus. The relevant passage of *Paradise Lost* had been quoted in an issue of the *Spectator* that satirized the attachment of women to mirrors and would thus have been especially familiar to Pope's early readers (see below, pp. 270). Eve would have remained at the pool-side indefinitely and "pin'd with vain desire" (4:466) had not a voice led her to Adam, whose superior beauty she immediately acknowledged and to whom she submitted. In spite of this first submission, it was Eve's vanity that later made her susceptible to the serpent's temptation, which Pope has already alluded to in Belinda's dream. Belinda's infatuation, we may speculate, will perhaps have proportionately serious consequences, especially since she is in no mood to submit to any man and since all she has for counsellors are the sylphs.

This speculation is encouraged when, at the climactic end of the sentence, the rites of the dressing table are assigned to Pride. It is one thing to be called a goddess by one's admirers; it is another to begin to act as if one believed the compliments. As the chain of allusion reaches farther, the shadows continue to deepen. Addison had devoted all of *Spectator* 73 (below, p. 260) to vain young ladies "wholly taken up in the Adorning of [their] Person." He called them idols, and evoked Milton's tremendous roll call of the fallen angels masquerading as pagan deities (1:356-507). In Belinda's dream, Pope had already alluded to the part of this passage which describes how the fallen angels can change their sex in order to seduce the faithful away from true worship. If these passages are relevant to ours — and one is never sure how much of another context a brief echo can be expected to evoke — then Belinda's idolatry runs deep indeed, and we may also recall, out of the many Old Testament denunciations of idolatry, the one in Psalm 115: "Their idols are silver and gold, the work of men's hands.... They that make them are like unto them; so is everyone that trusteth in them." Belinda's image is in part the work of her own hands and those of her maid; as she worships it she runs the risk of losing her substance and becoming more and more of an image. Or as Simone de Beauvoir might put it, she is collaborating in the objectification and depersonalization of herself that her society forces her into.

On a different tack, "trembling" at the beginning of line 128 may bring to mind another dressing table scene, the one in Dryden's translation of Juvenal's sixth satire (p. 221). The main relation here is one of contrast, however. Belinda is no aging "ghost of beauty," and Pope has already made it clear that his satire of womankind is far more subtle and nuancé than Juvenal's.

Belinda's table then becomes animated with a miraculous life of its own: treasures open, a casket unlocks, Arabia breathes, pins extend themselves in rows. Satire of the imports required to dress women in their finery usually emphasize the toil, risk, and expense of artisans and merchants (see *Spectator* 69, p. 258). Here the offerings simply present themselves as due tribute to the goddess; they are not articles of commerce at all. "Spoil," however, introduces the idea of conquest — epic heroes adorned themselves with armor captured in battle — and anticipates the military metaphor that will dominate the second half of the passage. The scene of the poem has expanded to encompass the whole world, as epics were required to do, and Belinda becomes correspondingly omniscient; she surveys this entire world, and is goddess of all she surveys.

Additional exotic offerings appear in the tortoise and elephant, united in their homage to Belinda. Pope's chiastic couplet leads these ponderous and ill-matched beasts through an elegant minuet. They are first separated by being named individually and for the moment presented as if they were live animals, then united as combs — domesticated and matched in size by the hand of man as they are joined at the end of the first line by a single word of the poet — then again separated by their visual aspects, speckled and white. Ovid himself would have envied such a metamorphosis. Still another hint may lie beneath these lines. There is a Hindu cosmological myth, mentioned twice by John Locke in his *Essay concerning Human Understanding*, according to which the earth rests on a giant elephant which in turn stands on a giant tortoise. If we admit the relevance of this myth (which the mention of India perhaps encourages), then the scale of the scene again increases enormously, far beyond India and Arabia, before it returns to the miniature. The foundation of Belinda's world is the combs that help hold her coiffure in place. A shaky foundation? Locke, in his common sense way, had of course wondered what the tortoise rested on.

With line 137 a military metaphor begins to replace the religious one, though we should remember that in the epics, and even more in the knightly romances, arming oneself was very often a religious act. The scale again expands, and the files and rows suggest perfect order — as neat as a pin. This order collapses in the justly famous following line, which not only rhymes imperfectly but is not even grammatically connected to the preceding one. We expect to find a single Bible on an altar; here, the use of the plural emphasizes these Bibles' contribution to the clutter and their probable function, for Belinda, as decorative objects — bibelots — rather than as copies of the one sacred book.

As we continue, Belinda herself becomes an epic warrior, arming for battle, though in her case, for the war of the sexes. "Awful" of course means "inspiring awe." Lightning darts from the eyes of both Petrarchan beauties and Homeric warriors. Belinda's arms are offensive, not defensive; she is going forth to conquer. The object of worship is still present in the mirror, lest we forget the implications of the first part of the passage: she *"sees...a purer Blush arise."* Belinda is beautiful to begin with, and she and her maid are consummate artists, lavishing as much skill on her image as Pope does on his poem. "Purer" is not merely ironic; Pope is also praising the artificial beauty of makeup, as Baudelaire was to do in the next century. "Keener," though, shifts the emphasis onto the pragmatic, thus strengthening the irony. As the rhyme of *arms* and *charms* emphasizes, her person and her makeup are the only weapons Belinda has in the particular war into which she's been drafted and from which there's no discharge. Whether she will use her weapons to compel worship of herself remains to be seen. This section is lighter and gayer than the preceding one; cosmetics are perhaps closer to weapons than to religion (we still sometimes call them "warpaint"), and the juxtaposition leans more toward amusement than censure.

The whole passage also mirrors Pope's *Iliad* (14:191-218, p. 68), where a real goddess, Juno, adorns herself in order to seduce Jove and distract his attention from the battle raging below on earth. Pope's revealing and rather arch note to this passage emphasizes the simplicity of Juno's adornments in contrast to those of modern ladies. Clearly, it takes more skill, art, and care to make oneself a goddess than to be born one. Finally, we may recall that Pope and the families for whom he wrote the original version of the poem were all Roman

Catholics, and that to them the altar scene could reasonably suggest the Catholic Mass. From this point of view Belinda is performing a parody of transubstantiation. The priest changes the substance of the bread and wine without altering their appearance; Belinda alters her appearance without changing her substance.

III

The contexts juxtaposed by verbal echo or similarity of situation act like the two terms of a metaphor. Belinda's table is (and is not) an altar; Belinda herself is (and is not) Eve. The difference between metaphor and allusion, between the table as altar and Belinda as Eve, is that in the latter case the reader has to discover the second term for himself. The poet of course runs the risk that the reader will either miss the signal or see signals where he shouldn't, as many will feel I have done in discussing the dressing table. But there are compensating advantages. Allusion is highly economical; a small echo can evoke a large and powerful second context at the same time that it is fulfilling its normal syntactic, melodic, imagistic, and other functions in its own context. The echo is a kind of synecdoche, a part standing for the whole of the second context; it can be a trivial thing of mighty poetic consequences. Another advantage is that the activity of looking for potential echoes and discovering their relevance or rejecting them as irrelevant involves the reader more actively than do most other kinds of reading.

The purpose of the present volume is to aid this activity. The ideal reader of *The Rape of the Lock* knows the *Iliad*, the *Aeneid*, *Paradise Lost*, *Le Comte de Gabalis*, and many other works intimately enough to catch Pope's glancing allusions as they occur. The discovery is all his own; he alone has made the connection. In practice, however, most readers usually discover Pope's allusions not in their own memories but in footnotes provided by editors, beginning with Pope himself. Useful and necessary as this method is, it lessens the surprise of discovery. If one could refresh his memory of some of the texts that Pope alludes to before reading or rereading *The Rape of the Lock*, he would be better equipped to make his own

8

discoveries. I have therefore tried to provide an abundant, though far from exhaustive, selection of such texts.

The limitations of such a project are obvious. It cannot give any sense of the plot, structure, or characterization of the epics, and only a very limited sense of the world view that informs them. It is merely a reminder or an introduction, not a substitute for a knowledge of the works in their entirety. It may tend to overemphasize Pope's dependence on his predecessors and to minimize the originality of his own genius, or even give the impression that a modern reader should not open the poem without a two-year course in "backgrounds." The aspects of the poem that it emphasizes are not negligible, however, and if properly used it should increase our enjoyment of them.

The texts included are related to Pope's poem in many different ways, examples of which have appeared in the discussion of the dressing table. Some are central to its meaning, some peripheral; some will probably strike some readers as totally irrelevant. Some are echoed almost word for word in Pope's poem, others illustrate themes, techniques, or ethical values more generally. Some bear primarily on Pope's style, some on his morality. Some are examples of commonplaces that occur in many works, some are unique. Some are fairly long, some are verbal tags occupying less than a line. With one major exception and a few minor ones noted below, all of them were available to Pope's readers when the poem appeared in 1714, though not all of them were well known. Very few of them are my own discoveries; *The Rape of the Lock* has been abundantly annotated. I have tried in headnotes to some passages both to provide a few hints about the significance the texts may have for the poem and to leave scope for the reader's independent discoveries. A key at the end identifies Pope's specific allusions in greater detail. If the headnote to a passage includes no reference to *The Rape of the Lock*, the lines have been included to illustrate one or more of these allusions, which may be located through the key.

9

IV

Bibliography

EDITIONS

The Rape of the Lock and Other Poems, ed. Geoffrey Tillotson. 3rd ed. *The Twickenham Edition of the Poems of Alexander Pope*, vol. 2. London: Methuen; New Haven: Yale University Press, 1960.

The Rape Observ'd, ed. Clarence Tracy. Toronto and Buffalo: University of Toronto Press, 1974. An illustrated edition which does for the material context of the poem what I have tried to do for the literary context.

COLLECTIONS OF POPE CRITICISM

These are referred to below by the names of their editors.

Hunt, John Dixon, ed. Alexander Pope, *The Rape of the Lock: A Casebook*. London: Macmillan, 1968.

Lougee, David G., and Robert W. McHenry, Jr., eds. Alexander Pope, *The Rape of the Lock*. The Merrill Literary Casebook Series. Columbus, Ohio: Charles E. Merrill, 1969.

Mack, Maynard, ed. *Essential Articles for the Study of Alexander Pope*. Hamden, Conn.: Archon Books, 1964; revised and enlarged, 1968.

Mack, Maynard, and James Winn, eds. *Pope: Recent Essays by Several Hands*. Hamden, Conn.: Archon Books, 1979.

Rousseau, G. S., ed. *Twentieth Century Interpretations of The Rape of the Lock*. Englewood Cliffs, N.J.: Prentice-Hall, 1969.

CRITICAL STUDIES

This list emphasizes studies of Pope's allusive techniques.

Babb, Lawrence. "The Cave of Spleen." *Review of English Studies* 12 (1936): 165-76.

Beyette, Kent. "Milton and Pope's *The Rape of the Lock*." *Studies in English Literature* 16 (1976): 421-36.

Brooks, Cleanth. "The Case of Miss Arabella Fermor: A Reexamination." *Sewanee Review* 51 (1943): 505-24. Also in Brooks' *The Well-Wrought Urn*. Rpt. in Rousseau, Hunt, Lougee, Mack.

Brower, Reuben. "Am'rous Causes." *Alexander Pope: The Poetry of Allusion*. Oxford: Clarendon Press, 1959. Rpt. in Rousseau (abridged), Hunt.

Brückmann, Patricia. "Pope's Shock and the Count of Gabalis." *English Language Notes* 1 (1964): 261-62.

Cohen, Murray. "Versions of the Lock: Readers of 'The Rape of the Lock'." *ELH* 43 (1976): 53-73.

Cohen, Ralph. "Transformation in *The Rape of the Lock*." *Eighteenth-Century Studies* 2 (1969): 205-24.

Cunningham, J. S. *Pope: The Rape of the Lock*. London: Edward Arnold, 1961.

Frost, William. "*The Rape of the Lock* and Pope's Homer." *Modern Language Quarterly* 8 (1947): 342-54. Rpt. in Mack.

Hardy, John P. "*The Rape of the Lock*." In *Reinterpretations: Essays on Poems by Milton, Pope, and Johnson*. London: Routledge and Kegan Paul, 1971, pp. 50-80.

Jack, Ian. "A Complex Mock-heroic: *The Rape of the Lock*." *Augustan Satire: Intention and Idiom in English Poetry 1660-1750*. Oxford: Clarendon Press, 1952. Slightly abridged in Rousseau.

Jackson, James L. "Pope's *Rape of the Lock* Considered as a Five-Act Epic." *PMLA* 65 (1950): 1283-87.

Keogh, J. G. "Pope's *The Rape of the Lock*, V, 75-102." *The Explicator* 30 (1971). Item 31.

Kinsley, William. "Ombre Replayed." *English Studies in Canada* 4 (1978): 255-63.

Landa, Louis A. "Pope's Belinda, the General Emporie of the World, and the Wondrous Worm." *South Atlantic Quarterly* 70 (1971): 215-35. Rpt. in Mack and Winn.

Mack, Maynard. " 'Wit and Poetry and Pope': Some Observations on His Imagery." *Pope and His Contemporaries: Essays Presented to George Sherburn*, ed. James L. Clifford and Louis A. Landa. Oxford: Clarendon Press, 1949, pp. 20-40. Rpt. in *Eighteenth-Century English Literature: Modern Essays in Criticism*, ed. James L. Clifford, and in *The Modern Critical Spectrum*, ed. G. J. and N. M. Goldberg.

Martin, L. C. "Lucretius and *The Rape of the Lock*." *Review of English Studies* 20 (1944): 299-303.

Price, Martin. "The Problem of Scale: The Game of Art." *To the Palace of Wisdom: Studies in Order and Energy from Dryden to Blake*. Garden City, N.Y.: Doubleday, 1964. Rpt. in Rousseau.

Reichard, Hugo M. "The Love Affair in Pope's *Rape of the Lock*." *PMLA* 69 (1954): 887-902. Rpt. in Hunt and Lougee.

Rudat, Wolfgang E. H. "Belinda's 'Painted Vessel': Allusive Technique in *The Rape of the Lock*." *Tennessee Studies in Literature* 19 (1974): 49-55.

_____. "The 'Mutual Commerce' in *The Rape of the Lock*: Pope and the Virgilian Tradition." *Etudes Anglaises* 29 (1976): 534-

44.

Wasserman, Earl R. "The Limits of Allusion in *The Rape of the Lock.*" *Journal of English and Germanic Philology* 65 (1966): 425-44. Rpt. in Rousseau (abridged) and in Mack and Winn.

Williams, Aubrey. "The 'Fall' of China and *The Rape of the Lock.*" *Philological Quarterly* 41 (1962): 412-25. Rpt. in Mack, Hunt, Lougee.

Wimsatt, W. K. "Belinda Ludens: Strife and Play in *The Rape of the Lock.*" *New Literary History* 4 (1973): 357-74. Rpt. in Mack and Winn.

V

A NOTE ON THE TEXTS

Many of the texts in this collection are facsimiles of the original editions. Readers unfamiliar with eighteenth-century typography should be forewarned about the "long s" in roman type and "long s" in italic, which can easily be confused with F.

PART I

Epic Theory and Practice

Joseph Addison, *Spectator* 267 (1712)

This essay is the first of Addison's long series of weekly papers on *Paradise Lost*. It is perhaps the best brief statement available of what the epic meant to Pope's contemporaries, and is all the more useful for us in that it was designed to instruct the kind of relatively unlearned readers that made up a large part of the potential audience for *The Rape of the Lock*. However imperfectly Addison's ideas may have been assimilated, the large circulation of the *Spectator* assured that they were at least widely disseminated. (See also the headnote to other selections from the *Spectator*, p. 248.)

1. Leda's Egg: Zeus, in the form of a swan, begot Helen of Troy on Leda, whose "egg" might thus be considered one of the starting points of the story of the Trojan war. Cf. W. B. Yeats' poem "Leda and the Swan."
2. Episode: an incidental narrative or digression, not part of the main story.
3. Original: origin.
4. *The Spanish Fryar, or the Double Discovery*: by John Dryden (published 1681). A present-day critic would be more likely to cite *King Lear* or *Henry IV*, Part 1, as an example of a double plot.

14

The SPECTATOR.

Cedite Romani Scriptores, cedite Graii. Propert.

Saturday, *January* 5. 17 2

THERE is nothing in Nature so irksom as general Discourses, especially when they turn chiefly upon Words. For this Reason I shall wave the Discussion of that Point which was started some Years since, Whether *Milton's Paradise Lost* may be called an Heroick Poem? Those who will not give it that Title, may call it (if they please) a Divine Poem. It will be sufficient to its Perfection, if it has in it all the Beauties of the highest kind of Poetry; and as for those who say it is not an Heroick Poem, they advance no more to the Diminution of it, than if they should say *Adam* is not *Æneas*, nor *Eve Helen.*

I shall therefore examine it by the Rules of Epic Poetry, and see whether it falls short of the *Iliad* or *Æneid* in the Beauties which are essential to that kind of Writing. The first thing to be considered in an Epic Poem, is the Fable, which is perfect or imperfect, according as the Action which it relates is more or less so. This Action should have three Qualifications in it. First, It should be but one Action. Secondly, It should be an entire Action; and Thirdly, It should be a great Action. To consider the Action of the *Iliad, Æneid,* and *Paradise Lost* in these three several Lights. *Homer* to preserve the Unity of his Action hastens into the midst of things, as *Horace* has observed: Had he gone

1 up to *Leda's* Egg, or begun much later, even at the Rape of *Helen,* or the Investing of *Troy,* it is manifest that the Story of the Poem would have been a Series of several Actions. He therefore opens his Poem with the Discord of his Princes, and with great Art interweaves in the several succeeding parts of it, an account of every thing which relates to the Story, and had passed before that fatal Dissension. After the same manner *Æneas* makes his first appearance in the *Tyrrhene* Seas, and within sight of *Italy,* because the Action proposed to be celebrated was that of his Settling himself in *Latium.* But because it was necessary for the Reader to know what had happened to him in the taking of *Troy,* and in the preceding parts of his Voyage, *Virgil* makes his

2 Hero relate it by way of Episode in the second and third Books of the *Æneis.* The Contents of both which Books come before those of the first Book in the Thread of the Story, tho' for the preserving of this Unity of Action, they follow them in the Disposition of the Poem. *Milton,* in Imitation of these two great Poets, opens his *Paradise Lost* with an Infernal Council plotting the Fall of Man, which is the Action he proposed to celebrate; and as for those great Actions which preceded in point of time, the Battel of the Angels, and the Creation of the World, (which would have entirely destroyed the Unity of his Principal Action, had he related them in the same Order that they happened) he cast them into the fifth, sixth and seventh Books, by way of Episode to this noble Poem.

Aristotle himself allows, that *Homer* has nothing to boast of as to the Unity of his Fable, tho' at the same time that great Critick and Philosopher endeavours to palliate this Imperfection in the *Greek* Poet, by imputing it in some Measure to the very Nature of an Epic Poem. Some have been of Opinion, that the *Æneid* labours also in this particular, and has Episodes which may be looked upon as Excrescencies rather than as Parts of the Action. On the contrary, the Poem which we have now under our Consideration, hath no other Episodes than such as naturally arise from the Subject, and yet is filled with such a multitude of astonishing Circumstances, that it gives us at the same time a Pleasure of the greatest Variety, and of the greatest Simplicity.

3 I must observe also, that as *Virgil* in the Poem which was designed to celebrate the Original of the *Roman* Empire, has described the Birth of its great Rival, the *Carthaginian* Commonwealth. *Milton* with the like Art in his Poem on the Fall of Man, has related the Fall of those Angels who are his professed Enemies. Besides the many other Beauties in such an Episode, it's running Parallel with the great Action of the Poem, hinders it from breaking the Unity so much as another Episode would have done, that had not so great an Affinity with the principal Subject. In short, this is the same kind of Beauty which the Criticks admire in the *Spanish Fryar,* or

4 the *Double Discovery,* where the two different Plots look like Counterparts and Copies of one another.

The second Qualification required in the Action of an Epic Poem is, that it should be an entire Action: An Action is entire when it is complete in all its Parts; or as *Aristotle* describes it, when it consists of a Beginning, a Middle, and an End. Nothing should go before it, be intermix'd with it, or follow after it, that is not related to it. As on the contrary, no single Step should be omitted in that just and regular Progress which it must be supposed to take from its Original to its Consummation. Thus we see the Anger of *Achilles* in its Birth, its Continuance and Effects; and *Æneas's* Settlement in *Italy,* carried on through all the Oppositions in his way to it both by Sea and Land. The Action in *Milton* excels (I think) both the former in this particular; we see it contrived in Hell, executed upon Earth, and punished by Heaven. The parts of it are told in the most distinct manner, and grow out of one another in the most natural Method.

The third Qualification of an Epic Poem is its *Greatness.* The Anger of *Achilles* was of such Consequence, that it embroiled the Kings of *Greece,* destroy'd the Heroes of *Troy,* and engaged all the Gods in Factions. *Æneas's* Settlement in *Italy* produced the *Cæsars,* and gave Birth to the *Roman* Empire. *Milton's* Subject was still greater than either of the former; it does not determine the Fate of single Persons or Nations, but of a whole Species. The
united

united Powers of Hell are joined together for the Destruction of Mankind, which they effected in part, and would have completed, had not Omnipotence it self interposed. The principal Actors are Man in his greatest Perfection, and Woman in her highest Beauty. Their Enemies are the fallen Angels: The Messiah their Friend, and the Almighty their Protector. In short, every thing that is great in the whole Circle of Being, whether within the Verge of Nature, or out of it, has a proper Part assigned it in this noble Poem.

In Poetry, as in Architecture, not only the whole, but the principal Members, and every part of them, should be Great. I will not presume to say, that the Book of Games in the *Æneid*, or that in the *Iliad*, are not of this nature, nor to reprehend *Virgil*'s Simile of a Top, and many other of the same nature in the *Iliad*, as liable to any Censure in this Particular; but I think we may say, without offence to those wonderful Performances, that there is an unquestionable Magnificence in every Part of *Paradise Lost*, and indeed a much greater than could have been formed upon any Pagan System.

But *Aristotle*, by the Greatness of the Action, does not only mean that it should be great in its Nature, but also in its Duration, or in other Words, that it should have a due length in it, as well as what we properly call Greatness. The just Measure of this kind of Magnitude, he explains by the following Similitude. An Animal, no bigger than a Mite, cannot appear perfect to the Eye, because the Sight takes it in at once, and has only a confused Idea of the whole, and not a distinct Idea of all its Parts; If on the contrary you should suppose an Animal of ten thousand Furlongs in length, the Eye would be so filled with a single Part of it, that it could not give the Mind an Idea of the whole. What these Animals are to the Eye, a very short or a very long Action would be to the Memory. The first would be, as it were, lost and swallowed up by it, and the other difficult to be contained in it. *Homer* and *Virgil* have shewn their principal Art in this Particular; the Action of the *Iliad*, and that of the *Æneid*, were in themselves exceeding short, but are so beautifully extended and diversified by the Intervention of *Episodes*, and the Machinery of Gods, with the like Poetical Ornaments, that they make up an agreeable Story sufficient to employ the Memory without overcharging it. *Milton*'s Action is enriched with such a variety of Circumstances, that I have taken as much Pleasure in reading the Contents of his Books, as in the best invented Story I ever met with. It is possible, that the Traditions on which the *Iliad* and *Æneid* were built, had more Circumstances in them than the History of *the Fall of Man*, as it is related in Scripture. Besides it was easier for *Homer* and *Virgil* to dash the Truth with Fiction, as they were in no danger of offending the Religion of their Country by it. But as for *Milton*, he had not only a very few Circumstances upon which to raise his Poem, but was also obliged to proceed with the greatest Caution in every thing that he added out of his own Invention. And, indeed, notwithstanding all the Restraints he was under, he has filled his Story with so many surprising Incidents, which bear so close an Analogy with what is delivered in Holy Writ, that it is capable of pleasing the most delicate Reader, without giving Offence to the most scrupulous.

The Modern Criticks have collected from several Hints in the *Iliad* and *Æneid* the Space of Time, which is taken up by the Action of each of those Poems; but as a great Part of *Milton*'s Story was transacted in Regions that lie out of the reach of the Sun and the Sphere of Day, it is impossible to gratify the Reader with such a Calculation, which indeed would be more curious than instructive, none of the Criticks, either Ancient or Modern, having laid down Rules to circumscribe the Action of an Epic Poem with any determined number of Years, Days or Hours.

This piece of Criticism on Milton's Paradise Lost, shall be carried on in following Papers.

LONDON: Printed for *Sam. Buckley*, at the *Dolphin* in *Little-Britain*; and Sold by *A. Baldwin* in *Warwick-Lane*; where Advertisements are taken in; as also by *Charles Lillie*, Perfumer, at the Corner of *Beauford-Buildings* in

5. Verge: limits.
6. Games: In the classical epic, athletic contests formed part of the funeral rites for dead heroes. See pp. 81ff.
7. Simile of the Top: In *Aeneid* 7:373-84, Amata, driven mad by Juno, runs wildly about the city. Her frenzied course is compared to the erratic motion of a boy's top, an object considered by some critics to be below the dignity of an epic poem.
8. Machinery: as a critical term, refers to gods or other superhuman beings who contribute to the action of the poem. The sylphs of course constitute the machinery of *The Rape of the Lock*.

Sir William Davenant, Preface to *Gondibert, an Heroick Poem* (Paris, 1650; London, 1651)

Davenant's preface offered an alternative to the traditional division of the epic into twelve or twenty-four books. Whether Davenant directly influenced Pope or not, it is suggestive that there is a heroic precedent for the five-canto structure of *The Rape of the Lock*.

I have now given you the accompt of such provisions as I made for this new Building ; and you may next pleafe(having examin'd the fubftance) to take a view of the forme; and obferve if I have methodically and with difcretion difpos'd of the materialls, which with fome curiofity I had collected. I cannot dilcerne by any help from reading, or learned men , (who have been to me the beft and briefeft Indexes of Books) that any Nation hath in reprefentment of great actions (either by *Heroicks* or *Dramaticks*) digefted Story into fo pleafant and inftructive a method as the Englifh by their *Drama* : and by that regular fpecies (though narratively and not in Dialogue) I have

have drawn the body of an Heroick Poem : In which I did not only obferve the Symmetry (proportioning five Books to five *Acts*, & *Canto's* to *Scenes*, (the *Scenes* having their number ever govern'd by occafion) but all the *fhadowings, happy ftrokes, fecret graces*, and even the *drapery* (which together make the fecond beauty) I have (I hope) exactly follow'd : and thofe compofitions of fecond beauty, I obferve in the *Drama* to be the under-walks, interweaving, or correfpondence of leffer defign in *Scenes*, not the great motion of the main plot, and coherence of the *Acts*.

Longinus, *On the Sublime (Peri Hupsos)*

One of the eighteenth century's favorite ancient critics, Longinus helped to counteract some of the more finicky tendencies of neo-classicism. Pope addressed him thus in *An Essay on Criticism*:

> Thee, bold *Longinus*! all the Nine inspire,
> And bless *their Critick* with a *Poet's Fire*.
>   . . .
> Whose *own Example* strengthens all his Laws,
> And *Is himself* that great *Sublime* he draws.   (675-80)

The following selections come from chapter seven (nine in modern editions), "Of the Sublimity of Thoughts." Their closest connection to *The Rape of the Lock* is the passage beginning "So when bold *Homer* makes the Gods engage" (5:45), though the conception of epic grandeur that they teach is relevant to the entire ethos of Pope's poem. Longinus' assimilation of the opening of Genesis to the epic tradition allows Belinda's naming of trumps to be heroic as well as biblical. The translation is based on Boileau's French version, and formed part of his English *Works* of 1712-13.

C H A P. VII.

Of the Sublimity of Thoughts.

THough of the Five Caufes I have mention'd, *A Natural Elevation of Wit*, the Firft and Chiefeft of 'em all, be rather a Gift of Heaven, than a Quality that may be acquir'd; yet we ought as much as we can, to accuftom our Thoughts to the Sublime, and keep 'em always full and puff'd up, as we may fay, with a certain Noble and Generous Boldnefs.

If 'tis demanded how it muft be effected; I have elfewhere faid, that this Elevation of Wit was an Image of a Greatnefs of Soul : For which Reafon, we fometimes admire the Thought only of a Man; tho' he does not fpeak on account of the great Courage we fee in him; As for Example, The Silence of *Ajax* in Hell, in the * *Odyffes* xx. For there's fomething Nobler in that Silence, than in any thing he could have faid.

Wherefore the Firft Qualification that is to be fuppos'd in a true Orator, is that his Wit be not Creeping; indeed 'tis impoffible that a Man, who all his Life time has been us'd to Mean and Servile Inclinations and Sentiments, fhould ever be able to produce any thing very *Marvellous*, or worthy of Pofterity. 'Tis not likely that any, but fuch as have Lofty and Solid Thoughts, fhou'd make Elevated Difcourfes; and Great Men particularly are thofe that fpeak extraordinary things; as for Inftance, *Alexander*'s Anfwer, when *Darius* offer'd him half
Afia

---

* *'Tis in the* xi *Book of the* Odyffes, *where* Ulyffes *makes his Submiffion to* Ajax; *but* Ajax *does not condefcend to anfwer him.*

Afia with his Daughter in Marriage. *As for me* faid Parmenio, *If I were* Alexander, *I wou'd have accepted of thofe Offers: And fo wou'd I,* reply'd that Prince, *If I had been* Parmenio. Who but *Alexander,* could have made fuch an Anfwer?

This was *Homer's* chief Excellence; *Homer,* whofe Thoughts were all Sublime, as may be feen by the Defcription of the Goddefs *Difcord*; Who, fays he,

Has in the Heav'ns her Head, on Earth her Feet.

For this Grandeur given by the Poet to *Difcord,* is lefs the Meafure of that Fury, than of the Capacity and Elevation of *Homer's* Wit. *Hefiod* has a Verfe in his Shield, quite different from this; if he was Author of that Poem, when fpeaking of the Goddefs of Darknefs, he fays;

A Filthy Humour from her Noftrils flow'd.

In effect, he does not properly render that Goddefs Terrible, but Odious and Shocking. See on the contrary, what Majefty *Homer* gives to the Gods.

What Space a Man can from a Lofty Rock,

On the Sea's Margin, in the Air behold;

Th' Intrepid Courfers of th' Immortal Gods

Leap at a Bound, *&c.* *Ilias* l. 5.

He meafures the Extent of their Leap by that of the Univerfe. Who is there, that when he fees the Magnificence of this Hyperbole, does not cry out: If the Horfes of the Gods were to have taken a Second Leap, there had not been Space enough in the World for them? When he Paints the Combat of the Gods, how Great are his Images! How Sublime is that when he fays; All

All Heaven refounded, and *Olympus* fhook.

Ilias l. 21.

And elfewhere ;

Hell at the Noife of *Neptune*'s Fury rofe,

And *Pluto* pale and howling left his Throne,

Afraid the God would reach thofe Dire Abodes,

To the World's Center with his Trident Strike ;

And thro' the gaping Earth admit the Day.

Thus leave the Defart Shoars of *Styx* expos'd ;

And to the Living fhew his Hated Realms,

Abhorr'd by Men, and dreaded ev'n by Gods.

Ilias l. 20.

There, my Dear *Terentianus,* you fee the Earth open'd to the Center, Hell is juft ready to appear, and the Machine of the World about to be deftroy'd and overturn'd. To fhew that in this Combat, Heaven, Hell, things Mortal and Immortal ; in a Word, all things combated with the Gods, and that there was nothing in Nature, but what was in Danger. However all thofe Thoughts muft be taken in an Allegorical Senfe ; otherwife they wou'd have fomething in 'em that is Frightful, Impious, and little agreeable to the Majefty of Gods. For my part, when I read in *Homer* of the Wounds, the Factions, the Sufferings, the Tears, the Imprifonments of the Gods, and all thofe Accidents which inceffantly befal 'em ; it feems to me, that he does his utmoft to make Gods of the Men, who were at the Siege of *Troy* ;

and

and on the contrary, of the Gods themfelves to
make Men: Indeed he puts 'em in a worfe Condition; for with refpect to us, when we are Miferable, we have Death at leaft, which is a certain
End to all our Miferies; whereas in reprefenting
the Gods in that Manner, he rather makes 'em
eternally Miferable than Immortal.

He fucceeds much better, when he Paints a God
fuch as he is, in his full Majefty and Grandeur;
without any Mixture of Mortal Imperfections, as in
that Paffage, which has been taken Notice of by
feveral before me; fpeaking of *Neptune*, he fays;

Neptune thus marching o'er thofe Boundlefs Plains,

Made the Hills Tremble, and the Forefts Shake.

Ilias l. 13

And in another Place;

He Proudly mounts on his Imperial Car,

And with it cleaves, where e'er he comes, the Waves,

When on the Liquid Plains he's feen to march,

The Heavy Whale grows Light, and leaps for Joy,

The Waters Dance beneath their Sov'raign God,

And feem, with Pleafure, to Confefs their King.

The Car thus flying, *&c.*

Thus the Law-giver of the Jews, who was no
Ordinary Man, having had a very juft Conception of the Greatnefs and Power of God, expreffes
it in all its Dignity, at the Beginning of his Laws,
by thefe Words; *God faid, Let there be Light; and
there was Light: Let the Earth be made; and the
Earth was made.*

～

Alexander Pope, *A Receit to Make an Epick Poem* (1713)

This mock-treatise appeared as the seventy-eighth number of the *Guardian,* and in a different form as the fifteenth chapter of *Peri Bathous or the Art of Sinking in Poetry* (1728), Pope's parody of Longinus. It bears somewhat the same relation to epic theory that *The Rape of the Lock* does to epic practice: that is, its main targets are modern poetasters with epic pretensions and minor critics who claim to establish rules by which poetry must be written. But at the same time it also reveals the dogmatic and potentially mechanical aspects of even the greatest neoclassical treatises on the epic. It does not embody the rhetoric of *The Rape of the Lock* as fully as *Peri Bathous* does that of the *Dunciad,* but it does help us to realize that *The Rape of the Lock* includes all the epic ingredients (suitably modified, of course) and that on one level it is very much a poem written to rule.

---

1. Docebo . . .: "I will teach the poet's office and duty; whence he draws his stories; what nurtures and fashions him" (Horace, *Ars Poetica*).
2. Arts and Sciences: Among the arts and sciences put on display in *The Rape of the Lock* are "theology," makeup, cards, and astrology.
3. Cluverius, Philip (1580-1623): geographer. The book referred to is probably a version of his *Introductionis ad generalem geographicam,* first published in 1624.

The GUARDIAN.

--------- *Docebo*
Unde parentur opes, quid alat, formetque Poetam. Hor.

Wednesday, June 10. 1713.

IT is no small Pleasure to me, who am zealous in the Interests of Learning, to think I may have the Honour of leading the Town into a very new and uncommon Road of Criticism. As that kind of Literature is at present carried on, it consists only in a Knowledge of Mechanick Rules, which contribute to the Structure of different sorts of Poetry, as the Receits of good Housewives do to the making Puddings of Flower, Oranges, Plumbs, or any other Ingredients. It would, methinks, make these my Instructions more easily intelligible to ordinary Readers, if I discoursed of these Matters in the Stile in which Ladies Learned in OEconomicks dictate to their Pupils for the Improvement of the Kitchin and Larder.

I shall begin with Epick Poetry, because the Criticks agree it is the greatest Work Human Nature is capable of. I know the *French* have already laid down many Mechanical Rules for Compositions of this Sort, but at the same time they cut off almost all Undertakers from the Possibility of ever performing them; for the first Qualification they unanimously require in a Poet, is a *Genius*. I shall here endeavour (for the Benefit of my Countrymen) to make it manifest, that Epick Poems may be made *without a Genius*, nay without Learning or much Reading. This must necessarily be of great Use to all those Poets who confess they never Read, and of whom the World is convinced they never Learn. What *Moliere* observes of making a Dinner, that any Man can do it *with Mony*, and if a profest Cook cannot *without*, he has his Art for nothing; the same may be said of making a Poem, 'tis easily brought about by him that *has* a Genius, but the Skill lies in doing it without one. In pursuance of this End, I shall present the Reader with a plain and certain *Recipe*, by which even Sonneteers and Ladies may be qualified for this grand Performance.

I know it will be objected, that one of the chief Qualifications of an Epick Poet, is to be knowing in all Arts and Sciences. But this ought not to discourage those that have no Learning, as long as Indexes and Dictionaries may be had, which are the Compendium of all Knowledge. Besides, since it

is an established Rule, that none of the Terms of those Arts and Sciences are to be made use of, one may venture to affirm, our Poet cannot impertinently offend in this Point. The Learning which will be more particularly necessary to him, is the ancient Geography of Towns, Mountains, and Rivers: For this let him take *Cluverius*, Value Fourpence.

Another Quality required is a compleat Skill in Languages. To this I answer, that it is notorious Persons of no Genius have been oftentimes great Linguists. To instance in the *Greek*, of which there are two Sorts ; the Original *Greek*, and that from which our Modern Authors translate. I should be unwilling to promise Impossibilities, but modestly speaking, this may be learned in about an Hour's time with Ease. I have known one, who became a sudden Professor of *Greek*, immediately upon Application of the Left-hand Page of the *Cambridge Homer* to his Eye. It is, in these Days, with Authors as with other Men, the well bred are familiarly acquainted with them at first Sight; and as it is sufficient for a good General to have *survey'd* the Ground he is to conquer, so it is enough for a good Poet to have *seen* the Author he is to be Master of. But to proceed to the Purpose of this Paper.

A Receit to make an *Epick* Poem.

For the *Fable*.

Take out of any old Poem, History-books, Romance, or Legend, (for instance Geffry of Monmouth or Don Belianis of Greece) those Parts of Story which afford most Scope for long Descriptions: Put these Pieces together, and throw all the Adventures you fancy into one Tale. Then take a Hero, whom you may chuse for the Sound of his Name, and put him into the midst of these Adventures: There let him work, for twelve Books ; at the end of which you may take him out, ready prepared to conquer or to marry; it being necessary that the Conclusion of an Epick Poem be fortunate.

To

(Price Two Pence.)

To make an Episode. Take *any remaining Adventure of your former Collection, in which you could no way involve your Hero; or any unfortunate Accident that was too good to be thrown away; and it will be of Use, applyed to any other Person; who may be lost and evaporate in the Course of the Work, without the least Damage to the Composition.*

For the Moral and Allegory. These *you may Extract out of the Fable afterwards at your Leisure: Be sure you strain them sufficiently.*

For the Manners.

For those of the Hero, take all the best Qualities you can find in all the best celebrated Heroes of Antiquity; if they will not be reduced to a Consistency, lay 'em all on a heap upon him. But be sure they are Qualities which your Patron would be thought to have; and to prevent any Mistake which the World may be subject to, select from the Alphabet those Capital Letters that compose his Name, and set them at the Head of a Dedication before your Poem. However, do not absolutely observe the exact Quantity of these Virtues, it not being determined whether or no it be necessary for the Hero of a Poem to be an honest Man — *For the Under-Characters, gather them from Homer and Virgil, and Change the Names as Occasion serves.*

For the Machines.

Take of Deities, Male and Female, as many as you can use. Separate them into two equal parts, and keep Jupiter in the middle. Let Juno put him in a Ferment, and Venus mollifie him. Remember on all Oc-
4 *sions to make use of Volatile Mercury. If you have need of Devils, draw them out of Milton's Paradise, and extract your Spirits from Tasso. The Use of these Machines is evident; for since no Epick Poem can possibly subsist without them, the wisest way is to reserve them for your greatest Necessities. When you cannot extricate your Hero by any Human Means, or your self by your own Wit, seek Relief from Heaven, and the Gods will do your Business very readily. This is according to the direct Prescription of Horace in his Art of Poetry.*

Nec Deus intersit, nisi dignus vindice *Nodus* Inciderit ——

That is to say, a Poet should never call upon the Gods for their Assistance, but when he is in great Perplexity.

For the Descriptions.

5 For a Tempest. *Take Eurus, Zephyr, Auster and Boreas, and cast them together in one Verse. Add to these of Rain, Lightning, and of Thunder (the*
6 *loudest you can) quantum sufficit. Mix your Clouds and Billows well together till they foam, and thicken your Description here and there with a Quicksand. Brew your Tempest well in your Head, before you set it a blowing.*

For a Battel. Pick a large quantity of *Images and Descriptions from* Homer's *Iliads, with a Spice or two of* Virgil, *and if there remain any Overplus, you may lay them by for a Skirmish. Season it well with Similes, and it will make an Excellent Battel.*

For a Burning Town. If *such a Description be necessary, because it is certain there is one in* Virgil, *Old* Troy *is ready burnt to your Hands. But if you fear That would be thought* borrowed, *a Chapter or two of the Theory of the* Conflagration, *well cir-* 7
cumstanced, and done into Verse, will be a good *Suc-* 8
cedaneum.

As for Similes and Metaphors, *they may be found all over the Creation, the most ignorant may gather them, but the danger is in applying them. For this,* advise with your Bookseller.

For the Language.

(I mean the Diction). *Here it will do well to be an Imitator of* Milton, *for you'll find it easier to imitate him in this than any thing else.* Hebraisms and Grecisms *are to be found in him, without the trouble of Learning the Languages. I knew a Painter, who (like our Poet) had no Genius, make his Dawbings be thought Originals by setting them in the Smoak: You may in the same manner give the venerable Air of Antiquity to your Piece, by darkening it up and down with Old English. With this you may be easily furnished upon any Occasion, by the Dictionary commonly Printed at the end of* Chaucer.

I must not conclude, without cautioning all Writers without Genius in one material Point; which is, never to be afraid of having *too much Fire* in their Works. I should advise rather to take their warmest Thoughts, and spread them abroad upon Paper; for they are observed to cool before they are read.

L O N D O N': Printed for *J. Tonson* in the *Strand*; and Sold by *A. Baldwin* in *Warwick-Lane*; where Advertisements are taken in. 1713.

---

4. Volatile: in the senses of "capable of flight" and "changeable, fickle."
5. Eurus...Boreas: respectively, the east, west, south, and north winds.
6. quantum sufficit: as much as is necessary; a formula used in medical prescriptions.
7. Conflagration: i.e., the end of the world.
8. Succedaneum: "a drug, frequently of inferior efficacy, substituted for another" (*OED*).

The Iliad

Homer's *Iliad* provides the main classical foundation for *The Rape of the Lock*, the sense of great men engaging in great actions, the backdrop of fatality and heroism against which the modern beaux and belles are diminished. The simple but dignified manners of Homer's heroes provide another kind of standard by which to judge the fopperies and affectations of Hampton Court. But these juxtapositions may also have different implications. Homer is an unsurpassable poet, but his heroes are far from being morally irreproachable. Pope imitates epic decorum so skillfully that the distance between his subject and Homer's seems to decrease a little, and we are led to suspect that ancient warriors may not have been as completely different from modern ladies as their received reputation suggests. The Trojan War, after all, was the consequence of a dire offence that had sprung from an amorous cause: the abduction of Helen, Menelaus' wife, by Paris. A modification of this view has recently been advanced: Pope may be ridiculing his contemporaries for living their lives according to forms that no longer have any function, for refusing to admit that ancient standards are not automatically applicable to modern life. All these ironic discrepancies, whomever they ridicule, are primarily comic, though serious purposes can underlie the comedy.

Pope's own translation of the *Iliad* appears here, even though it was not completed until 1720 and thus, unlike most of the other texts in this volume, was not available to the first readers of *The Rape of the Lock*. Two factors justify this exception. First, no version existed in 1714 that satisfied contemporary taste, Chapman's and Hobbes' having long since fallen out of favor. More important, Pope's text and copious notes obviously embody more clearly than any other version the conception of classical epic against which he set his mock-epic.

Pope was not content, however, with merely producing an adequate eighteenth-century embodiment of the *Iliad*; perhaps as a compensation for Greekless readers who had to wait a few years to appreciate fully the role of the *Iliad* in Belinda's adventures, he appears to have translated several passages so as to provide specific epic contexts for certain passages of his already existent mock-epic, thus achieving a kind of "parody in reverse time."

BOOK I

The opening of the poem sketches rather elliptically the background of the quarrel between Achilles and Agamemnon. Chryses, a Trojan priest, begs Agamemnon to release his daughter, taken captive in a Greek victory. Agamemnon finally gives her up, but confiscates Achilles' captive in recompense. As a result Achilles refuses to fight for the Greeks while Agamemnon remains in command. Some of Pope's notes suggest how the theme of the *Iliad* may parallel that of *The Rape of the Lock*.

---

7. Atrides: son of Atreus, i.e., Agamemnon. Homeric heroes are frequently referred to by such patronymics; thus Achilles is Pelides, son of Peleus.
11. Latona's Son: Apollo.

THE Wrath of *Peleus'* Son, the direful Spring
  Of all the *Grecian* Woes, O Goddefs, fing!
That Wrath which hurl'd to *Pluto's* gloomy Reign
The Souls of mighty Chiefs untimely flain;
Whofe Limbs unbury'd on the naked Shore   5
Devouring Dogs and hungry Vultures tore.
Since Great *Achilles* and *Atrides* ftrove,   7
Such was the Sov'reign Doom and fuch the Will of *Jove*.

  Declare, O Mufe! in what ill-fated Hour
Sprung the fierce Strife, from what offended Pow'r?   10
Latona's Son a dire Contagion fpread,   11
And heap'd the Camp with Mountains of the Dead;

A   The

The King of Men his Rev'rend Prieſt defy'd,
And, for the King's Offence, the People dy'd.
15 For *Chryſes* ſought with coſtly Gifts to gain
His Captive Daughter from the Victor's Chain.
Suppliant the Venerable Father ſtands,
Apollo's awful Enſigns grace his Hands :
By theſe he begs ; and lowly bending down,
20 Extends the Sceptre and the Laurel Crown.
He ſu'd to All, but chief implor'd for Grace
The Brother-Kings, of *Atreus*' Royal Race.
    Ye Kings and Warriors ! may your Vows be crown'd,
And *Troy's* proud Walls lie level with the Ground.
25 May *Jove* reſtore you, when your Toils are o'er,
Safe to the Pleaſures of your native Shore.
But oh ! relieve a wretched Parent's Pain,
And give *Chruſeïs* to theſe Arms again ;
If Mercy fail, yet let my Preſents move,
30 And dread avenging *Phœbus*, Son of *Jove*.
    The *Greeks* in Shouts their joint Aſſent declare
The Prieſt to rev'rence, and releaſe the Fair.
Not ſo *Atrides* : He, with Kingly Pride,
Repuls'd the ſacred Sire, and thus reply'd.

                                        Hence

---

30. Phoebus: another name for Apollo.

Hence on thy Life, and fly thefe hoftile Plains,   35
Nor ask, Prefumptuous, what the King detains;
Hence, with thy Laurel Crown, and Golden Rod,
Nor truft too far thofe Enfigns of thy God.
Mine is thy Daughter, Prieft, and fhall remain;
And Pray'rs, and Tears, and Bribes fhall plead in vain; 40
'Till Time fhall rifle ev'ry youthful Grace,
And Age difmifs her from my cold Embrace,
In daily Labours of the Loom employ'd,
Or doom'd to deck the Bed fhe once enjoy'd.
Hence then: to *Argos* fhall the Maid retire;   45
Far from her native Soil, and weeping Sire.

The trembling Prieft along the Shore return'd,
And in the Anguifh of a Father mourn'd.
Difconfolate, nor daring to complain,
Silent he wander'd by the founding Main: 50
'Till, fafe at diftance, to his God he prays,
The God who darts around the World his Rays.

Apollo hears the prayer of Chryses and devastates the Greek camp with a plague. Calchas, a priest, reveals to the Greeks that the plague will not end until Agamemnon returns Chryses' daughter. In Pope, there is similar concern about the return of Belinda's lock.

The Prophet fpoke; when with a gloomy Frown,
The Monarch ftarted from his fhining Throne;
Black Choler fill'd his Breaft that boil'd with Ire,
And from his Eyeballs flafh'd the living Fire.   130
Augur accurft! denouncing Mifchief ftill,
Prophet of Plagues, for ever boding Ill!
Still muft that Tongue fome wounding Meffage bring,
And ftill thy Prieftly Pride provoke thy King?
For this are *Phœbus'* Oracles explor'd,   135
To teach the *Greeks* to murmur at their Lord?
For this with Falfhoods is my Honour ftain'd;
Is Heav'n offended, and a Prieft profan'd,
Becaufe my Prize, my beauteous Maid I hold,
And heav'nly Charms prefer to proffer'd Gold?   140
A Maid, unmatch'd in Manners as in Face,
Skill'd in each Art, and crown'd with ev'ry Grace.
Not half fo dear were *Clytemneftra's* Charms,
When firft her blooming Beauties bleft my Arms.

Yet

145 Yet if the Gods demand her, let her fail;
Our Cares are only for the Publick Weal :
Let me be deem'd the hateful Caufe of all,
And fuffer, rather than my People fall.
The Prize, the beauteous Prize I will refign,
150 So dearly valu'd, and fo juftly mine.
But fince for common Good I yield the Fair,
My private Lofs let grateful *Greece* repair ;
Nor unrewarded let your Prince complain,
That He alone has fought and bled in vain.
155   Infatiate King (*Achilles* thus replies)
Fond of the Pow'r, but fonder of the Prize !
Would'ft thou the *Greeks* their lawful Prey fhou'd yield,
The due Reward of many a well-fought Field ?
The Spoils of Cities raz'd, and Warriors flain,
160 We fhare with Juftice, as with Toil we gain :
But to refume whate'er thy Av'rice craves,
(That Trick of Tyrants) may be born by Slaves.
Yet if our Chief for Plunder only fight,
The Spoils of *Ilion* fhall thy Lofs requite,
165 Whene'er, by *Jove*'s Decree, our conqu'ring Pow'rs
Shall humble to the Duft her lofty Tow'rs.

Then

Then thus the King.   Shall I my Prize refign
With tame Content, and Thou poffeft of thine ?
Great as thou art, and like a God in Fight,
Think not to rob me of a Soldier's Right.   170
At thy Demand fhall I reftore the Maid ?
Firft let the juft Equivalent be paid ;
Such as a King might ask ; and let it be
A Treafure worthy Her, and worthy Me.
Or grant me this, or with a Monarch's Claim   175
This Hand fhall feize fome other Captive Dame.
The mighty *Ajax* fhall his Prize refign,
Ulyffes' Spoils, or ev'n thy own be mine.
The Man who fuffers, loudly may complain ;
And rage he may, but he fhall rage in vain.   180
But this when Time requires——It now remains
We launch a Bark to plow the watry Plains,
And waft the Sacrifice to *Chryfa*'s Shores,
With chofen Pilots, and with lab'ring Oars.
Soon fhall the Fair the fable Ship afcend,   185
And fome deputed Prince the Charge attend ;
This *Creta*'s King, or *Ajax* fhall fulfill,
Or wife *Ulyffes* fee perform'd our Will,

C   Or,

37

Or, if our Royal Pleafure fhall ordain,
190 *Achilles* felf conduct her o'er the Main;
Let fierce *Achilles*, dreadful in his Rage,
192 The God propitiate, and the Peft affwage.

At this, *Pelides* frowning ftern, reply'd:
O Tyrant, arm'd with Infolence and Pride!
195 Inglorious Slave to Int'reft, ever join'd
With Fraud, unworthy of a Royal Mind.
What gen'rous *Greek* obedient to thy Word,
Shall form an Ambufh, or fhall lift the Sword?
What Caufe have I to war at thy Decree?
200 The diftant *Trojans* never injur'd me.

To *Pthia*'s Realms no hoftile Troops they led;
Safe in her Vales my warlike Courfers fed:
Far hence remov'd, the hoarfe-refounding Main
And Walls of Rocks, fecure my native Reign,
205 Whofe fruitful Soil luxuriant Harvefts grace,
Rich in her Fruits, and in her martial Race.
Hither we fail'd, a voluntary Throng,
T' avenge a private, not a publick Wrong:
What elfe to *Troy* th' affembled Nations draws,
210 But thine, Ungrateful, and thy Brother's Caufe?

Is

Is this the Pay our Blood and Toils deserve,

Disgrac'd and injur'd by the Man we serve?

And dar'st thou threat to snatch my Prize away,   213

Due to the Deeds of many a dreadful Day?

A Prize as small, O Tyrant! match'd with thine,   215

As thy own Actions if compar'd to mine.

Thine in each Conquest is the wealthy Prey,

Tho' mine the Sweat and Danger of the Day.

Some trivial Present to my Ships I bear,

Or barren Praises pay the Wounds of War.   220

But know, proud Monarch, I'm thy Slave no more;

My Fleet shall waft me to *Thessalia's* Shore.

Left by *Achilles* on the *Trojan* Plain,

What Spoils, what Conquests shall *Atrides* gain?

    To this the King: Fly, mighty Warriour! fly, 225

Thy Aid we need not, and thy Threats defy.

---

192. Pest: plague; asswage: assuage, bring relief from.

210. thy Brother's Cause: Agamemnon and Menelaus were brothers.

213. Nothing is finer than the Moral shewn us in this Quarrel, of the Blindness and Partiality of Mankind to their own Faults: The *Græcians* make a War to recover a Woman that was ravish'd, and are in danger to fail in the Attempt by a Dispute about another. *Agamemnon* while he is revenging a Rape, commits one; and *Achilles* while he is in the utmost Fury himself, reproaches *Agamemnon* for his Passionate Temper. [Pope's note.]

Minerva (Reason) descends and persuades Achilles not to draw his sword on Agamemnon, but she cannot moderate his verbal attack.

295   Nor yet the Rage his boiling Breaſt forſook,
Which thus redoubling on the Monarch broke.
O Monſter, mix'd of Inſolence and Fear,
Thou Dog in Forehead, but in Heart a Deer!

When

When wert thou known in ambufh'd Fights to dare,

Or nobly face the horrid Front of War?   300

'Tis ours, the Chance of fighting Fields to try,

Thine to look on, and bid the Valiant dye.

So much 'tis fafer thro' the Camp to go,

And rob a Subject, than defpoil a Foe.

Scourge of thy People, violent and bafe!   305

Sent in *Jove's* Anger on a flavifh Race,

Who loft to Senfe of gen'rous Freedom paft

Are tam'd to Wrongs, or this had been thy laft.

Now by this facred Sceptre, hear me fwear,

Which never more fhall Leaves or Bloffoms bear, 310

Which fever'd from the Trunk (as I from thee)

On the bare Mountains left its Parent Tree;

This Sceptre, form'd by temper'd Steel to prove

An Enfign of the Delegates of *Jove,*

From whom the Pow'r of Laws and Juftice fprings: 315

(Tremendous Oath! inviolate to Kings)

By this I fwear, when bleeding *Greece* again

Shall call *Achilles,* fhe fhall call in vain.

When flufh'd with Slaughter, *Hector* comes, to fpread 319

The purpled Shore with Mountains of the Dead, 320

           Then

---

319. Hector: chief warrior of the Trojans.

Then shalt thou mourn th'Affront thy Madnefs gave,

Forc'd to deplore, when impotent to fave:

Then rage in Bitternefs of Soul, to know

This Act has made the braveft *Greek* thy Foe.

Nestor, oldest and wisest of the Greeks, tries in vain to compose the quarrel as Sir Plume intervenes with the Baron in *The Rape of the Lock.*

This faid, he ceas'd: The King of Men replies;

Thy Years are awful, and thy Words are wife.

But that imperious, that unconquer'd Soul,

No Laws can limit, no Refpect controul.

380 Before his Pride muft his Superiors fall,

His Word the Law, and He the Lord of all?

Him muft our Hofts, our Chiefs, our Self obey?

What King can bear a Rival in his Sway?

Grant that the Gods his matchlefs Force have giv'n;

385 Has foul Reproach a Privilege from Heav'n?

Here

42

Here on the Monarch's Speech *Achilles* broke,
And furious, thus, and interrupting fpoke.
Tyrant, I well deferv'd thy galling Chain,
To live thy Slave, and ftill to ferve in vain,
Should I fubmit to each unjuft Decree :   390
Command thy Vaffals, but command not Me.
Seize on *Brifeïs*, whom the *Grecians* doom'd
My Prize of War, yet tamely fee refum'd ;
And feize fecure ; No more *Achilles* draws
His conqu'ring Sword in any Woman's Caufe.   395
The Gods command me to forgive the paft ;
But let this firft Invafion be the laft :
For know, thy Blood, when next thou dar'ft invade,
Shall ftream in Vengeance on my reeking Blade.
   At this, they ceas'd ; the ftern Debate expir'd :   400
The Chiefs in fullen Majefty retir'd.

---

395. When *Achilles* promises not to contest for *Briseïs*, he expresses it in a sharp
despising Air, *I will not fight for the sake of a Woman*: by which he glances at *Helena*,
and casts an oblique Reflection upon those Commanders whom he is about to leave at
the Siege for her Cause. One may observe how well it is fancy'd of the Poet, to make one
Woman the ground of a Quarrel which breaks an Alliance that was only form'd upon
account of another: and how much the Circumstance thus consider'd contributes to
keep up the Anger of *Achilles*, for carrying on the Poem beyond this Dissolution of the
Council. For (as he himself argues with *Ulysses* in the *9th Iliad*) it is as reasonable for
him to retain his Anger upon the account of *Briseïs*, as for the Brothers with all *Greece*
to carry on a War upon the score of *Helena*. I do not know that any Commentator has
taken notice of this Sarcasm of *Achilles*, which I think a very obvious one. [Pope's
note.]

Book V

Diomedes, a Greek, is the most prominent warrior in this book. He kills Pallarus, whose body Aeneas rushes to defend against despoliation. Aeneas in turn is wounded, and Venus, his goddess mother, tries to rescue him. The incongruity of the goddess of love on a battlefield may have been one germ of some of the mock-epic incongruities of Pope's drawing room battles.

He fpoke, and rifing hurl'd his forceful Dart,
Which driv'n by *Pallas*, pierc'd a vital Part;   352
Full in his Face it enter'd, and betwixt
The Nofe and Eye-ball the proud *Lycian* fixt;
Crafh'd all his Jaws, and cleft the Tongue within,   355
'Till the bright Point look'd out beneath the Chin.
Headlong he falls, his Helmet knocks the Ground;
Earth groans beneath him, and his Arms refound;
The ftarting Courfers tremble with Affright;
The Soul indignant feeks the Realms of Night.   360
   To guard his flaughter'd Friend, *Æneas* flies,
His Spear extending where the Carcafs lies;

I   Watchful

---

352. Pallas: Athena, fighting on the side of the Greeks.

Watchful he wheels, protects it ev'ry way,
As the grim Lyon ftalks around his Prey.
365 O'er the fall'n Trunk his ample Shield difplay'd,
He hides the Hero with his mighty Shade.
And threats aloud : The *Greeks* with longing Eyes
Behold at diftance, but forbear the Prize.
369 Then fierce *Tydides* ftoops; and from the Fields
370 Heav'd with vaft Force, a Rocky Fragment wields.
Not two ftrong Men th' enormous Weight could raife,
Such Men as live in thefe degen'rate Days.
He fwung it round; and gath'ring Strength to throw,
Difcharg'd the pond'rous Ruin at the Foe.
375 Where to the Hip th' inferted Thigh unites,
Full on the Bone the pointed Marble lights;
Thro' both the Tendons broke the rugged Stone,
And ftripp'd the Skin, and crack'd the folid Bone.
Sunk on his Knees and ftagg'ring with his Pains,
380 His falling Bulk his bended Arm fuftains;
Loft in a dizzy Mift the Warrior lies;
A fudden Cloud comes fwimming o'er his Eyes.
There the brave Chief who mighty Numbers fway'd
Opprefs'd had funk to Death's Eternal Shade,

4

But

369. Tydides: Diomedes.

But Heav'nly *Venus*, mindful of the Love   385
She bore *Anchifes* in th' *Idæan* Grove,
His Danger views with Anguish and Despair,
And guards her Offspring with a Mother's Care.
About her much-lov'd Son her Arms she throws,
Her Arms whose Whiteness match'd the falling Snows. 390
Screen'd from the Foe behind her shining Veil,
The Swords wave harmless, and the Javelins fail:
Safe thro' the rushing Horse and feather'd Flight
Of founding Shafts, she bears him from the Fight.

   Nor *Sthenelus*, with unassisting Hands,   395
Remain'd unheedful of his Lord's Commands:
His panting Steeds, remov'd from out the War,
He fix'd with straiten'd Traces to the Car.
Next rushing to the *Dardan* Spoil, detains
The heav'nly Courfers with the flowing Manes.   400
These in proud Triumph to the Fleet convey'd,
No longer now a *Trojan* Lord obey'd.
That Charge to bold *Deipylus* he gave,
(Whom most he lov'd, as brave Men love the Brave)
Then mounting on his Car, resum'd the Rein,   405
And follow'd where *Tydides* swept the Plain.
                                        Meanwhile

Meanwhile (his Conqueſt raviſh'd from his Eyes)
The raging Chief in chace of *Venus* flies:
No Goddeſs She, commiſſion'd to the Field,
410 Like *Pallas* dreadful with her ſable Shield,
Or fierce *Bellona* thund'ring at the Wall,
While Flames aſcend, and mighty Ruins fall.
He knew ſoft Combates ſuit the tender Dame,
New to the Field, and ſtill a Foe to Fame.
415 Thro' breaking Ranks his furious Courſe he bends,
And at the Goddeſs his broad Lance extends;
Thro' her bright Veil the daring Weapon drove
Th' Ambroſial Veil which all the Graces wove:
Her ſnowie Hand the razing Steel profan'd,
420 And the tranſparent Skin with Crimſon ſtain'd.
From the clear Vein a Stream immortal flow'd,
422 Such Stream as iſſues from a wounded God;
Pure Emanation! uncorrupted Flood;
Unlike our groſs, diſeas'd, terreſtrial Blood:
425 (For not the Bread of Man their Life ſuſtains,
Nor Wine's inflaming Juice ſupplies their Veins.)
With tender Shrieks the Goddeſs fill'd the Place,
And dropt her Offspring from her weak Embrace.

4   Him

---

422. See page 51.

Him *Phœbus* took: He cafts a Cloud around
The fainting Chief, and wards the mortal Wound. 430
   Then with a Voice that fhook the vaulted Skies,
The King infults the Goddefs as fhe flies.
Ill with *Jove's* Daughter bloody Fights agree,
The Field of Combate is no Scene for thee:
Go, let thy own foft Sex employ thy Care,   435
Go lull the Coward, or delude the Fair.
Taught by this Stroke, renounce the War's Alarms,
And learn to tremble at the Name of Arms.
   Tydides thus. The Goddefs, feiz'd with Dread,
Confus'd, diftracted, from the Conflict fled.   440
To aid her, fwift the winged *Iris* flew,
Wrapt in a Mift above the warring Crew.
The Queen of Love with faded Charms fhe found,
Pale was her Cheek, and livid look'd the Wound.
To *Mars*, who fate remote, they bent their way; 445
Far on the left, with Clouds involv'd, he lay;
Befide him ftood his Lance, diftain'd with Gore,
And, rein'd with Gold, his foaming Steeds before.
Low at his Knee, fhe begg'd, with ftreaming Eyes,
Her Brother's Car, to mount the diftant Skies,   450
               K   And

And fhew'd the Wound by fierce *Tydides* giv'n,
A mortal Man, who dares encounter Heav'n.

Stern *Mars* attentive hears the Queen complain,
And to her Hand commits the golden Rein :
455 She mounts the Seat opprefs'd with filent Woe,
Driv'n by the Goddefs of the painted Bow.
The Lafh refounds, the rapid Chariot flies,
And in a Moment fcales the lofty Skies.
There ftopp'd the Car, and there the Courfers ftood,
460 Fed by fair *Iris* with Ambrofial Food.
Before her Mother Love's bright Queen appears,
O'erwhelm'd with Anguifh and diffolv'd in Tears;
She rais'd her in her Arms, beheld her bleed,
And ask'd, what God had wrought this guilty Deed?
465   Then fhe : This Infult from no God I found,
An impious Mortal gave the daring Wound!
Behold the Deed of haughty *Diomed*!
'Twas in the Son's Defence the Mother bled.
The War with *Troy* no more the *Grecians* wage;
470 But with the Gods (th' immortal Gods) engage.
Dione then. Thy Wrongs with Patience bear,
And fhare thofe Griefs inferior Pow'rs muft fhare;
Unnum-

Book V. *HOMER's ILIAD.*

Unnumber'd Woes Mankind from us fuſtain,
And Men with Woes afflict the Gods again.

---

422. This is one of the Passages in *Homer* which have given occasion to that famous
Censure of *Tully* and *Longinus, That he makes Gods of his Heroes, and Mortals of his
Gods.* This, taken in a general Sense, appear'd the highest Impiety to *Plato* and
Pythagoras; one of whom has banish'd *Homer* from his Commonwealth, and the other
said he was tortured in Hell, for Fictions of this Nature. But if a due Distinction be
made of a difference among Beings superior to Mankind, which both the Pagans and
Christians have allowed, these Fables may be easily accounted for. *Wounds inflicted on
the Dragon, Bruising the Serpent's Head,* and other such metaphorical Images are
consecrated in holy Writ, and apply'd to Angelical and incorporeal Natures. But in our
Author's Days they had a Notion of Gods that were corporeal, to whom they ascribed
Bodies, tho' of a more subtil Kind than those of Mortals. So in this very Place he
supposes them to have Blood, but Blood of a finer or superior Nature. Notwithstanding
the foregoing Censures, *Milton* has not scrupled to imitate and apply this to Angels in
the Christian System, when *Satan* is wounded by *Michael* in his sixth Book.

> — *Then* Satan *first knew Pain,*
> *And writh'd him to and fro convolv'd; so sore*
> *The griding Sword with discontinuous Wound*
> *Pass'd thro' him; but th' Ætherial Substance clos'd,*
> *Not long divisible, and from the gash*
> *A Stream of Nectarous Humour issuing flow'd.*
> *Sanguin, such as Celestial Spirits may bleed —* [327-33]

> . . . .
> *Yet soon he heal'd, for Spirits that live throughout,*
> *Vital in ev'ry Part, not as frail Man*
> *In Entrails, Head or Heart, Liver or Reins,*
> *Cannot but by annihilating die.* [344-47]

— [Pope's note. He had, of course, already used these passages in *The Rape of the Lock,*
3:152, and Addison had discussed Milton's use of Homer in *Spectator* 333.]

Book VIII

Jove commands the gods to leave the battlefield, and the fighting breaks out again. His threats to disobedient gods served as one model for Ariel's threats to careless sylphs.

I L I A D.

AURORA now, fair Daughter of the Dawn,
Sprinkled with rofy Light the dewy Lawn.
When *Jove* conven'd the Senate of the Skies,
Where high *Olympus'* cloudy Tops arife.
The Sire of Gods his awful Silence broke ;   5
The Heav'ns attentive trembled as he fpoke.

   Celeftial States, Immortal Gods! give ear,
Hear our Decree, and rev'rence what ye hear ;
The fix'd Decree which not all Heav'n can move ;
Thou Fate! fulfill it; and ye Pow'rs! approve.   10
What God but enters yon' forbidden Field,
Who yields Affiftance, or but wills to yield ;

Q q q

Back

53

Back to the Skies with Shame he fhall be driv'n,
Gafh'd with difhoneft Wounds, the Scorn of Heav'n:
15 Or far, oh far from fteep *Olympus* thrown,
Low in the dark, *Tartarean* Gulf fhall groan,
With burning Chains fix'd to the Brazen Floors,
And lock'd by Hell's inexorable Doors;
As deep beneath th' Infernal Centre hurl'd,
20 As from that Centre to th' Æthereal World.
Let him who tempts me, dread thofe dire Abodes;
And know, th' Almighty is the God of Gods.
League all your Forces then, ye Pow'rs above,
Join all, and try th' Omnipotence of *Jove:*
25 Let down our golden everlafting Chain,
Whofe ftrong Embrace holds Heav'n, and Earth, and
Main:
Strive all, of mortal and immortal Birth,
To drag, by this, the Thund'rer down to Earth:
Ye ftrive in vain! If I but ftretch this Hand,
30 I heave the Gods, the Ocean, and the Land,
I fix the Chain to great *Olympus'* Height,
And the vaft World hangs trembling in my Sight!

For

54

For fuch I reign, unbounded and above ;
And fuch are Men, and Gods, compar'd to *Jove*,

Th' Almighty fpoke, nor durft the Pow'rs reply, 35
A rev'rend Horror filenc'd all the Sky ;
Trembling they ftood before their Sov'reign's Look;
At length his Beft-belov'd, the Pow'r of *Wifdom*, fpoke.

Oh Firft and Greateft! God by Gods ador'd!
We own thy Might, our Father and our Lord!   40
But ah! permit to pity human State ;
If not to help, at leaft lament their Fate.
From Fields forbidden we fubmifs refrain,
With Arms unaiding mourn our *Argives* flain;   44
Yet grant my Counfels ftill their Breafts may move, 45
Or all muft perifh in the Wrath of *Jove*.

The Cloud-compelling God her Suit approv'd,
And fmil'd fuperior on his Beft-belov'd.
Then call'd his Courfers, and his Chariot took ;
The ftedfaft Firmament beneath them fhook :   50
Rapt by th' Æthereal Steeds the Chariot roll'd ;
Brafs were their Hoofs, their curling Manes of Gold.
Of Heav'ns undroffy Gold the God's Array
Refulgent, flafh'd intolerable Day.

                                        High

---

44. Argives: Greeks.

55 High on the Thröne he ſhines: His Courſers fly,
Between th' extended Earth and ſtarry Sky.
But when to *Ida*'s topmoſt Height he came,
(Fair Nurſe of Fountains, and of Savage Game)
Where o'er her pointed Summits proudly rais'd,
60 His Fane breath'd Odours, and his Altar blaz'd:
There, from his radiant Car, the ſacred Sire
Of Gods and Men releas'd the Steeds of Fire:
Blue ambient Miſts th' immortal Steeds embrac'd;
High on the cloudy Point his Seat he plac'd.
65 Thence his broad Eye the ſubject World ſurveys,
The Town, the Tents, and navigable Seas.
   Now had the *Grecians* ſnatch'd a ſhort Repaſte,
And buckled on their ſhining Arms with Haſte.
Troy rowz'd as ſoon; for on this dreadful Day
70 The Fate of Fathers, Wives, and Infants lay.
The Gates unfolding pour forth all their Train;
Squadrons on Squadrons cloud the dusky Plain:
Men, Steeds, and Chariots ſhake the trembling Ground;
The Tumult thickens, and the Skies reſound.
75 And now with Shouts the ſhocking Armies clos'd,
To Lances, Lances, Shields to Shields oppos'd,

                                              Hoſt

---

60. Fane: temple.

Hoſt againſt Hoſt with ſhadowy Legions drew,
The ſounding Darts in Iron Tempeſts flew,
Victors and Vanquiſh'd join promiſcuous Cries,
Triumphant Shouts and dying Groans ariſe;   80
With ſtreaming Blood the ſlipp'ry Fields are dy'd,
And ſlaughter'd Heroes ſwell the dreadful Tide.
Long as the Morning Beams encreaſing bright,
O'er Heav'ns clear Azure ſpread the ſacred Light;
Commutual Death the Fate of War confounds,   85
Each adverſe Battel goar'd with equal Wounds.
But when the Sun the Height of Heav'n aſcends;
The Sire of Gods his golden Scales ſuſpends,
With equal Hand: In theſe explor'd the Fate
Of *Greece* and *Troy*, and pois'd the mighty Weight. 90
Prefs'd with its Load the *Grecian* Balance lies
Low ſunk on Earth, the *Trojan* ſtrikes the Skies.

Book XII

Hector, the Trojan leader ("he" in line 295), rouses his troops, and the two Ajaxes do likewise for the Greeks. Sarpedon's speech (371-96) is one of the most celebrated expressions of the heroic code and the direct model for Clarissa's speech in canto 5. Pope had already published a version of it in Tonson's *Miscellanies* of 1709. Sir John Denham's version of the same passage, published in 1668, also seems to have given a hint or two to Clarissa.

295   Furious he fpóke, and rufhing to the Wall,
Calls on his Hoft; his Hoft obey the Call;
With Ardour follow, where their Leader flies:
Redoubling Clamóurs thunder in the Skies.

1   *Jove*

Jove breaths a Whirlwind from the Hills of *Ide*,
And Drifts of Duſt the clouded Navy hide: 300
He fills the *Greeks* with Terror and Diſmay,
And gives great *Hector* the predeſtin'd Day.
Strong in themſelves, but ſtronger in his Aid,
Cloſe to the Works their rigid Siege they laid.
In vain the Mounds and maſſy Beams defend,   305
While theſe they undermine, and thoſe they rend;
Upheave the Piles that prop the ſolid Wall;
And Heaps on Heaps the ſmoaky Ruins fall.
Greece on her Ramparts ſtands the fierce Alarms;
The crowded Bulwarks blaze with waving Arms,   310
Shield touching Shield, a long-refulgent Row;
Whence hiſſing Darts, inceſſant, rain below.
The bold *Ajaces* fly from Tow'r to Tow'r,
And rouze, with Flame divine, the *Grecian* Pow'r.
The gen'rous Impulſe ev'ry *Greek* obeys;   315
Threats urge the fearful, and the valiant, Praiſe.

    Fellows in Arms! whoſe Deeds are known to Fame,
And you whoſe Ardour hopes an equal Name!
Since not alike endu'd with Force or Art,
Behold a Day when each may act his Part!   320

P p p   **A Day**

A Day to fire the brave, and warm the cold,
To gain new Glories, or augment the old.
Urge thofe who ftand, and thofe who faint excite;
Drown *Hector's* Vaunts in loud Exhorts of Fight;
325 Conqueft, not Safety, fill the Thoughts of all;
Seek not your Fleet, but fally from the Wall;
So *Jove* once more may drive their routed Train,
And *Troy* lie trembling in her Walls again.

Their Ardour kindles all the *Grecian* Pow'rs;
330 And now the Stones defcend in heavier Show'rs.
As when high *Jove* his fharp Artill'ry forms,
And opes his cloudy Magazine of Storms;
In Winter's bleak, uncomfortable Reign,
A Snowy Inundation hides the Plain;
335 He ftills the Winds, and bids the Skies to fleep;
Then pours the filent Tempeft, thick, and deep:
And firft the Mountain Tops are cover'd o'er,
Then the green Fields, and then the fandy Shore;
Bent with the Weight the nodding Woods are feen,
340 And one bright Wafte hides all the Works of Men:
The circling Seas alone abforbing all,
Drink the diffolving Fleeces as they fall.

So

So from each fide increas'd the ftony Rain,
And the white Ruin rifes o'er the Plain.

   Thus God-like *Hector* and his Troops contend   345
To force the Ramparts, and the Gates to rend;
Nor *Troy* could conquer, nor the *Greeks* would yield,
Till great *Sarpedon* tow'r'd amid the Field;
For mighty *Jove* infpir'd with martial Flame
His matchlefs Son, and urg'd him on to Fame.   350
In Arms he fhines, confpicuous from afar,
And bears aloft his ample Shield in Air;
Within whofe Orb the thick Bull-Hides were roll'd,
Pond'rous with Brafs, and bound with ductile Gold:
And while two pointed Javelins arm his Hands,   355
Majeftick moves along, and leads his *Lycian* Bands.

   So prefs'd with Hunger, from the Mountain's Brow
Defcends a Lion on the Flocks below;
So ftalks the lordly Savage o'er the Plain,
In fullen Majefty, and ftern Difdain: 360
In vain loud Maftives bay him from from afar,
And Shepherds gaul him with an Iron War;
Regardlefs, furious, he purfues his way;
He foams, he roars, he rends the panting Prey.

                              Refolv'd

365 Refolv'd alike, divine *Sarpedon* glows
With gen'rous Rage that drives him on the Foes.
He views the Tow'rs, and meditates their Fall,
To fure Deftruction dooms th' afpiring Wall;
Then cafting on his Friend an ardent Look,
370 Fir'd with the Thirft of Glory, thus he fpoke.
    Why boaft we, *Glaucus!* our extended Reign,
Where *Xanthus*' Streams enrich the *Lycian* Plain,
Our num'rous Herds that range the fruitful Field,
And Hills where Vines their purple Harveft yield,
375 Our foaming Bowls with purer Nectar crown'd,
Our Feafts enhanc'd with Mufic's fprightly Sound?
Why on thofe Shores are we with Joy furvey'd,
Admir'd as Heroes, and as Gods obey'd?
Unlefs great Acts fuperior Merit prove,
380 And vindicate the bount'ous Pow'rs above.
    'Tis ours, the Dignity they give, to grace;
The firft in Valour, as the firft in Place.
That when with wond'ring Eyes our martial Bands
Behold our Deeds tranfcending our Commands,
385 Such, they may cry, deferve the fov'reign State,
Whom thofe that envy, dare not imitate!

Could

Could all our Care elude the gloomy Grave,
Which claims no lefs the fearful than the brave,
For Luft of Fame I fhould not vainly dare
In fighting Fields, nor urge thy Soul to War.   390
But fince, alas! ignoble Age muft come,
Difeafe, and Death's inexorable Doom;
The Life which others pay, let us beftow,
And give to Fame what we to Nature owe;
Brave tho' we fall, and honour'd if we live,   395
Or let us Glory gain, or Glory give!

   He faid; his Words the lift'ning Chief infpire
With equal Warmth, and rouze the Warrior's Fire;
The Troops purfue their Leaders with Delight,
Rufh to the Foe, and claim the promis'd Fight.   400

Sarpedon's *Speech to* Glaucus *in the* 12th *of* Homer.

Thus to *Glaucus* spake

Divine *Sarpedon*, since he did not find
Others as great in Place, as great in Mind.
Above the rest, why is our Pomp, our Power?
Our flocks, our herds, and our possessions more?
Why all the Tributes Land and Sea affords
Heap'd in great Chargers, load our sumptuous
    boards?
Our chearful Guests carowse the sparkling tears
Of the rich Grape, whilst Musick charms their
    ears.
Why as we pass, do those on *Xanthus* shore,
As Gods behold us, and as Gods adore?
But that as well in danger, as degree,
We stand the first; that when our *Lycians* see
                                    Our

Our brave examples, they admiring say,

Behold our Gallant Leaders! These are They

Deserve the Greatness; and un-envied stand :

Since what they act, transcends what they command.

Could the declining of this Fate (oh friend)

Our Date to Immortality extend ?

Or if Death sought not them, who seek not
  Death,

Would I advance? Or should my vainer breath

With such a Glorious Folly thee inspire ?

But since with Fortune Nature doth conspire,

Since Age, Disease, or some less noble End,

Though not less certain, doth our days attend;

Since 'tis decreed, and to this period lead,

A thousand ways the noblest path we'll tread ;

And bravely on, till they, or we, or all,

A common Sacrifice to honour fall.

Martial.

Book XIV

War yields to love as Juno prepares to distract Jove, who has proved too partial to the Trojans for her liking, from the affairs of men. Her love, like Belinda's, is also a form of warfare.

She fees her *Jove*, and trembles at the Sight.

Jove to deceive, what Methods fhall fhe try,   185

What Arts, to blind his all-beholding Eye?

D d   At

At length she trusts her Pow'r; resolv'd to prove
' The old, yet still succefsful, Cheat of Love;
Against his Wisdom to oppose her Charms,
190 And lull the Lord of Thunders in her Arms.
   Swift to her bright Apartment she repairs,
Sacred to Drefs, and Beauty's pleasing Cares:
With Skill divine had *Vulcan* form'd the Bow'r,
Safe from Accefs of each intruding Pow'r.
195 Touch'd with her secret Key, the Doors unfold;
Self-clos'd behind her shut the Valves of Gold.
Here first she bathes; and round her Body pours
Soft Oils of Fragrance, and ambrosial Show'rs:
The Winds perfum'd, the balmy Gale convey
200 Thro' Heav'n, thro' Earth, and all th'aerial Way;
Spirit divine! whose Exhalation greets
The Sense of Gods with more than mortal Sweets.
203 Thus while she breath'd of Heav'n, with decent Pride
Her artful Hands the radiant Treffes ty'd;
2 5 Part on her Head in shining Ringlets roll'd,
Part o'er her Shoulders wav'd like melted Gold.
Around her next a heav'nly Mantle flow'd,
That rich with *Pallas*' labour'd Colours glow'd;

                                           Large

203 See page 72.

Large Clafps of Gold the Foldings gather'd round,
A golden Zone her fwelling Bofom bound.   210
Far-beaming Pendants tremble in her Ear,
Each Gemm illumin'd with a triple Star.
Then o'er her Head fhe cafts a Veil more white
Than new fal'n Snow, and dazling as the Light.
Laft her fair Feet celeftial Sandals grace.   215
Thus iffuing radiant, with majeftic Pace,   216
Forth from the Dome th'Imperial Goddefs moves,
And calls the Mother of the *Smiles* and *Loves.*

How long (to *Venus* thus apart fhe cry'd)
Shall human Strifes celeftial Minds divide?   220
Ah yet, will *Venus* aid *Saturnia's* Joy,
And fet afide the Caufe of *Greece* and *Troy?*

Let Heav'n's dread Emprefs *(Cytheræa* faid)
Speak her Requeft, and deem her Will obey'd.
Then grant me (faid the Queen) thofe conqu'ring 225
   Charms,
That Pow'r, which Mortals and Immortals warms,
That Love, which melts Mankind in fierce Defires,
And burns the Sons of Heav'n with facred Fires!

For

---

210 See page 72.
216 See page 72.

69

For lo! I hafte to thofe remote Abodes,
230 Where the great Parents (facred Source of Gods!)
Ocean and *Tethys* their old Empire keep,
On the laft Limits of the Land and Deep.
In their kind Arms my tender Years were paft;
What-time old *Saturn*, from *Olympus* caft,
235 Of upper Heav'n to *Jove* refign'd the Reign,
Whelm'd under the huge Mafs of Earth and Main.
For Strife, I hear, has made the Union ceafe,
Which held fo long that ancient Pair in Peace.
What Honour, and what Love fhall I obtain,
240 If I compofe thofe fatal Feuds again?
Once more their Minds in mutual Ties engage,
And what my Youth has ow'd, repay their Age.
 She faid. With Awe divine the Queen of Love
Obey'd the Sifter and the Wife of *Jove*:
245 And from her fragrant Breaft the Zone unbrac'd,
With various Skill and high Embroid'ry grac'd.
In this was ev'ry Art, and ev'ry Charm,
To win the wifeft, and the coldeft warm:
Fond Love, the gentle Vow, the gay Defire,
250 The kind Deceit, the ftill-reviving Fire,

Perfuafive

Perſuaſive Speech, and more perſuaſive Sighs,
Silence that ſpoke, and Eloquence of Eyes.
This on her Hand the *Cyprian* Goddeſs lay'd ;
Take this, and with it all thy Wiſh, ſhe ſaid:
With Smiles ſhe took the Charm ; and ſmiling preſt 255
The pow'rful *Ceſtus* to her ſnowy Breaſt.   256

---

256 See page 72.

203. We have here a compleat Picture from Head to Foot of the Dress of the Fair Sex, and of the Mode between two and three thousand Years ago. May I have leave to observe the great Simplicity of *Juno's* Dress, in Comparison with the innumerable Equipage of a modern Toilette? The Goddess, even when she is setting herself out on the greatest Occasion, has only her own Locks to tie, a white Veil to cast over them, a Mantle to dress her whole Body, her Pendants, and her Sandals. This the Poet expresly says was *all her Dress*, and one may reasonably conclude it was all that was used by the greatest Princesses and finest Beauties of those Times. The good *Eustathius* is ravish'd to find, that here are no Washes for the Face, no Dies for the Hair, and none of those artificial Embellishments since in Practice; he also rejoices not a little, that *Juno* has no Looking-Glass, Tire-Woman, or waiting Maid. One may preach till Doomsday on this Subject, but all the Commentators in the World will never prevail upon a Lady to stick one Pin the less in her Gown, except she can be convinced, that the ancient Dress will better set off her Person.

As the *Asiaticks* always surpass'd the *Grecians* in whatever regarded Magnificence and Luxury, so we find their Women far gone in the contrary Extreme of Dress. There is a Passage in *Isaiah*, Ch. 3. [18-23] that gives us a Particular of their Wardrobe, with the Number and Uselessness of their Ornaments; and which I think appears very well in Contrast to this of *Homer*. *The Bravery of their tinkling Ornaments about their Feet, and their Cauls, and their round Tires like the Moon: The Chains, and the Bracelets, and the Mufflers, the Bonnets, and the Ornaments of the Legs, and the Headbands, and the Tablets, and the Ear-rings, the Rings and Nose-jewels, the changeable Suits of Apparel, and the Mantles, and the Wimples, and the Crisping-Pins, the Glasses, and the fine Linen, and the Hoods, and the Veils.*

I could be glad to ask the Ladies, which they should like best to imitate, the *Greeks*, or the *Asiaticks*? I would desire those that are handsome and well-made, to consider, that the Dress of *Juno* (which is the same they see in *Statues*) has manifestly the Advantage of the present, in displaying whatever is beautiful: That the Charms of the *Neck* and *Breast* are not less laid open, than by the modern Stays; and that those of the *Leg* are more gracefully discover'd, than even by the Hoop-petticoat: That the fine Turn of the *Arms* is better observ'd: and that several natural Graces of the *Shape* and *Body* appear much more conspicuous. It is not to be deny'd but the *Asiatic* and our present Modes were better contriv'd to conceal some People's *Defects*, but I don't speak to such People: I speak only to Ladies of that Beauty, who can make any Fashion prevail by their being seen in it; and who put others of their Sex under the wretched Necessity of being like them in their Habits, or not being like them at all. As for the rest, let 'em follow the Mode of *Judæa*, and be content with the Name of *Asiaticks*. [Pope's note.]

210. Zone: normally a poetic word for a belt or sash, here one that covers and contains the breasts.

216. Thus the Goddess comes from her Apartment against her Spouse in compleat Armour. The Pleasures of Women mostly prevail by pure cunning, and the artful Management of their Persons; For there is but one way for the weak to subdue the mighty, and that is by Pleasure. The Poet shews at the same time, that Men of Understanding are not master'd, without a great deal of Artifice and Address. There are but three ways, whereby to overcome another, by Violence, by Persuasion, or by Craft: *Jupiter* was invincible by main Force; to think of persuading was as fruitless, after he had pass'd his Nod to *Achilles*; therefore *Juno* was obliged of necessity to turn her Thoughts entirely upon Craft; and by the Force of Pleasure it is, that she insnares and manages the God. *Eustathius.* [Pope's note.]

256. Cestus: the magical girdle just described.

Book XIX

Having finally decided to return to the war, Achilles arms
himself. Belinda does likewise for her contest at Hampton Court.

Full in the midſt, high tow'ring o'er the reſt, 390
His Limbs in Arms divine *Achilles* dreſt;
Arms which the Father of the Fire beſtow'd,
Forg'd on th'Eternal Anvils of the God.
Grief and Revenge his furious Heart inſpire,
His glowing Eye-balls roll with living Fire, 395
He grinds his Teeth, and furious with Delay
O'erlooks th'embattled Hoſt, and hopes the bloody Day.
The ſilver Cuiſhes firſt his Thighs infold;
Then o'er his Breaſt was brac'd the hollow Gold:
The brazen Sword a various Baldrick ty'd, 400
That, ſtarr'd with Gems, hung glitt'ring at his ſide;
And like the Moon, the broad refulgent Shield
Blaz'd with long Rays, and gleam'd athwart the Field.
So to Night-wand'ring Sailors, pale with Fears,
Wide o'er the wat'ry Waſte, a Light appears, 405
Which on the far-ſeen Mountain blazing high,
Streams from ſome lonely Watch-tow'r to the Sky:

Y y   With

73

With mournful Eyes they gaze, and gaze again;
Loud howls the Storm, and drives them o'er the Main.
412   Next, his high Head the Helmet grac'd ; behind
The fweepy Creft hung floating in the Wind :
Like the red Star, that from his flaming Hair
Shakes down Difeafes, Peftilence and War:
414 So ftream'd the golden Honours from his Head,
415 Trembled the fparklingPlumes,and the loofeGlories fhed
  The Chief beholds himfelf with wond'ring eyes;
His Arms he poifes, and his Motions tries;
Buoy'd by fome inward Force, he feems to fwim,
And feels a Pinion lifting ev'ry Limb.
420 And now he fhakes his great paternal Spear,
Pond'rous and huge! which not a *Greek* could rear.
From *Pelion's* cloudy Top an Afh entire
Old *Chiron* fell'd, and fhap'd it for his Sire ;
A Spear which ftern *Achilles* only wields,
425 The Death of Heroes, and the Dread of Fields.
Automedon and *Alcimus* prepare
427 Th'immortal Courfers, and the radiant Car,
(The filver Traces fweeping at their fide)
Their fiery Mouths refplendent Bridles ty'd,
                        The

---

414. Honours: epic vocabulary for "hair."
427. Car: chariot.

The Iv'ry ſtudded Reins, return'd behind,   430
Wav'd o'er their Backs, and to the Chariot join'd.
The Charioteer then whirl'd the Laſh around,
And ſwift aſcended at one active Bound.
All bright in heav'nly Arms, above his Squire
Achilles mounts, and ſets the Field on Fire;   435
Not brighter, *Phœbus* in th'Æthereal Way,
Flames from his Chariot, and reſtores the Day.
High o'er the Hoſt, all terrible he ſtands,
And thunders to his Steeds theſe dread Commands.

BOOK XX

With Achilles' return to the battle the odds are too heavily weighted against the Trojans, so Jove allows the gods to fight actively again. Their confrontation was singled out by Longinus as a preeminent example of the sublime (above, p. 24): Pope quotes extensively from Longinus in his notes to this passage and refers to it specifically in canto 5.

'Tis true (the Cloud-compelling Pow'r replies)
30 This Day, we call the Council of the Skies
In Care of human Race; ev'n *Jove*'s own Eye
Sees with Regret unhappy Mortals die.
Far on *Olympus'* Top in secret State
Ourself will sit, and see the Hand of Fate

Work

Work out our Will. Celeſtial Pow'rs! deſcend, 35
And as your Minds direct, your Succour lend
To either Hoſt. *Troy* ſoon muſt lye o'erthrown,
If uncontroll'd *Achilles* fights alone:
Their Troops but lately durſt not meet his Eyes;
What can they now, if in his Rage he riſe? 40
Aſſiſt them Gods! or *Ilion*'s ſacred Wall 41
May fall this Day, tho' Fate forbids the Fall.

He ſaid, and fir'd their heav'nly Breaſts with Rage:
On adverſe Parts the warring Gods engage. 44
Heav'ns awful Queen; and He whoſe azure Round 45
Girds the vaſt Globe; the Maid in Arms renown'd;
Hermes, of profitable Arts the Sire,
And *Vulcan*, the black Sov'reign of the Fire:
Theſe to the Fleet repair with inſtant Flight,
The Veſſels tremble as the Gods alight. 50
In aid of *Troy*, *Latona*, *Phœbus* came,
Mars fiery-helm'd, the Laughter-loving Dame,
Xanthus whoſe Streams in golden Currents flow,
And the chaſt Huntreſs of the ſilver Bow.
E'er yet the Gods their various Aid employ, 55
Each *Argive* Boſom ſwell'd with manly Joy,

E e e   While

---

41. Ilion: Troy.
44. warring Gods: Precise identification of each deity in the following passage isn't essential.

While great *Achilles*, (Terror of the Plain)
Long loft to Battel, fhone in Arms again.
Dreadful he ftood in Front of all his Hoft;
60 Pale *Troy* beheld, and feem'd already loft;
Her braveft Heroes pant with inward Fear,
And trembling fee another God of War.

But when the Pow'rs defcending fwell'd the Fight,
Then Tumult rofe; fierce Rage and pale Affright
65 Vary'd each Face; then Difcord founds Alarms,
Earth echoes, and the Nations rufh to Arms.
Now thro' the trembling Shores *Minerva* calls.
And now fhe thunders from the *Grecian* Walls.
Mars hov'ring o'er his *Troy*, his Terror fhrouds
70 In gloomy Tempefts, and a Night of Clouds:
Now thro' each *Trojan* Heart he Fury pours
With Voice divine from *Ilion*'s topmoft Towr's,
Now fhouts to *Simois*, from her beauteous * Hill;
The Mountain fhook, the rapid Stream ftood ftill.
75 Above, the Sire of Gods his Thunder rolls,
And Peals on Peals redoubled rend the Poles.
Beneath, ftern *Neptune* fhakes the folid Ground,
The Forefts wave, the Mountains nod around;

ſ   Thro'

Thro' all their Summits tremble *Ida's* Woods,
And from their Sources boil her hundred Floods. 80
Troy's Turrets totter on the rocking Plain;
And the tofs'd Navies beat the heaving Main.
Deep in the difmal Regions of the Dead,
Th'infernal Monarch rear'd his horrid Head,
Leap'd from his Throne, left *Neptunes* Arm fhould lay 85
His dark Dominions open to the Day,
And pour in Light on *Pluto's* drear Abodes,
Abhorr'd by Men, and dreadful ev'n to Gods.

Such War th'Immortals wage: Such Horrors rend
The World's vaft Concave, when the Gods contend. 90
Firft filver-fhafted *Phœbus* took the Plain
Againft blue *Neptune,* Monarch of the Main:
The God of Arms his Giant Bulk difplay'd,
Oppos'd to *Pallas,* War's triumphant Maid.
Againft *Latona* march'd the Son of *May;*   95
The quiver'd *Dian,* Sifter of the Day,
(Her golden Arrows founding at her fide)
Saturnia, Majefty of Heav'n, defy'd.
With fiery *Vulcan* laft in Battle ftands
The facred Flood that rolls on golden Sands;   100

Xanthus

Xanthus his Name with thofe of heavenly Birth,
But call'd *Scamander* by the Sons of Earth.
  While thus the Gods in various League engage,
Achilles glow'd with more than mortal Rage:

Neptune chides Aeneas for trying to meet Achilles in single combat.
The same fate awaits coquettes and heroes: dust.

  What Pow'r, O Prince, with Force inferior far,
Urg'd thee to meet *Achilles'* Arm in War?
Henceforth beware, nor antedate thy Doom,
Defrauding Fate of all thy Fame to come.

  But when the **Day** decreed (for come it muft)   185
Shall lay this dreadful **Hero** in the **Duft**,
Let then the **Furies** of that **Arm** be known,
Secure, no **Grecian** Force tranfcends thy own.

BOOK XXIII

Part of the funeral celebration that Achilles arranges for Patroclus consists of athletic events — chariot racing, foot racing, javelin throwing, etc. — with valuable prizes for the winners. Boxing and wrestling occupy the selection presented here. Such games became a convention of the epic; by the time the convention reaches Belinda's card table, the sweat, strain, and dust have disappeared, and the contestants have dwindled to playing cards.

The Prizes next are order'd to the Field

For the bold Champions who the *Cæstus* wield. 753

A ſtately Mule, as yet by Toils unbroke,

Of ſix years Age, unconſcious of the Yoke, 755

Is

---

753. Cæstus: the ancient equivalent of the boxing glove, but much more an offensive weapon. It consisted of strips of leather, usually (as here — see line 793) reinforced with iron.

81

756 Is to the *Circus* led, and firmly bound;
   Next ftands a Goblet, maffy, large and round.
   Achilles rifing, thus: Let *Greece* excite
   Two Heroes equal to this hardy Fight;
760 Who dares his Foe with lifted Arms provoke,
   And rufh beneath the long-defcending Stroke?
   On whom *Apollo* fhall the Palm beftow,
   And whom the *Greeks* fupreme by Conqueft know,
   This Mule his dauntlefs Labours fhall repay;
765 The Vanquifh'd bear the maffy Bowl away.

   This dreadful Combate great *Epæus* chofe,
   High o'er the Crowd, enormous Bulk! he rofe,
   And feiz'd the Beaft, and thus began to fay:
   Stand forth fome Man, to bear the Bowl away!
770 (Price of his Ruin:) For who dares deny
   This Mule my right? th'undoubted Victor I.
   Others 'tis own'd, in Fields of Battle fhine,
   But the firft Honours of this Fight are mine;
   For who excells in all? Then let my Foe
775 Draw near, but firft his certain Fortune know,
   Secure, this Hand fhall his whole Frame confound,
   Mafh all his Bones, and all his Body pound:

                                    6
                                        So
───────────
756. Circus: the boxing ring.

So let his Friends be nigh, a needful Train
To heave the batter'd Carcase off the Plain.
   The Giant spoke; and in a stupid Gaze   780
The Host beheld him, silent with Amaze!
'Twas thou, *Euryalus!* who durst aspire
To meet his Might, and emulate thy Sire,
The great *Mecistheus*; who in Days of yore
In *Theban* Games the noblest Trophy bore,   785
(The Games ordain'd dead *Oedipus* to grace)
And singly vanquish'd the *Cadmæan* Race.
Him great *Tydides* urges to contend,
Warm with the Hopes of Conquest for his Friend,
Officious with the Cincture girds him round;   790
And to his Wrists the Gloves of Death are bound.
Amid the Circle now each Champion stands,
And poises high in Air his Iron Hands;
With clashing Gantlets now they fiercely close,
Their crackling Jaws re-echoe to the Blows,   795
And painful Sweat from all their Members flows.
At length *Epæus* dealt a weighty Blow
Full on the Cheek of his unwary Foe;

C c   Beneath

Beneath that pond'rous Arm's refiftlefs Sway
800 Down dropt he, nervelefs, and extended lay.
As a large Fifh, when Winds and Waters roar,
By fome huge Billow dafh'd againft the Shore,
Lies panting: Not lefs batter'd with his Wound,
The bleeding Hero pants upon the Ground.
805 To rear his fallen Foe, the Victor lends
Scornful, his Hand; and gives him to his Friends;
Whofe Arms fupport him, reeling thro' the Throng,
And dragging his difabled Legs along;
Nodding, his Head hangs down his Shoulder o'er;
810 His Mouth and Noftrils pour the clotted Gore;
Wrapt round in Mifts he lies, and loft to Thought:
His Friends receive the Bowl, too dearly bought.
The third bold Game *Achilles* next demands,
And calls the Wreftlers to the level Sands:
815 A maffy Tripod for the Victor lies,
Of twice fix Oxen its reputed Price;
And next, the Lofers Spirits to reftore,
818 A female Captive, valu'd but at four.
Scarce did the Chief the vig'rous Strife propofe,
820 When tow'r-like *Ajax* and *Ulyffes* rofe.

Amid

---

818. four: i.e., four oxen. At least from the time of Mme. Dacier, Pope's contemporary, feminists have objected.

Amid the Ring each nervous Rival ſtands,

Embracing rigid with implicit Hands: 822

Cloſe lock'd above, their Heads and Arms are mixt;

Below, their planted Feet at diſtance fixt:

Like two ſtrong Rafters which the Builder forms   825

Proof to the wintry Winds and howling Storms,

Their Tops connected, but at wider ſpace

Fixt on the Center ſtands their ſolid Baſe.

Now to the Graſp each manly Body bends;

The humid Sweat from ev'ry Pore deſcends;   830

Their Bones reſound with Blows: Sides, Shoulders, Thighs

Swell to each Gripe, and bloody Tumours riſe.   832

Nor could *Ulyſſes*, for his Art renown'd,

O'erturn the Strength of *Ajax* on the Ground;

Nor could the Strength of *Ajax* overthrow   835

The watchful Caution of his artful Foe.

While the long Strife ev'n tir'd the Lookers-on,

Thus to *Ulyſſes* ſpoke great *Telamon.*

Or let me lift thee, Chief, or lift thou me:

Prove we our Force, and *Jove* the reſt decree.   840

He ſaid; and ſtraining, heav'd him off the Ground

With matchleſs Strength; that time *Ulyſſes* found

                                                                    The

---

822. implicit: tightly folded, clenched.
832. Gripe: grip.

The Strength t'evade, and where the Nerves combine,

His Ankle ſtrook: The Giant fell ſupine:

845 *Ulyſſes* following, on his Boſom lies;

Shouts of Applauſe run rattling thro the Skies.

Ajax to lift, *Ulyſſes* next eſſays,

He barely ſtirr'd him, but he could not raiſe:

His Knee lock'd faſt the Foe's Attempt deny'd;

850 And grappling cloſe, they tumble ſide by ſide.

Defil'd with honourable Duſt, they roll,

Still breathing Strife, and unſubdu'd of Soul:

Again they rage, again to Combat riſe;

When great *Achilles* thus divides the Prize.

855 Your noble Vigour, oh my Friends reſtrain;

Nor weary out your gen'rous Strength in vain.

Ye both have won: Let others who excell

Now prove that Prowefs you have prov'd ſo well.

  The Hero's Words the willing Chiefs obey, ⎫
860 From their tir'd Bodies wipe the Duſt away, ⎬
  And, cloth'd anew, the following Games ſurvey. ⎭

The Aeneid

For Virgil's *Aeneid*, Pope found a worthy English version ready
to hand; Dryden's translation of 1697 had achieved almost universal
acclaim by 1714, and allusions to Virgil were thus within the reach of
readers (especially women) who had no Latin. *The Rape of the Lock*
owes another, less direct, debt to Dryden's version as well, since
Pope's *Iliad* depends heavily on Dryden's example as an epic
translator. The main ethical focus of the *Aeneid*, politics and empire
building, was less relevant to Pope's needs than the more individ-
ualistic heroism of the *Iliad*, and his use of Virgil's poem, though
extensive, is more incidental and fragmentary. The major exception
to this generalization is the love story of Aeneas and Dido, which
provides an example of heroic and tragic love against which to set
Belinda's teasing and coquetry. However one judges Dido morally —
sympathies were divided in Pope's day — she at least committed
herself wholeheartedly to another person. One might also point out
the amorous causes of Juno's hatred of Troy and Aeneas: Jove's many
infidelities and Paris' choice of Venus over herself in a beauty contest
(1:36-43 and note).

Virgil's Æneis.

The First Book of the Æneis.

The Argument.

The Trojans, *after a seven Years Voyage, set sail for* Italy, *but are overtaken by a dreadful Storm, which Æolus raises at* Juno's *Request. The Tempest sinks one, and scatters the rest :* Neptune *drives off the Winds and calms the Sea. Æneas with his own Ship, and six more, arrives safe at an* Affrican *Port.* Venus *complains to* Jupiter *of her Son's Misfortunes.* Jupiter *comforts her, and sends* Mercury *to procure him a kind Reception among the* Carthaginians. *Æneas going out to discover the Country, meets his Mother in the Shape of an Huntreß, who conveys him in a Cloud to* Carthage; *where he sees his Friends whom he thought lost, and receives a kind Entertainment from the Queen.* Dido *by a device of* Venus *begins to have a Paßion for him, and after some Discourse with him, desires the History of his Adventures since the Siege of* Troy, *which is the Subject of the two following Books.*

Rms, and the Man I sing, who, forc'd by Fate,
And haughty *Juno's* unrelenting Hate ;
Expell'd and exil'd, left the *Trojan* Shoar:
Long Labours, both by Sea and Land he bore;
5 And in the doubtful War, before he won
6 The *Latian* Realm, and built the destin'd Town :
His banish'd Gods restor'd to Rites Divine,
And setl'd sure Succeßion in his Line :
From whence the Race of *Alban* Fathers come,
10 And the long Glories of Majestick *Rome.*
O Muse! the Causes and the Crimes relate,
What Goddeß was provok'd, and whence her hate :

6. Latian: Italian.

A a   For

89

For what Offence the Queen of Heav'n began
To perfecute fo brave, fo juft a Man!
15 Involv'd his anxious Life in endlefs Cares,
Expos'd to Wants, and hurry'd into Wars!
Can Heav'nly Minds fuch high refentment fhow;
Or exercife their Spight in Human Woe?
    Againft the *Tiber*'s Mouth, but far away,
20 An ancient Town was feated on the Sea:
A *Tyrian* Colony; the People made
Stout for the War, and ftudious of their Trade.
Carthage the Name, belov'd by *Juno* more
Than her own *Argos*, or the *Samian* Shoar.
25 Here ftood her Chariot, here, if Heav'n were kind,
The Seat of awful Empire fhe defign'd.
Yet fhe had heard an ancient Rumour fly,
(Long cited by the People of the Sky;)
That times to come fhou'd fee the *Trojan* Race
30 Her *Carthage* ruin, and her Tow'rs deface:
Nor thus confin'd, the Yoke of Sov'raign Sway,
Should on the Necks of all the Nations lay.
She ponder'd this, and fear'd it was in Fate;
Nor cou'd forget the War fhe wag'd of late,.
35 For conq'ring *Greece* againft the *Trojan* State.
Befides long Caufes working in her Mind,
And fecret Seeds of Envy lay behind.
Deep graven in her Heart, the Doom. remain'd
39 Of partial *Paris*, and her Form difdain'd:
40 The Grace beftow'd on ravifh'd *Ganimed,*
41 *Electra*'s Glories, and her injur'd Bed.
Each was a Caufe alone, and all combin'd
To kindle Vengeance in her haughty Mind.
For this, far diftant from the *Latian* Coaft,
45 She drove the Remnants of the *Trojan* Hoaft:

         And

And fev'n long Years th' unhappy wand'ring Train,
Were tofs'd by Storms, and fcatter'd through the Main.
Such Time, fuch Toil requir'd the *Roman* Name,
Such length of Labour for fo vaft a Frame.

---

39. partial Paris: When Eris (Strife) once threw down an apple inscribed "for the
fairest," Paris, as the handsomest of mortal men, was assigned to adjudicate the claims
of Venus, Juno, and Minerva, who tried to bribe him respectively with the world's
loveliest woman, greatness, and military success. Paris chose Venus, thereby earning
the lasting enmity of Juno as well as the hand of Helen of Troy. This "Judgement of
Paris" is thus another cause of the Trojan War.
41. Electra's Glories: The kings of Troy were descended from the union of Jove with
Electra (not to be confused with the daughter of Agamemnon), which gave Juno
another reason for hating the Trojans.

Book IV

After a shipwreck Aeneas arrives at Carthage, whose queen, Dido, soon falls in love with him despite her vow to remain a widow after the death of her first husband, Sichaeus. Belinda also experiences "anxious Cares" at the beginning of her fourth book.

The Fourth Book of the Æneis.

The Argument.

Dido *difcovers to her Sifter her Paffion for* Æneas, *and her thoughts of marrying him. She prepares a Hunting-Match for his Entertainment.* Juno *by* Venus's *confent raifes a Storm, which feparates the Hunters, and drives* Æneas *and* Dido *into the fame Cave, where their Marriage is fuppos'd to be compleated.* Jupiter *difpatches* Mercury *to* Æneas, *to warn him from* Carthage; Æneas *fecretly prepares for his Voyage:* Dido *finds out his Defign, and to put a ftop to it, makes ufe of her own, and her Sifter's Entreaties, and difcovers all the variety of Paffions that are incident to a neglected Lover: When nothing wou'd prevail upon him, fhe contrives her own Death, with which this Book concludes.*

BUT anxious Cares already feiz'd the Queen:
   She fed within her Veins a Flame unfeen:
The Heroe's Valour, Acts, and Birth infpire
Her Soul with Love, and fann the fecret Fire.
5 His Words, his Looks imprinted in her Heart,
Improve the Paffion, and increafe the Smart.
Now, when the Purple Morn had chas'd away
The dewy Shadows, and reftor'd the Day;
Her Sifter firft, with early Care fhe fought,
10 And thus in mournful Accents eas'd her Thought.
My deareft *Anna*, what new Dreams affright
My lab'ring Soul; what Vifions of the Night
Difturb my Quiet, and diftract my Breaft,
With ftrange Ideas of our *Trojan* Gueft?
15 His Worth, his Actions, and Majeftick Air,
A Man defcended from the Gods declare:
Fear never harbours in a Noble Mind,
But Modefty, with juft Affurance join'd.

Then

Then, what he suffer'd, when by Fate betray'd,
20 What brave Attempts for falling *Troy* he made!
Such were his Looks, so gracefully he spoke,
That were I not resolv'd against the Yoke
Of hapless Marriage; never to be curs'd
With second Love, so fatal was my first;
25 To this one Error I might yield again:
For since *Sichæus* was untimely slain,
This onely Man, is able to subvert
The fix'd Foundations of my stubborn Heart.
And to confess my Frailty, to my shame,
30 Somewhat I find within, if not the same,
Too like the Sparkles of my former Flame.
    But first let yawning Earth a Passage rend;
And let me through the dark Abyss descend;
First let avenging *Jove*, with Flames from high,
35 Drive down this Body, to the neather Sky,
Condemn'd with Ghosts in endless Night to lye;
Before I break the plighted Faith I gave;
No; he who had my Vows, shall ever have;
For whom I lov'd on Earth, I worship in the Grave.
40 She said; the Tears ran gushing from her Eyes,
And stop'd her Speech: her Sister thus replies.
O dearer than the vital Air I breath,
Will you to Grief, our blooming Years bequeath?
Condem'd to wast in Woes, your lonely Life,
45 Without the Joys of Mother, or of Wife.
Think you these Tears, this pompous Train of Woe,
Are known, or valu'd by the Ghosts below?
I grant, that while your Sorrows yet were green,
It well became a Woman, and a Queen,
50 The Vows of *Tyrian* Princes to neglect,
To scorn *Hyarbas*, and his Love reject;

With all the *Lybian* Lords of mighty Name,
But will you fight againſt a pleaſing Flame!
This little Spot of Land, which Heav'n beſtows,
55 On ev'ry ſide is hemm'd with warlike Foes:
Getulian Cities here are ſpread around;
And fierce *Numidians* there your Frontiers bound;
Here lies a barren Waſt of thirſty Land,
And there the *Syrtes* raiſe the moving Sand:
60 *Barcæan* Troops beſiege the narrow Shore;
And from the Sea *Pigmalion* threatens more.
Propitious Heav'n, and gracious *Juno,* lead
This wand'ring Navy to your needful Aid:
How will your Empire ſpread, your City riſe
65 From ſuch an Union, and with ſuch Allies!
Implore the Favour of the Pow'rs above;
And leave the Conduct of the reſt to Love.
Continue ſtill your hoſpitable way,
And ſtill invent occaſions of their Stay;
70 'Till Storms, and winter Winds, ſhall ceaſe to threat,
And Plancks and Oars, repair their ſhatter'd Fleet.

    Theſe Words, which from a Friend, and Siſter came,
With Eaſe reſolv'd the Scruples of her Fame;   }
And added Fury to the kindled Flame.

75 Inſpir'd with Hope, the Project they purſue;
On ev'ry Altar Sacrifice renew;
A choſen Ewe of two Years old they pay
To *Ceres, Bacchus,* and the God of Day:
Preferring *Juno's* Pow'r: For *Juno* ties
80 The Nuptial Knot, and makes the Marriage Joys.
The beauteous Queen before her Altar ſtands,
And holds the Golden Goblet in her Hands:
A milk-white Heifar ſhe with Flow'rs adorns,
And pours the ruddy Wine betwixt her Horns;

                                           And

85 And while the Priefts with Pray'r the Gods invoke,
    She feeds their Altars with *Sabæan* Smoke.
    With hourly Care the Sacrifice renews,
    And anxioufly the panting Entrails Views.
    What Prieftly Rites, alas! what Pious Art,
90 What Vows avail to cure a bleeding Heart!
    A gentle Fire fhe feeds within her Veins;
    Where the foft God fecure in filence reigns.
        Sick with defire, and feeking him fhe loves,
    From Street to Street, the raving *Dido* roves.
95 So when the watchful Shepherd, from the Blind,
    Wounds with a random Shaft the carelefs Hind;
    Diftracted with her pain fhe flies the Woods,
    Bounds o're the Lawn, and feeks the filent Floods;
    With fruitlefs Care; for ftill the fatal Dart
100 Sticks in her fide; and ranckles in her Heart.
    And now fhe leads the *Trojan* Chief, along
    The lofty Walls, amidft the buifie Throng;
    Difplays her *Tyrian* Wealth, and rifing Town,
    Which Love, without his Labour, makes his own.
105 This Pomp fhe fhows to tempt her wond'ring Gueft;
    Her falt'ring Tongue forbids to fpeak the reft.
    When Day declines, and Feafts renew the Night,
    Still on his Face fhe feeds her famifh'd fight;
    She longs again to hear the Prince relate
110 His own Adventures, and the *Trojan* Fate:
    He tells it o're and o're; but ftill in vain;
    For ftill fhe begs to hear it, once again.

During a splendid hunting party arranged by Dido, Juno causes a violent thunderstorm. Dido and Aeneas take shelter in a cave, where her ill-fated love is consummated.

The rofy Morn was rifen from the Main,
And Horns and Hounds awake the Princely Train:
They iffue early through the City Gate,
¹⁸⁵ Where the more wakeful Huntfmen ready wait,

With

97

With Nets, and Toils, and Darts, beſide the force
Of *Spartan* Dogs, and ſwift *Maſſylian* Horſe.
The *Tyrian* Peers, and Officers of State,
For the ſlow Queen, in Anti-Chambers wait :
190 Her lofty Courſer, in the Court below,
(Who his Majeſtick Rider ſeems to know,)
Proud of his Purple Trappings, paws the Ground ;
And champs the Golden Bitt ; and ſpreads the Foam around.
The Queen at length appears: On either Hand
195 The brawny Guards in Martial Order ſtand.
196 A flow'rd Cymarr, with Golden Fringe, ſhe wore ;
And at her Back a Golden Quiver bore :
198 Her flowing Hair, a Golden Caul reſtrains ;
A golden Claſp, the *Tyrian* Robe ſuſtains.
200 Then young *Aſcanius*, with a ſprightly Grace,
Leads on the *Trojan* Youth to view the Chace.
But far above the reſt in beauty ſhines
The great *Æneas*, when the Troop he joins :
Like fair *Apollo*, when he leaves the froſt
205 Of wintry *Xanthus*, and the *Lycian* Coaſt ;
When to his Native *Delos* he reſorts,
Ordains the Dances, and renews the Sports :
Where painted *Scythians*, mix'd with *Cretan* Bands,
Before the joyful Altars join their Hands.
210 Himſelf, on *Cynthus* walking, ſees below
The merry Madneſs of the ſacred Show.
Green Wreaths of Bays his length of Hair incloſe,
213 A Golden Fillet binds his awful Brows :
His Quiver ſounds : Not leſs the Prince is ſeen
215 In manly Preſence, or in lofty Meen.
     Now had they reach'd the Hills, and ſtorm'd the Seat
Of ſalvage Beaſts, in Dens, their laſt Retreat ;
The Cry purſues the Mountain-Goats ; they bound
From Rock to Rock, and keep the craggy Ground:

Quite

220 Quite otherwise the Stags, a trembling Train,
    In Herds unfingl'd, scour the dusty Plain;
    And a long Chace, in open view, maintain.
    The glad *Ascanius*, as his Courser guides,
    Spurs through the Vale; and these and those outrides.
225 His Horses flanks and sides are forc'd to feel
    The clanking lash, and goring of the Steel.
    Impatiently he views the feeble Prey,
    Wishing some Nobler Beast to cross his way.
    And rather wou'd the tusky Boar attend,
230 Or fee the Lyon from the Hills defcend.
      Mean time, the gath'ring Clouds obfcure the Skies;
    From Pole to Pole the forky Lightning flies;
    The ratling Thunders rowl; and *Juno* pours
    A wintry Deluge down; and founding Show'rs.
235 The Company difpers'd, to Coverts ride,
    And feek the homely Cotts, or Mountains hollow fide.
    The rapid Rains, defcending from the Hills,
    To rowling Torrents raife the creeping Rills.
    The Queen and Prince, as Love or Fortune guides,
240 One common Cavern in her Bofom hides.
    Then firft the trembling Earth the fignal gave ;
    And flafhing Fires enlighten all the Cave :
    Hell from below, and *Juno* from above,
    And howling Nymphs, were confcious to their Love.
245 From this ill Omend Hour, in Time arofe
    Debate and Death, and all fucceeding woes.
      The Queen whom fenfe of Honour cou'd not move
    No longer made a Secret of her Love ;
    But call'd it Marriage, by that fpecious Name,
250 To veil the Crime and fanctifie the Shame.

---

196. Cymarr: a loose flowing robe.
198. Caul: a close-fitting cap or helmet.
200. Ascanius: Aeneas' son.
213. Fillet: headband.

Despite the love and concern for Dido that he genuinely feels, Aeneas remains firmly committed to his vocation to build a new Troy in Italy. Dido finally resigns herself to his ultimate departure, but sends Anna to beg him to delay a little. In *The Rape of the Lock* it is the Baron who inherits Aeneas' firmness (5:1ff.).

What Pangs the tender Breast of *Dido* tore,
When, from the Tow'r, she saw the cover'd Shore,
And heard the Shouts of Sailors from afar,
Mix'd with the Murmurs of the wat'ry War?
595 All pow'rful Love, what Changes canst thou cause
In Human Hearts, subjected to thy Laws!
Once more her haughty Soul the Tyrant bends;
To Pray'rs and mean Submissions she descends.
No female Arts or Aids she left untry'd,
600 Nor Counsels unexplor'd, before she dy'd.
Look, *Anna*, look; the *Trojans* crowd to Sea,
They spread their Canvas, and their Anchors weigh.
The shouting Crew, their Ships with Garlands binds;
Invoke the Sea-Gods, and invite the Winds.
605 Cou'd I have thought this threatning Blow so near,
My tender Soul had been forewarn'd to bear.
But do not you my last Request deny,
With yon perfidious Man your Int'rest try;
And bring me News, if I must live or dye.
610 You are his Fav'rite, you alone can find
The dark recesses of his inmost Mind:
In all his trusted Secrets you have part,
And know the soft Approaches to his Heart.
Haste then, and humbly seek my haughty Foe;
615 Tell him, I did not with the *Grecians* goe;
Nor did my Fleet against his Friends employ,
Nor swore the Ruin of unhappy *Troy*.
Nor mov'd with Hands prophane his Father's Dust;
Why shou'd he then reject a suit so just!
620 Whom does he shun, and whither would he fly;
Can he this last, this only Pray'r deny!
Let him at least his dang'rous Flight delay,
Wait better Winds, and hope a calmer Sea.

The

100

The Nuptials he difclaims I urge no more;
625 Let him purfue the promis'd *Latian* Shore.
A fhort delay is all I ask him now,
A paufe of Grief; an interval from Woe:
'Till my foft Soul be temper'd to fuftain
Accuftom'd Sorrows, and inur'd to Pain.
630 If you in Pity grant this one Requeft,
My Death fhall leave you of my Crown poffefs'd.
This mournful meffage, Pious *Anna* bears,
And feconds, with her own, her Sifter's Tears:
But all her Arts are ftill employ'd in vain;
635 Again fhe comes, and is refus'd again.
His harden'd Heart nor Pray'rs nor Threatnings move;
Fate, and the God, had ftop'd his Ears to Love.
    As when the Winds their airy Quarrel try;
Juftling from ev'ry quarter of the Sky;
640 This way and that, the Mountain Oak they bend,
His Boughs they fhatter, and his Branches rend;
642 With Leaves, and falling Maft, they fpread the Ground,
The hollow Vallies echo to the Sound:
Unmov'd, the Royal Plant their Fury mocks;
645 Or fhaken, clings more clofely to the Rocks:
Far as he fhoots his tow'ring Head on high,
So deep in Earth his fix'd Foundations lye.
No lefs a Storm the *Trojan* Heroe bears;
Thick Meffages and loud Complaints he hears; }
650 And bandy'd Words, ftill beating on his Ears. }
Sighs, Groans and Tears, proclaim his inward Pains,
But the firm purpofe of his Heart remains.
    The wretched Queen, purfu'd by cruel Fate,
Begins at length the light of Heav'n to hate:
655 And loaths to live: Then dire Portents fhe fees,
To haften on the Death her Soul decrees.

642. Mast: acorns.

Strange to relate: for when before the Shrine
She pours, in Sacrifice, the Purple Wine,
The Purple Wine is turn'd to putrid Blood:
660 And the white offer'd Milk, converts to Mud.
This dire Prefage, to her alone reveal'd,
From all, and ev'n her Sifter, fhe conceal'd.

After Aeneas has finally left, Dido prepares her suicide. It is usually the "thread" of life that is cut by the fates (the sisters of line 1,001) to signify the final end; here, however, it is a lock of hair. Since the dead were considered a sacrifice to the gods, this unusual image may also refer to the rite of clipping a few hairs from the forehead of sacrificial animals.

> This said, within her anxious Mind she weighs
> The Means of cutting short her odious Days.
> Then to Sichaeus's Nurse, she briefly said,
> (For when she left her Country, hers was dead)
> 910 Go Barce, call my Sifter ; let her Care
> The folemn Rites of Sacrifice prepare :
> The Sheep, and all th' attoneing Off'rings bring ;
> Sprinkling her Body from the Cryftal Spring
> With living Drops : then let her come, and thou
> 915 With facred Fillets, bind thy hoary Brow.
> Thus will I pay my Vows, to Stygian Jove ;
> And end the Cares of my difaftrous Love.
> Then caft the Trojan Image on the Fire ;
> And as that burns, my Paffion fhall expire.
> 920 The Nurfe moves onward, with officious Care,
> And all the fpeed her aged Limbs can bear.
> But furious Dido, with dark Thoughts involv'd,
> Shook at the mighty Mifchief fhe refolv'd.

With

With livid Spots diftinguifh'd was her Face,
925 Red were her rowling Eyes, and difcompos'd her Pace:
Ghaftly fhe gaz'd, with Pain fhe drew her Breath,
And Nature fhiver'd at approaching Death.
    Then fwiftly to the fatal place fhe pafs'd;
And mounts the Fun'ral Pile, with furious hafte.
930 Unfheaths the Sword the *Trojan* left behind,
(Not for fo dire an Enterprife defign'd,)
But when fhe view'd the Garments loofely fpred,
Which once he wore, and faw the confcious Bed,
She paus'd, and, with a Sigh, the Robes embrac'd;
935 Then on the Couch her trembling Body caft,
Reprefs'd the ready Tears, and fpoke her laft.
Dear Pledges of my Love, while Heav'n fo pleas'd,
Receive a Soul, of Mortal Anguifh eas'd:
My fatal Courfe is finifh'd; and I go
940 A glorious Name, among the Ghofts below.
A lofty City by my Hands is rais'd;
Pygmalion punifh'd, and my Lord appeas'd.
What cou'd my Fortune have afforded more,
Had the falfe *Trojan* never touch'd my Shore!
945 Then kifs'd the Couch; and muft I die, fhe faid;
And unreveng'd; 'tis doubly to be dead!
Yet ev'n this Death with Pleafure I receive;
On any Terms, 'tis better than to live.
Thefe Flames, from far, may the falfe *Trojan* view;
950 Thefe boding Omens his bafe flight purfue.
She faid, and ftruck: Deep enter'd in her fide
The piercing Steel, with reeking Purple dy'd:
Clog'd in the Wound the cruel Weapon ftands;
The fpouting Blood came ftreaming on her Hands.
955 Her fad Attendants faw the deadly Stroke,
And with loud Cries the founding Palace fhook.

Diftracted

Diftracted from the fatal fight they fled;
And thro the Town the difmal Rumor fpread.
Firft from the frighted Court, the Yell began,
960 Redoubled thence from Houfe to Houfe it ran:
The groans of Men, with Shrieks, Laments, and Cries
Of mixing Women, mount the vaulted Skies.
Not lefs the Clamour, than if ancient *Tyre*,
Or the new *Carthage*, fet by Foes on Fire,
965 The rowling Ruin, with their lov'd Abodes,
Involv'd the blazing Temples of their Gods.
Her Sifter hears, and, furious with Defpair,
She beats her Breaft, and rends her yellow Hair:
And calling on *Eliza*'s Name aloud,
970 Runs breathlefs to the Place, and breaks the Crowd.
Was all that Pomp of Woe for this prepar'd,
Thefe Fires, this Fun'ral Pile, thefe Altars rear'd;
Was all this Train of Plots contriv'd, faid fhe,
All only to deceive unhappy me?
975 Which is the worft, didft thou in Death pretend
To fcorn thy Sifter, or delude thy Friend!
Thy fummon'd Sifter, and thy Friend had come:
One Sword had ferv'd us both, one common Tomb.
Was I to raife the Pile, the Pow'rs invoke,
980 Not to be prefent at the fatal Stroke?
At once thou haft deftroy'd thy felf and me;
Thy Town, thy Senate, and thy Colony!
Bring Water, bathe the Wound; while I in death
Lay clofe my Lips to hers; and catch the flying Breath.
985 This faid, fhe mounts the Pile with eager hafte;
And in her Arms the gafping Queen embrac'd:
Her Temples chaf'd; and her own Garments tore
To ftanch the ftreaming Blood, and cleanfe the Gore.
Thrice *Dido* try'd to raife her drooping Head,
990 And fainting thrice, fell grov'ling on the Bed.

                                        Thrice

Thrice op'd her heavy Eyes, and fought the Light,
But having found it, ficken'd at the fight ;
And clos'd her Lids at laft, in endlefs Night.
Then *Juno*, grieving that fhe fhou'd fuftain
995 A Death fo ling'ring, and fo full of Pain ;
Sent *Iris* down, to free her from the Strife
Of lab'ring Nature, and diffolve her Life.
For fince fhe dy'd, not doom'd by Heav'ns Decree,
Or her own Crime ; but Human Cafualty ;
1000 And rage of Love, that plung'd her in Defpair,
The Sifters had not cut the topmoft Hair ;
Which *Proferpine*, and they can only know ;
Nor made her facred to the Shades below.
Downward the various Goddefs took her flight ;
1005 And drew a thoufand Colours from the Light :
Then ftood above the dying Lover's Head,
And faid, I thus devote thee to the dead.
This Off'ring to the Infernal Gods I bear :
Thus while fhe fpoke, fhe cut the fatal Hair ;
1010 The ftrugling Soul was loos'd ; and Life diffolv'd in Air.

Book VI

In this book Aeneas visits the underworld, guided by the sibyl and protected by a magical golden bough that he carries, in order to obtain from his dead father a vision of the future of Rome. Umbriel, protected by a branch of spleenwort, performs this kind of journey in *The Rape of the Lock*.

These Rites perform'd, the Prince, without delay,
Haftes to the neather World, his deftin'd Way.
Deep was the Cave; and downward as it went
From the wide Mouth, a rocky rough Defcent;
340 And here th' accefs a gloomy Grove defends;
And there th' unnavigable Lake extends.
O're whofe unhappy Waters, void of Light,
No Bird prefumes to fteer his Airy Flight;
Such deadly Stenches from the depth arife,
345 And fteaming Sulphur, that infects the Skies.
From hence the *Grecian* Bards their Legends make,
And give the name *Avernus* to the Lake.
Four fable Bullocks, in the Yoke untaught,
For Sacrifice the pious Heroe brought.
350 The Prieftefs pours the Wine betwixt their Horns:
Then cuts the curling Hair; that firft Oblation burns.
Invoking *Hecate* hither to repair;
(A pow'rful Name in Hell, and upper Air.)
The facred Priefts with ready Knives bereave
355 The Beafts of Life; and in full Bowls receive

The

108

The ſtreaming Blood: A Lamb to Hell and Night,
(The ſable Wool without a ſtreak of white)
Æneas offers: And, by Fates decree,
A barren Heifar, *Proſerpine* to thee.
360 With Holocauſts he *Pluto*'s Altar fills:
Sev'n brawny Bulls with his own Hand he kills:
Then on the broiling Entrails Oyl he pours,
Which, ointed thus, the raging Flame devours.
Late, the Nocturnal Sacrifice begun;
365 Nor ended, 'till the next returning Sun.
Then Earth began to bellow, Trees to dance;
And howling Dogs in glimm'ring Light advance;
E're *Hecate* came: Far hence be Souls prophane,
The Sibyl cry'd, and from the Grove abſtain.
370 Now, *Trojan*, take the way thy Fates afford:
Aſſume thy Courage, and unſheath thy Sword.
She ſaid, and paſs'd along the gloomy Space:
The Prince purſu'd her Steps with equal pace.
Ye Realms, yet unreveal'd to human ſight,
375 Ye Gods, who rule the Regions of the Night,
Ye gliding Ghoſts, permit me to relate
The myſtick Wonders of your ſilent State.
Obſcure they went thro dreery Shades, that led
Along the waſte Dominions of the dead:
380 Thus wander Travellers in Woods by Night,
By the Moon's doubtful, and malignant Light:
When *Jove* in dusky Clouds involves the Skies;
And the faint Creſcent ſhoots by fits before their Eyes.
Juſt in the Gate, and in the Jaws of Hell,
385 Revengeful Cares, and ſullen Sorrows dwell;
And pale Diſeaſes, and repining Age;
Want, Fear, and Famine's unreſiſted rage.
Here Toils, and Death, and Death's half-brother, Sleep,
Forms terrible to view, their Centry keep:

With

109

390 With anxious Pleasures of a guilty Mind,
    Deep Frauds before, and open Force behind :
    The Furies Iron Beds, and Strife that shakes
    Her hissing Tresses, and unfolds her Snakes.
    Full in the midst of this infernal Road,
395 An Elm displays her dusky Arms abroad ;
    The God of Sleep there hides his heavy Head :
    And empty Dreams on ev'ry Leaf are spread.
    Of various Forms unnumber'd Specters more ;
    Centaurs, and double Shapes, besiege the Door :
400 Before the Passage horrid *Hydra* stands,
    And *Briareus* with all his hundred Hands :
    Gorgons, *Geryon* with his triple Frame;
    And vain *Chimæra* vomits empty Flame.
    The Chief unsheath'd his shining Steel, prepar'd,
405 Tho seiz'd with sudden Fear, to force the Guard.
    Off'ring his brandish'd Weapon at their Face;
    Had not the Sibyl stop'd his eager Pace,
    And told him what those empty Fantomes were;
    Forms without Bodies, and impassive Air.

• • •

    Assaracus and *Ilus* here enjoy
885 Perpetual Fame, with him who founded *Troy*.
    The Chief beheld their Chariots from afar;
    Their shining Arms, and Coursers train'd to War :
    Their Lances fix'd in Earth, their Steeds around,
    Free from their Harness, graze the flow'ry Ground.
890 The love of Horses which they had, alive,
    And care of Chariots, after Death survive.

                                    Some

Some chearful Souls, were feasting on the Plain ;
Some did the Song, and some the Choir maintain.
Beneath a Laurel Shade, where mighty *Po*
895 Mounts up to Woods above, and hides his Head below.
Here Patriots live, who, for their Countries good,
In fighting Fields, were prodigal of Blood :
Priests of unblemish'd Lives here make Abode ;
And Poets worthy their inspiring God :
900 And searching Wits, of more Mechanick parts,
Who grac'd their Age with new invented Arts.
Those who, to worth, their Bounty did extend ;
And those who knew that Bounty to commend.
The Heads of these with holy Fillets bound ;
905 And all their Temples were with Garlands crown'd.

John Milton, *Paradise Lost* (1667)

Paradise Lost was the great native epic of Pope's country, and mock-epic convention alone would have assured its presence in *The Rape of the Lock*. There is also an intriguing similarity in the action of the two poems: like Belinda's lock, Eve's apple is a trivial object endowed with great significance by a particular context. *Paradise Lost* operates in *The Rape of the Lock* primarily as a source of moral and religious perspectives which most of Pope's audience would consider more immediately relevant to themselves and certainly more binding than Homer's heroic code or Virgil's empire building. Pride was sinful for Milton and Pope in a way that it was not for Homer. Belinda can't be expected to emulate Hector's virtues, but she ought at least to strive to avoid Eve's failings. Occasionally Pope has some fun with one of Milton's partially unsolved problems; for example, the airy sylph who regenerates himself after being severed by the scissors may reveal the latent absurdity of making invulnerable angels fight epic battles (but cf. Pope's note to his *Iliad*, 5:422, p. 51). Most of the extensive allusions to *Paradise Lost*, though, are relatively serious; they darken the tone of the poem and intimate that Belinda's failings may be graver than they seem.

Paradise Lost *

BOOK I

Of Man's First Disobedience, and the Fruit
Of that Forbidden Tree, whose mortal taste
Brought Death into the World, and all our woe,
With loss of *Eden*, till one greater Man°   4
Restore us, and regain the blissful Seat,   5
Sing Heav'nly Muse, that on the secret top
Of *Oreb*, or of *Sinai*, didst inspire
That Shepherd,° who first taught the chosen Seed,   8
In the Beginning how the Heav'ns and Earth
Rose out of *Chaos:* Or if *Sion* Hill°   10
Delight thee more, and *Siloa's* Brook that flow'd
Fast by the Oracle of God; I thence
Invoke thy aid to my advent'rous Song,
That with no middle flight intends to soar
Above th' *Aonian* Mount,° while it pursues   15
Things unattempted yet in Prose or Rhyme.
And chiefly Thou O Spirit, that dost prefer
Before all Temples th' upright heart and pure,
Instruct me, for Thou know'st; Thou from the first
Wast present, and with mighty wings outspread   20
Dove-like satst brooding on the vast Abyss°   21
And mad'st it pregnant: What in me is dark
Illumine, what is low raise and support;
That to the highth of this great Argument
I may assert Eternal Providence,   25
And justify the ways of God to men.
    Say first, for Heav'n hides nothing from thy view
Nor the deep Tract of Hell, say first what cause
Mov'd our Grand Parents in that happy State,
Favor'd of Heav'n so highly, to fall off   30
From thir Creator, and transgress his Will
For one restraint, Lords of the World besides?
Who first seduc'd them to that foul revolt?

---

*This learned poem calls for abundant annotation, and several fully annotated editions are available. Here I have tried to keep notes to a minimum, merely supplying the information needed to keep readers from going seriously astray or to elucidate points particularly relevant to *The Rape of the Lock.*

4. greater Man: Jesus.
8. that Shepherd: Moses.
10. Sion's Hill: Mount Zion, in Jerusalem, site of the Temple.
15. Aonian Mount: Helicon, sacred to the Muses.
21. vast Abyss: See the opening of the book of Genesis.

Book I continues to describe Satan and his host of followers scattered on a burning lake at the bottom of hell. He rouses himself and then rallies his forces. The roll call of the fallen angels, who are identified with the heathen deities that seduced the ancient Jews from the worship of the true God, is one of the best-known parts of *Paradise Lost* and one of the most important for *The Rape of the Lock*. When Ariel declares to Belinda that "Spirits, freed from mortal Laws, with ease Assume what sexes and what shapes they please" (1:69-70), Pope is clearly alluding to Milton's lines 423ff. Since the purpose of the demonic sex shifting is to seduce Israel from the worship of their God, Pope may imply that the love offered by the sylphs is another kind of misdirection and idolatry. See also *Spectator* 73 (below, p. 259).

He call'd so loud, that all the hollow Deep	
Of Hell resounded. Princes, Potentates,	315
Warriors, the Flow'r of Heav'n, once yours, now lost,	
If such astonishment as this can seize	
Eternal spirits; or have ye chos'n this place	
After the toil of Battle to repose	
Your wearied virtue, for the ease you find	320
To slumber here, as in the Vales of Heav'n?	
Or in this abject posture have ye sworn	
To adore the Conqueror? who now beholds	
Cherub and Seraph rolling in the Flood	
With scatter'd Arms and Ensigns, till anon	325
His swift pursuers from Heav'n Gates discern	
Th' advantage, and descending tread us down	
Thus drooping, or with linked Thunderbolts	
Transfix us to the bottom of this Gulf.	
Awake, arise, or be for ever fall'n.	330
They heard, and were abasht, and up they sprung	
Upon the wing; as when men wont to watch	
On duty, sleeping found by whom they dread,	
Rouse and bestir themselves ere well awake.	
Nor did they not perceive the evil plight	335
In which they were, or the fierce pains not feel;	
Yet to thir General's Voice they soon obey'd	
Innumerable. As when the potent Rod	
Of *Amram's Son°* in *Egypt's* evil day	339
Wav'd round the Coast, up call'd a pitchy cloud	340
Of *Locusts*, warping on the Eastern Wind,	
That o'er the Realm of impious *Pharaoh* hung	
Like Night, and darken'd all the Land of *Nile:*	
So numberless were those bad Angels seen	
Hovering on wing under the Cope of Hell	345
'Twixt upper, nether, and surrounding Fires;	
Till, as a signal giv'n, th' uplifted Spear	

---

339. Amram's Son: Moses. See Exodus 10.

Of thir great Sultan waving to direct
Thir course, in even balance down they light
On the firm brimstone, and fill all the Plain;   350
A multitude, like which the populous North
Pour'd never from her frozen loins, to pass
Rhene or the *Danaw*, when her barbarous Sons
Came like a Deluge on the South, and spread
Beneath *Gibraltar* to the *Lybian* sands.   355
Forthwith from every Squadron and each Band
The Heads and Leaders thither haste where stood
Thir great Commander; Godlike shapes and forms
Excelling human, Princely Dignities,
And Powers that erst in Heaven sat on Thrones;   360
Though of thir Names in heav'nly Records now
Be no memorial, blotted out and ras'd
By thir Rebellion, from the Books of Life.
Nor had they yet among the Sons of *Eve*
Got them new Names, till wand'ring o'er the Earth,   365
Through God's high sufferance for the trial of man,
By falsities and lies the greatest part
Of Mankind they corrupted to forsake
God thir Creator, and th' invisible
Glory of him that made them, to transform   370
Oft to the Image of a Brute, adorn'd
With gay Religions full of Pomp and Gold,
And Devils to adore for Deities:
Then were they known to men by various Names,
And various Idols through the Heathen World.   375
Say, Muse, thir Names then known, who first, who last,
Rous'd from the slumber on that fiery Couch,
At thir great Emperor's call, as next in worth
Came singly where he stood on the bare strand,
While the promiscuous crowd stood yet aloof?   380
The chief were those who from the Pit of Hell
Roaming to seek thir prey on earth, durst fix
Thir Seats long after next the Seat of God,
Thir Altars by his Altar, Gods ador'd
Among the Nations round, and durst abide   385
Jehovah thund'ring out of *Sion*, thron'd
Between the Cherubim; yea, often plac'd
Within his Sanctuary itself thir Shrines,
Abominations; and with cursed things
His holy Rites, and solemn Feasts profan'd   390
And with thir darkness durst affront his light.
First *Moloch*, horrid King besmear'd with blood
Of human sacrifice, and parents' tears,
Though for the noise of Drums and Timbrels loud
Thir children's cries unheard, that pass'd through fire   395
To his grim Idol. Him the *Ammonite*
Worshipt in *Rabba* and her wat'ry Plain,
In *Argob* and in *Basan*, to the stream
Of utmost *Arnon*. Nor content with such
Audacious neighborhood, the wisest heart   400

Of *Solomon* he led by fraud to build
His Temple right against the Temple of God
On that opprobrious Hill, and made his Grove
The pleasant Valley of *Hinnom*, *Tophet* thence
And black *Gehenna* call'd, the Type of Hell.   405
Next *Chemos*, th' obscene dread of *Moab's* Sons,
From *Aroar* to *Nebo*, and the wild
Of Southmost *Abarim*; in *Hesebon*
And *Horonaim*, *Seon's* Realm, beyond
The flow'ry Dale of *Sibma* clad with Vines   410
And *Eleale* to th' *Asphaltic* Pool.
Peor his other Name, when he entic'd
Israel in *Sittim* on thir march from *Nile*
To do him wanton rites, which cost them woe.
Yet thence his lustful Orgies he enlarg'd   415
Even to that Hill of scandal, by the Grove
Of *Moloch* homicide, lust hard by hate;
Till good *Josiah* drove them thence to Hell.
With these came they, who from the bord'ring flood
Of old *Euphrates* to the Brook that parts   420
Egypt from *Syrian* ground, had general Names
Of *Baalim* and *Ashtaroth*, those male,
These Feminine. For Spirits when they please
Can either Sex assume, or both; so soft
And uncompounded is thir Essence pure,   425
Not ti'd or manacl'd with joint or limb,
Nor founded on the brittle strength of bones,
Like cumbrous flesh; but in what shape they choose
Dilated or condens't, bright or obscure,
Can execute thir aery purposes,   430
And works of love or enmity fulfil.
For those the Race of *Israel* oft forsook
Thir living strength, and unfrequented left
His righteous Altar, bowing lowly down
To bestial Gods; for which thir heads as low   435
Bow'd down in Battle, sunk before the Spear
Of despicable foes. With these in troop
Came *Astoreth*, whom the *Phoenicians* call'd
Astarte, Queen of Heav'n, with crescent Horns;
To whose bright Image nightly by the Moon   440
Sidonian Virgins paid thir Vows and Songs,
In *Sion* also not unsung, where stood
Her Temple on th' offensive Mountain, built
By that uxorious King,° whose heart though large,   444
Beguil'd by fair Idolatresses, fell
To Idols foul. *Thammuz* came next behind,
Whose annual wound in *Lebanon* allur'd
The *Syrian* Damsels to lament his fate
In amorous ditties all a Summer's day,
While smooth *Adonis* from his native Rock   450

---

444. uxorious King: Solomon; see line 401.

Ran purple to the Sea, suppos'd with blood
Of *Thammuz* yearly wounded: the Love-tale
Infected *Sion's* daughters with like heat,
Whose wanton passions in the sacred Porch
Ezekiel saw, when by the Vision led   455
His eye survey'd the dark Idolatries
Of alienated *Judah*. Next came one
Who mourn'd in earnest, when the Captive Ark
Maim'd his brute Image, head and hands lopt off
In his own Temple, on the grunsel edge,   460
Where he fell flat, and sham'd his Worshippers:
Dagon° his Name, Sea Monster, upward Man   462
And downward Fish: yet had his Temple high
Rear'd in *Azotus*, dreaded through the Coast
Of *Palestine*, in *Gath* and *Ascalon*,   465
And *Accaron* and *Gaza's* frontier bounds.
Him follow'd *Rimmon*, whose delightful Seat
Was fair *Damascus*, on the fertile Banks
Of *Abbana* and *Pharphar*, lucid streams.
He also against the house of God was bold: 470
A Leper once he lost and gain'd a King,
Ahaz his sottish Conqueror, whom he drew
God's Altar to disparage and displace
For one of *Syrian* mode, whereon to burn
His odious off'rings, and adore the Gods   475
Whom he had vanquisht. After these appear'd
A crew who under Names of old Renown,
Osiris, Isis, Orus and thir Train
With monstrous shapes and sorceries abus'd
Fanatic *Egypt* and her Priests, to seek   480
Thir wand'ring Gods disguis'd in brutish forms
Rather than human. Nor did *Israel* scape
Th' infection when thir borrow'd Gold compos'd
The Calf in *Oreb*:° and the Rebel King   484
Doubl'd that sin in *Bethel* and in *Dan*,   485
Lik'ning his Maker to the Grazed Ox,
Jehovah, who in one Night when he pass'd
From *Egypt* marching, equall'd with one stroke
Both her first born and all her bleating Gods.
Belial came last, than whom a Spirit more lewd   490
Fell not from Heaven, or more gross to love
Vice for itself: To him no Temple stood
Or Altar smok'd; yet who more oft than hee
In Temples and at Altars, when the Priest
Turns Atheist, as did *Ely's* Sons, who fill'd   495
With lust and violence the house of God:
In courts and Palaces he also Reigns
And in luxurious Cities, where the noise
Of riot ascends above thir loftiest Tow'rs,

---

462. Dagon: See 1 Samuel 5.
484. The Calf in Oreb: The story of the Golden Calf is told in Exodus 32.

And injury and outrage: And when Night   500
Darkens the Streets, then wander forth the Sons
Of *Belial*, flown with insolence and wine.
Witness the Streets of *Sodom*, and that night
In *Gibeah*, when the hospitable door
Expos'd a Matron to avoid worse rape.   505
These were the prime in order and in might;
The rest were long to tell, though far renown'd,

Satan addresses the fallen angels in an epic manner that Ariel
imitates:

O Myriads of immortal Spirits, O Powers
Matchless, but with th' Almighty, and that strife
Was not inglorious, though th' event was dire,
At this place testifies, and this dire change   625
Hateful to utter: but what power of mind
Foreseeing or presaging, from the Depth
Of knowledge past or present, could have fear'd
How such united force of Gods, how such
As stood like these, could ever know repulse?   630
For who can yet believe, though after loss,
That all these puissant Legions, whose exile
Hath emptied Heav'n, shall fail to re-ascend
Self-rais'd, and repossess thir native seat?
For mee be witness all the Host of heav'n,   635
If counsels different, or danger shunn'd
By me, have lost our hopes. But he who reigns
Monarch in Heav'n, till then as one secure
Sat on his Throne, upheld by old repute,
Consent or custom, and his Regal State   640
Put forth at full, but still his strength conceal'd,
Which tempted our attempt, and wrought our fall.
Henceforth his might we know, and know our own
So as not either to provoke, or dread
New War, provok't; our better part remains   645
To work in close design, by fraud or guile
What force effected not:

BOOK III

Milton's "Limbo of Vanities," like Pope's "Lunar Sphere," owes a debt to Ariosto (see below, p. 222).

<pre>
Alone, for other Creature in this place
Living or lifeless to be found was none,
None yet, but store hereafter from the earth
Up hither like Aereal vapors flew   445
Of all things transitory and vain, when Sin
With vanity had fill'd the works of men:
Both all things vain, and all who in vain things
Built thir fond hopes of Glory or lasting fame,
Or happiness in this or th' other life;   450
All who have thir reward on Earth, the fruits
Of painful Superstition and blind Zeal,
Naught seeking but the praise of men, here find
Fit retribution, empty as thir deeds;
All th' unaccomplisht works of Nature's hand,   455
Abortive, monstrous, or unkindly mixt,
Dissolv'd on Earth, fleet hither, and in vain,
Till final dissolution, wander here,
Not in the neighboring Moon, as some have dream'd;
Those argent Fields more likely habitants,   460
Translated Saints, or middle Spirits hold
Betwixt th' Angelical and Human kind:
Hither of ill-join'd Sons and Daughters born
First from the ancient World those Giants came
With many a vain exploit, though then renown'd: 465
The builders next of Babel on the Plain
Of Sennaar, and still with vain design
New Babels°, had they wherewithal, would build: 468
Others came single; he who to be deem'd
A God, leap'd fondly into Ætna flames,   470
Empedocles, and hee who to enjoy
Plato's Elysium, leap'd into the Sea,
Cleombrotus, and many more too long,
Embryos, and Idiots, Eremites and Friars
White, Black and Grey, with all thir trumpery.   475
Here Pilgrims roam, that stray'd so far to seek
In Golgotha° him dead, who lives in Heav'n;   477
And they who to be sure of Paradise
Dying put on the weeds of Dominic,
Or in Franciscan think to pass disguis'd;   480
They pass the Planets seven, and pass the fixt,
And that Crystalline Sphere whose balance weighs
</pre>

---

468. Babels: See Genesis 11.
477. Golgotha: site of the crucifixion of Jesus.

The Trepidation talkt, and that first mov'd;
And now Saint *Peter* at Heav'n's Wicket seems
To wait them with his Keys, and now at foot   485
Of Heav'n's ascent they lift thir Feet, when lo
A violent cross wind from either Coast
Blows them transverse ten thousand Leagues awry
Into the devious Air; then might ye see
Cowls, Hoods and Habits with thir wearers tost   490
And flutter'd into Rags, then Reliques, Beads,
Indulgences, Dispenses, Pardons, Bulls,°   492
The sport of Winds: all these upwhirl'd aloft
Fly o'er the backside of the World far off
Into a *Limbo* large and broad, since call'd   495
The Paradise of Fools,

BOOK V

Eve recounts the dream that Satan whispered into her ear while
she slept. For discussion, see headnote to *Spectator* 327 (p. 272).
Belinda, too, awakes from a dream.

Now Morn her rosy steps in th' Eastern Clime
Advancing, sow'd the Earth with Orient Pearl,
When *Adam* wak't, so custom'd, for his sleep
Was Aery light, from pure digestion bred,
And temperate vapors bland, which th' only sound°   5
Of leaves and fuming rills, *Aurora's* fan,
Lightly dispers'd, and the shrill Matin Song
Of Birds on every bough; so much the more
His wonder was to find unwak'n'd *Eve*
With Tresses discompos'd, and glowing Cheek,   10
As through unquiet rest: hee on his side
Leaning half-rais'd, with looks of cordial Love
Hung over her enamor'd, and beheld
Beauty, which whether waking or asleep,
Shot forth peculiar graces; then with voice   15
Mild, as when *Zephyrus* on *Flora* breathes,
Her hand soft touching, whisper'd thus. Awake
My fairest, my espous'd, my latest found,
Heav'n's last best gift, my ever new delight.
Awake, the morning shines, and the fresh field   20
Calls us; we lose the prime, to mark how spring

---

492. Bulls: i.e., Papal Bulls, official communications from the Pope (from Latin *bulla*,
the seal used on the documents).

5. this only sound... : i.e., the soft sound mentioned was by itself enough to wake
Adam.

Our tended Plants, how blows the Citron Grove,
What drops the Myrrh, and what the balmy Reed,
How Nature paints her colors, how the Bee
Sits on the Bloom extracting liquid sweet.   25
    Such whispering wak'd her, but with startl'd eye
On *Adam*, whom imbracing, thus she spake.
    O Sole in whom my thoughts find all repose,
My Glory, my Perfection, glad I see
Thy face, and Morn return'd, for I this Night,   30
Such night till this I never pass'd, have dream'd,
If dream'd, not as I oft am wont, of thee,
Works of day past, or morrow's next design,
But of offense and trouble, which my mind
Knew never till this irksome night; methought   35
Close at mine ear one call'd me forth to walk
With gentle voice, I thought it thine; it said,
Why sleep'st thou *Eve?* now is the pleasant time,
The cool, the silent, save where silence yields
To the night-warbling Bird, that now awake   40
Tunes sweetest his love-labor'd song; now reigns
Full Orb'd the Moon, and with more pleasing light
Shadowy sets off the face of things; in vain,
If none regard; Heav'n wakes with all his eyes,
Whom to behold but thee, Nature's desire,   45
In whose sight all things joy, with ravishment
Attracted by thy beauty still to gaze.
I rose as at thy call, but found thee not;
To find thee I directed then my walk;
And on, methought, alone I pass'd through ways   50
That brought me on a sudden to the Tree
Of interdicted Knowledge: fair it seem'd,
Much fairer to my Fancy than by day:
And as I wond'ring lookt, beside it stood
One shap'd and wing'd like one of those from Heav'n   55
By us oft seen; his dewy locks distill'd
Ambrosia; on that Tree he also gaz'd;
And O fair Plant, said he, with fruit surcharg'd,
Deigns none to ease thy load and taste thy sweet,
Nor God, nor Man; is Knowledge so despis'd?   60
Or envy, or what reserve forbids to taste?
Forbid who will, none shall from me withhold
Longer thy offer'd good, why else set here?
This said he paus'd not, but with vent'rous Arm
He pluckt, he tasted; mee damp horror chill'd   65
At such bold words voucht with a deed so bold:
But he thus overjoy'd, O Fruit Divine,
Sweet of thyself, but much more sweet thus cropt,
Forbidd'n here, it seems, as only fit
For Gods, yet able to make Gods of Men: 70
And why not Gods of Men, since good, the more
Communicated, more abundant grows,
The Author not impair'd, but honor'd more?
Here, happy Creature, fair Angelic *Eve*,

Partake thou also; happy though thou art,   75
Happier thou may'st be, worthier canst not be:
Taste this, and be henceforth among the Gods
Thyself a Goddess, not to Earth confin'd,
But sometimes in the Air, as wee, sometimes
Ascend to Heav'n, by merit thine, and see   80
What life the Gods live there, and such live thou.
So saying, he drew nigh, and to me held,
Even to my mouth of that same fruit held part
Which he had pluckt; the pleasant savory smell
So quick'n'd appetite, that I, methought,   85
Could not but taste. Forthwith up to the Clouds
With him I flew, and underneath beheld
The Earth outstretcht immense, a prospect wide
And various: wond'ring at my flight and change
To this high exaltation; suddenly   90
My Guide was gone, and I, methought, sunk down,
And fell asleep; but O how glad I wak'd
To find this but a dream!

"He" in the following passage is the archangel Raphael, sent by
God to instruct and reassure Adam and Eve: his role as teacher has
resemblances to that of Ariel.

At once on th' Eastern cliff of Paradise   275
He lights, and to his proper shape returns
A Seraph wing'd; six wings he wore, to shade
His lineaments Divine; the pair that clad
Each shoulder broad, came mantling o'er his breast
With regal Ornament; the middle pair   280
Girt like a Starry Zone his waist, and round
Skirted his loins and thighs with downy Gold
And colors dipt in Heav'n; the third his feet
Shadow'd from either heel with feather'd mail°   284
Sky-tinctur'd grain.° Like *Maia's* son° he stood,   285
And shook his Plumes

At Adam's request, Raphael recounts Satan's rebellion, beginning with an assembly of angels convoked by God for the purpose of
proclaiming his son viceroy of heaven: there may be a hint of this in
Ariel's message to Belinda about the spirits that surround her and in
his speech to the other sylphs.

---

284. mail: The meaning seems to be that the feathers have the appearance of links of
chain mail.
285. grain: color.
    Maia's son: Mercury.

As yet this World was not, and *Chaos* wild
Reign'd where these Heav'ns now roll, where Earth now rests
Upon her Centre pois'd, when on a day
(For Time, though in Eternity, appli'd   580
To motion, measures all things durable
By present, past, and future) on such day
As Heav'n's great Year brings forth, th' Empyreal Host
Of Angels by Imperial summons call'd,
Innumerable before th' Almighty's Throne   585
Forthwith from all the ends of Heav'n appear'd
Under thir Hierarchs in orders bright;
Ten thousand thousand Ensigns high advanc'd,
Standards and Gonfalons, twixt Van and Rear
Stream in the Air, and for distinction serve   590
Of Hierarchies, of Orders, and Degrees;
Or in thir glittering Tissues bear imblaz'd
Holy Memorials, acts of Zeal and Love
Recorded eminent. Thus when in Orbs
Of circuit inexpressible they stood,   595
Orb within Orb, the Father infinite,
By whom in bliss imbosom'd sat the Son,
Amidst as from a flaming Mount, whose top
Brightness had made invisible, thus spake.
　　Hear all ye Angels, Progeny of Light,   600
Thrones, Dominations, Princedoms, Virtues, Powers,
Hear my Decree, which unrevok't shall stand.
This day I have begot whom I declare
My only Son, and on this holy Hill
Him have anointed, whom ye now behold   605
At my right hand; your Head I him appoint;
And by my Self have sworn to him shall bow
All knees in Heav'n, and shall confess him Lord:
Under his great Vice-gerent Reign abide
United as one individual Soul   610
For ever happy: him who disobeys
Mee disobeys, breaks union, and that day
Cast out from God and blessed vision, falls
Into utter darkness, deep ingulft, his place
Ordain'd without redemption, without end.   615

BOOK VI

　　Satan and the archangel Michael, in single combat, begin the
battle in heaven between Satan's rebels and the loyal angels. (Lines
320-34 were quoted in *Spectator* 333.) Both single combat and general
melee occur in *The Rape of the Lock*.

123

They ended parle, and both address'd for fight
Unspeakable; for who, though with the tongue
Of Angels, can relate, or to what things
Liken on Earth conspicuous, that may lift
Human imagination to such highth   300
Of Godlike Power: for likest Gods they seem'd,
Stood they or mov'd, in stature, motion, arms
Fit to decide the Empire of great Heav'n.
Now wav'd thir fiery Swords, and in the Air
Made horrid Circles; two broad Suns thir Shields   305
Blaz'd opposite, while expectation stood
In horror; from each hand with speed retir'd
Where erst was thickest fight, th' Angelic throng,
And left large field, unsafe within the wind
Of such commotion, such as, to set forth   310
Great things by small, if Nature's concord broke,
Among the Constellations war were sprung,
Two Planets rushing from aspect malign
Of fiercest opposition in mid Sky,
Should combat, and thir jarring Spheres confound.   315
Together both with next to Almighty Arm,
Uplifted imminent one stroke they aim'd
That might determine, and not need repeat,
As not of power, at once; nor odds appear'd
In might or swift prevention; but the sword   320
Of *Michael* from the Armory of God
Was giv'n him temper'd so, that neither keen
Nor solid might resist that edge: it met
The sword of *Satan* with steep force to smite
Descending, and in half cut sheer, nor stay'd,   325
But with swift wheel reverse, deep ent'ring shear'd
All his right side; then *Satan* first knew pain,
And writh'd him to and fro convolv'd; so sore
The griding sword with discontinuous° wound   329
Pass'd through him, but th' Ethereal substance clos'd   330
Not long divisible, and from the gash
A stream of Nectarous humor issuing flow'd
Sanguine, such as Celestial Spirits may bleed,
And all his Armor stain'd erewhile so bright.
Forthwith on all sides to his aid was run   335
By Angels many and strong, who interpos'd
Defense, while others bore him on thir Shields
Back to his Chariot, where it stood retir'd
From off the files of war: there they him laid
Gnashing for anguish and despite and shame   340
To find himself not matchless, and his pride
Humbl'd by such rebuke, so far beneath
His confidence to equal God in power.
Yet soon he heal'd; for Spirits that live throughout
Vital in every part, not as frail man   345

---

329. discontinuous: breaking the continuity of (i.e., of Satan's body).

In Entrails, Heart or Head, Liver or Reins,
Cannot but by annihilating die;
Nor in thir liquid texture mortal wound
Receive, no more than can the fluid Air:
All Heart they live, all Head, all Eye, all Ear,   350
All Intellect, all Sense, and as they please,
They Limb themselves, and color, shape or size
Assume, as likes them best, condense or rare.

BOOK IX

Satan prepares and carries out the temptation of Eve. Ariel seems
to have learned some flattering tricks from him.

    So spake the Enemy of Mankind, enclos'd
In Serpent, Inmate bad, and toward *Eve*   495
Address'd his way, not with indented wave,
Prone on the ground, as since, but on his rear,
Circular base of rising folds, that tow'r'd
Fold above fold a surging Maze, his Head
Crested aloft, and Carbuncle° his Eyes;   500
With burnisht Neck of verdant Gold, erect
Amidst his circling Spires, that on the grass
Floated redundant:° pleasing was his shape,   503
        . . . .
His gentle dumb expression turn'd at length
The Eye of *Eve* to mark his play; he glad
Of her attention gain'd, with Serpent Tongue
Organic, or impulse of vocal Air,   530
His fraudulent temptation thus began.
    Wonder not, sovran Mistress, if perhaps
Thou canst, who are sole Wonder, much less arm
Thy looks, the Heav'n of mildness, with disdain,
Displeas'd that I approach thee thus, and gaze   535
Insatiate, I thus single, nor have fear'd
Thy awful° brow, more awful thus retir'd.   537
Fairest resemblance of thy Maker fair,
Thee all things living gaze on, all things thine
By gift, and thy Celestial Beauty adore   540
With ravishment beheld, there best beheld
Where universally admir'd: but here
In this enclosure wild, these Beasts among,
Beholders rude, and shallow to discern

---

500. carbuncle: any of several gems of a red or fiery color, such as the ruby or garnet.
503. redundant: abundant; floating, wavelike.
537. awful: awe-inspiring.

Half what in thee is fair, one man except,   545
Who sees thee? (and what is one?) who shouldst be seen
A Goddess among Gods, ador'd and serv'd
By Angels numberless, thy daily Train.

. . . .

Thenceforth to Speculations high or deep
I turn'd my thoughts, and with capacious mind
Consider'd all things visible in Heav'n,
Or Earth, or Middle, all things fair and good;   605
But all that fair and good in thy Divine
Semblance, and in thy Beauty's heav'nly Ray
United I beheld; no Fair to thine
Equivalent or second, which compell'd
Mee thus, though importune perhaps, to come   610
And gaze, and worship thee of right declar'd
Sovran of Creatures, universal Dame.

After the fall, Adam and Eve awake and begin to comprehend
their plight. Like the loss of Belinda's lock, the eating of the apple is
irremediable.

Soon as the force of that fallacious Fruit,
That with exhilarating vapor bland
About thir spirits had play'd, and inmost powers
Made err, was now exhal'd, and grosser sleep
Bred of unkindly fumes, with conscious dreams   1050
Encumber'd, now had left them, up they rose
As from unrest, and each the other viewing,
Soon found thir Eyes how op'n'd, and thir minds
How dark'n'd; innocence, that as a veil
Had shadow'd them from knowing ill, was gone,   1055
Just confidence, and native righteousness,
And honor from about them, naked left
To guilty shame: hee cover'd, but his Robe
Uncover'd more. So rose the *Danite* strong
Herculean Samson from the Harlot-lap   1060
Of *Philistean Dalilah*, and wak'd
Shorn of his strength,° They destitute and bare   1062
Of all thir virtue: silent, and in face
Confounded long they sat, as struck'n mute,
Till *Adam*, though not less than *Eve* abasht,   1065
At length gave utterance to these words constrain'd.
     O *Eve*, in evil hour thou didst give ear
To that false Worm, of whomsoever taught
To counterfeit Man's voice, true in our Fall,
False in our promis'd Rising; since our Eyes   1070

1059-62: Samson's strength lay in his hair, which the treacherous Delilah shaved off
while he slept after she had persuaded him to reveal its secret (Judges 16:16-22).

Op'n'd we find indeed, and find we know
Both Good and Evil, Good lost, and Evil got,
Bad Fruit of Knowledge, if this be to know,
Which leaves us naked thus, of Honor void,
Of Innocence, of Faith, of Purity,   1075
Our wonted Ornaments now soil'd and stain'd,
And in our Faces evident the signs
Of foul concupiscence; whence evil store;
Even shame, the last of evils; of the first
Be sure then. How shall I behold the face   1080
Henceforth of God or Angel, erst with joy
And rapture so oft beheld? those heav'nly shapes
Will dazzle now this earthly, with thir blaze
Insufferably bright. O might I here
In solitude live savage, in some glade   1085
Obscur'd, where highest Woods impenetrable
To Star or Sun-light, spread thir umbrage broad,
And brown as Evening: Cover me ye Pines,
Ye Cedars, with innumerable boughs
Hide me, where I may never see them more.   1090
But let us now, as in bad plight, devise
What best may for the present serve to hide
The Parts of each from other, that seem most
To shame obnoxious, and unseemliest seen,
Some Tree whose broad smooth Leaves together sew'd,   1095
And girded on our loins, may cover round
Those middle parts, that this new comer, Shame,
There sit not, and reproach us as unclean.
    So counsell'd hee, and both together went
Into the thickest Wood, there soon they chose   1100
The Figtree, not that kind for Fruit renown'd,
But such as at this day to *Indians* known
In *Malabar* or *Decan* spreads her Arms
Branching so broad and long, that in the ground
The bended Twigs take root, and Daughters grow   1105
About the Mother Tree, a Pillar'd shade
High overarch't, and echoing Walks between;
There oft the *Indian* Herdsman shunning heat
Shelters in cool, and tends his pasturing Herds
At Loopholes cut through thickest shade: Those Leaves   1110
They gather'd, broad as *Amazonian* Targe,°
And with what skill they had, together sew'd,
To gird thir waist, vain Covering if to hide
Thir guilt and dreaded shame; O how unlike
To that first naked Glory. Such of late   1115
Columbus found th' *American* so girt
With feather'd Cincture, naked else and wild
Among the Trees on Isles and woody Shores.
Thus fenc't, and as they thought, thir shame in part
Cover'd, but not at rest or ease of Mind,   1120

1111. Targe: shield.

They sat them down to weep, nor only Tears
Rain'd at thir Eyes, but high Winds worse within
Began to rise, high Passions, Anger, Hate,
Mistrust, Suspicion, Discord, and shook sore
Thir inward State of Mind, calm Region once   1125
And full of Peace, now toss't and turbulent:
For Understanding rul'd not, and the Will
Heard not her lore, both in subjection now
To sensual Appetite,

———————————

PART II

The Mock-Epic Tradition

As what might be called a second-generation mock-epic, *The Rape of the Lock* not only refracts the epic tradition directly but also refracts previous mock-epic refractions, thus becoming imitative on two levels. The earlier mock-epics that were most useful for Pope were Boileau's *Le Lutrin* and Samuel Garth's *Dispensary*. So dependent are these mock-epics on each other and on the epic tradition that it is sometimes possible to trace an episode invented by Homer through successive modifications in Virgil, Milton, Boileau, Garth, and Pope. Both *Le Lutrin* and *The Dispensary*, like true epics, are masculine poems, but instead of the larger-than-life heroic world they depict the world of Jonsonian comedy: coarse, crass, materialistic, middle-class, life-size. Pope's main modification of the mock-epic tradition as it came to him was to transpose it into an upper-class feminine world, further reducing its scale but heightening its beauty and charm.

Nicolas Boileau, *Le Lutrin*

The intramural ecclesiastical quarrel on which Boileau based *Le Lutrin* occurred in Paris in 1667. The treasurer of the Sainte-Chapelle had a huge pulpit ("lutrin") installed in the choir in such a way that it concealed the choir-leader, or "chanter," from the congregation. Indignantly refusing to sing in obscurity, the choir-leader had the pulpit removed. Further replacements and removals ensued until the treasurer finally triumphed and the pulpit remained. After telling Boileau the story, Guillaume de Lamoignon, chief justice of the supreme court of Paris, challenged him to produce a heroic poem on that subject, and *Le Lutrin* was the result. The unauthorized publication of fragments of the poem in 1673 led Boileau to publish the first four cantos in 1674; the last two did not appear until 1683. The poem is dominated by two sets of opposed passions: sloth and gluttony contend against vanity and pride of place.

In his preface, Boileau enunciated the principle of the "high burlesque" mode that he was following and that Pope in turn would follow: instead of making Dido and Aeneas talk like fishwives and porters, as Paul Scarron and other earlier French writers had done, he boasts that he has made a clockmaker and his wife talk like Dido and Aeneas. *Le Lutrin* was very popular in England: a translation of the first four cantos by "N. O." appeared in 1682, and the complete poem was rendered by John Crowne in 1692 and John Ozell in 1708. N. O.'s version is used for the selection from canto 1 below, and Ozell's less lively version for canto 5.

Canto I

Like Virgil before him and Pope after, Boileau's rhetorical questions ironically profess surprise at finding unworthy passions where they don't belong. The treasurer is as fond of sleep as Belinda and her sleepless lovers.

131

IMmortal feuds, and more than Civil Warrs,
And Fights thô fierce, disfigur'd with no Scarrs
I sing ! And thee *Great Prelate*, who of late,
Maugre the Chanter, and Reluctant Fate
Didst raise at length a *Pulpit* in the Quire,
Th' immortal Trophee of thy Mortal Ire.
7   Twice the *Pragmatick Chanter*, thô in vain,
Presum'd to discompose thy peaceful Reign;
Twice with Schismatick Pride did enterprize
To force the *Chapter* in Rebellion rise ;
As oft the *Dean* him swoln with envious rage,
Hurl'd Headlong from high hopes; and by the sage
Sexton:

7. Pragmatick: here, interfering, meddling.

132

Sexton affifted, terrify'd the People
  Who durft difpute the Title to his *Steeple.*
Inftruct me *Mufe,* for thou canft tell, what Thirft
Of fweet Revenge, thô Dire, engaged firft
Religious Souls to break the Sacred Tye
Of bleffed Peace and heaven-born Amitie,
To make old Friends new Rivals; *can there reft
Such bitter Gall in a Religious Breaft?*
  And thou Great *Heroe,* whofe wife conduct ftifled   21
The growing Schifme which elfe thy Church had rifled,.
With favour influence my Advent'rous Verfe,
Nor dare to laugh, whileft I thy Acts rehearfe..
  In melting Pleafures of Fraternal Peace
An ancient *Abbey* long had dwelt at eafe,
Whofe Scarlet *Prebends* blear'd poor Mortals eyes,
Whofe *Ermines,* Winters Froft, and Snow defies;
Basking in fat, and Wealth, themfelves they Blefs
In fweet Repofe of *Sacred Idlenefs:*
Thus Stretcht at length on downy Featherbeds,
To chaunt their Matines ne're lift up their Heads,
But before Dinner wak'd; for they could fmell
The Kitchin Steams, though Deaf to th' Prayer-bell;.
When Eyes and Ears Nights leaden Key compofes,
Kind Sleep yet open left their fubtle Nofes;
Thefe alwaies *Eat in Perfon,* but did praife
Their God *by Proxie,* in Harmonious Layes,
Pawning the *Chanters,* and Poor Singing-boyes
Condemn'd to thofe inferiour Drudgeries.
  When *Difcord* dappled o're with thoufand Crimes,
The Villanies of our Debauched times
Quitting the humble Seat of Parifh Churches,
On a Magnificent *Cathedral* Perches,
The hideous clang of her hate-bearing wing
Peace trembled: whilft the Fiend arm'd with her Sting:

A 3   Allight-

---

21. Great Heroe: Lamoignon, the chief justice.

Allighting fwift before the Pompous Pile
48 Of her proud Pallace, ftood and paws'd a while.
   Thence with obferving eye, her Empire viewing,
Fomented Feuds and Warrs thereon enfuing,
Hatred, and variance, her felf fhe bleffes,
Applauds her Wit in thefe Atchiev'd fucceffes;
53 From *Norwich* there, and *Briftol* Coaches, fhe
Legions of *Tories* dear, arriv'd might fee,
And could her Vaffals boaft of all Degrees,
Cittizens, Nobles, Clerks, Prieſs, Dignities;
But above all her Feats renown'd in ftories,
In this fhe Prides her felf, in this fhe Glories,
That Troops of *Barr-gowns* rang'd under her Banner
60 Had routed *Themes,* and now Triumph't on her;
   And yet fhe faw, and rag'd, and Griev'd to fee
One *Church* difturb this rare Felicity,
One *Church* to brave her triumphs; *one Alone*
Threaten to fhake the firmnefs of her Throne,
That amidft all thefe *Herricanes* and *Scuffles*
No breath of Stormy Wind it's Quiet ruffles.
   Needs muft fo Odious a fight as this
Awake her Rage, make all her Serpents hifs;
69 With *Stygian Aconite* her mouth fhe fills,
From glaring eyes fhe ftreams of Flame diftills:
   "What? (faid fhe with a tone made windows Quiver,)
"Have I been able hitherto to Shiver
"The Union 'twixt *Cordeliers, Carmelites,*
" *Dominicans, Francifcans, Minorites,*
"Betwixt the *Molinifts,* the *Celeftines,*
"*Janfenifts, Jefuites,* and *Auguftines?*
"Have I by fecreet Arts, nourifht *the Stickle*
78 "*Between the Church-men, and the Conventicle?*
"And fhall one *Paultry Chappel* dare to Brave me;
"Nay hope in time to it's nice Laws t' inflave me?
                                              And

---

48. Pallace: Palace of Justice, or courthouse.
53ff. Norwich, Bristol: The translator often provides English equivalents for Boileau's proper names.
60. Themis: goddess of Justice.
69. Aconite: a genus of poisonous plants, including wolf'sbane and monk'shood..
78. Church-men and Conventicle: i.e., the Established Church of England and the Dissenters. The preceding list, though, refers to French religious orders and ecclesiastical factions.

" And am I *Difcord* ftill? *who any more*
" *With Incenfe will my Sacred Shrines Adore?*
 Thus fpoke the Hagg! And in a trice unfeen
Of an *Old Chawer* takes the fhape and meen:
A corner'd Cap her Snake-wigg'd Head did cover,
Her rich Face fparkling Rubies ftudded over,
Her Nofe, embofs'd with Carbuncles Divine
Before her fteps did like a Flamboy fhine;   88
Accoutred thus, with Red-coat Soldiers pace
Haughty fhe march't to find the *Prelates* Grace.
 A Stately Bed, the Pofts moft richly Gilt,
Cover'd with Sumptuous Crimfon Damask Quilt,
Enclos'd with Double Curtains, fcorning light
Of mid-day Sun, and counterfeiting Night,
Stood clofe in an Appartment like a Cell
Where Sweet Repofe and Silence chofe to Dwell;
The Tefter was all fac'd with Looking-Glafs,
The rare Invention of this Golden Afs,
Contriv'd myfterioufly that he might peep
And fee how Blithe he lookt, when faft a-fleep.
 Here lay the *Mitred Head*! in flumber drown'd,
Whilft gentle fumes his Dreaming Temples Crown'd;
A Sprightly Air adorns his Youthful Face,
His double Chin hangs down with goodly Grace;
The Claret fhin'd through the tranfparent Skin,
A broad conjeĉture where he late had been;
And his Fat comely Corps, fo thick and fhort
Made the Soft Pillows groan under his Port:
Here, in Sack-poffet arm'd, without repining
He waits in patience the bleft hour of Dining.
 The Goddefs entring, faw the Table fpread,
And all within doors rarely ordered,
Then Softly marching to his lodging, took him
Profoundly napping, and thus fhe befpoke him.
          " Sleep'ft:

---

88. Flamboy: flambeau, or torch.

" Sleep'ſt thou, *Great Prelate?* Sleep'ſt thou then Supine?
" And to *the Chanter* mean'ſt thy Place Reſign?
" Whilſt he ſings *Oremus,* makes Grave Proceſſions,
"And hurls about by whole-ſale Vows and Bleſſings?
" Sleep'ſt thou ſecurely, till the *Chanter* come,
" And without *Bull,* or *Brief* procur'd from *Rome,*
" Whilſt thou'rt wrapt up in ſloath, and free from Fears,
122 " *Rotchet* and *Surplice* ſhall pluck o're thy Ears?
" Sluggard, awake, ariſe, beſtir thee quick,
" Renounce thy Eaſe, or quit thy *Biſhoprick!*
She ſpoke; and from her Poyſonous Mouth did fling
Into his Soul the *Zeal of Quarrelling.*
The *Dean* awakes; The choler in his breaſt
Fermented boils; yet he the Fury Bleſt!
Have you not ſeen *a Bull* by Gad-fly ſtung,
When his tormented pride flownc'd, kick't, and flung?
The vexed Air, with *Ecchoes* frighted rings!
Whilſt he exhales his Rage in Bellowings!
So ſtorm'd the *Prelate,* with his Dream o're-heated,
Poor Page, and Chambermaid were rudely treated;
His mettle mov'd with conceiv'd Indignation,
Needs will he go to'th' *Quire* before *Collation.*
When Prudent *Gilotin* his Almoner
With grave Advice ſtept into ſtint the Stir;
Shews him the Danger of that Raſh Deſign,
How mad to go to Prayers, before he Dine;
" What Rage (quoth he) is this? what head-ſtrong crotchet?
" Pray Sir, regard the Honour of your *Rotchet!*
" He that for *Chappel* lets warm Dinner cool,
" May think himſelf Devout, I'le think him Fool!
"Does our Church conſecrate *Prelates* to Pray?
" For ſhame, this Zeal unſeaſonable allay!
" Shall all your Learning e're make me believe,
"That this is *Lent,* or any *Saints dayes* Eve?

Theſe

---

122. Rotchet: a vestment similar to a surplice, usually worn by bishops and abbots.

"Then Reaffume your felf, forbear to Doat,
"Meat heated twice, is not worth half a Groat!
  Thus reafon'd *Gilotin*, and very loath
T' adjourn a Meal, bad 'em ferve in the broath.
The *Prelate* ftood a while in deep fufpence,
He ey'd the *Soupe* with *Holy Reverence*;
O'recome at laft with Reafon and good Nature
He yields, and fits him down *to taft the Creature*:
'Yet inward Rage did all the while provoke him,
Twas fear'd each Morfel would go near to choke him;
Gilotin faw't, and figh'd! in Zeal he rifes
T' acquaint his party with thefe Enterprifes;
Tells them with Grief of Heart, what rude Affronters
Of Lawn-fleev'd Grandeur were thefe Sawcy *Chanters*;
Protefts they'd vex't his *Lordfhip* fo that day
His Meat went down like *Orts*, or *old chopt Hay*!
Nay I may fafely fay't without Prefumption,
This Courfe muft bring him int' a Deep Confumption!
  Now might you fee whole troops of *Chanons*, all
To *Rendevouz* in the great Pallace-hall!
So have you feen perhaps Legions of *Cranes*,
Marching on Wing o're *Strymons* Spacious plains,
When the proud *Pygmies*, muft'ring their warlike Nation
Defign againft them an Unjuft Invafion!
  Surpriz'd at fight of this great friendly Rabble,
The Sweetned Prelate rifes from the Table;
Nodding he Touch't his Hat, to keep *Decorum*;
Nor feem'd to *flight*, nor bafely to *Adore 'um*!
His face no longer fhone with Orient Flame,
But pleas'd, recalls the good *Weftphalia-Ham*;
Then takes himfelf a lufty Beer-bowl brimmer
Of *Racy Claret*, and Commends a Swimmer
To the good Company; they with joint confent
Follow the *Prelates gracious Precedent*;
                    B   And

Canto V

Awaking to find the pulpit removed again, the canons decide to beg their sibyl, Chicanery, to foretell the final outcome of the dispute. The setting bears some resemblance to the Cave of Spleen in *The Rape of the Lock*.

CANTO V.

Amidſt thoſe *Gothic Pillars*, which ſupport
The formidable *Hall*, and auful Court
Of *Common Pleas* ; a Famous *Fabrick*'s rear'd,
Ador'd by *Lawyers* and by *Clients* fear'd.
Here Fools and Knaves each *Term* in Shoals repair,
Thin'd with the Diet of *Litigious* Air,
Beneath a Hill of *Briefs*, *Green Bags*, and *Scroles*,   39
Here every Morn a *Hectic Sibyl* howls.
Vain are the Tears of *Orphans*, vain their Cries,
To that *foul Monſter*, void of Ears and Eyes,
Call'd *Chicanry*, in learned Modern ſtyle,
Bulky with Ruin, and o'ergrown with Spoil.
While the wrong'd Widow want of Juſtice mourns,
And the vex'd *Air* each empty Groan returns ;
Pale *Want* and *Famine*, like ſome *injur'd Ghoſt*,
Stalk o'er the Ground and weep their Treaſures loſt.
Infamous *Poverty*, Devouring *Care*,
And Everlaſting *Toil*, and lean *Deſpair*,
And black *Chagrin*, Compleat the Mournful Part ;
The wretched Off-ſpring of her *curſed Art* !
Caſe-Books and *Codes* the Buſie Hag Conſume,
And Dies her ſelf to dig another's Tomb :

At

---

39. Green Bags: used by lawyers to carry their papers.

At every Meal, the hungry *Fury* Eats
Fair *Palaces*, ftrong *Caftles*, *Country Seats*:

57 The bubbl'd *Suitors* at their Fate repine;
Gull'd with *Superfluous Reams* for *Solid Coin*.

A Hundred times has *Juftice* turn'd her Scales;
So oft her guilty Influence prevails.

Inceffantly from Trick to Trick fhe runs;
And fometimes *like an Owl*, the Day-light fhuns.

Now, like a *Lion* Lafhing his dull Sides,
She ftalks with fiery Eyes, and frightful Strides:
Now like a *Serpent* thro' the *Herbage* glides.

Long has the jufteft *Monarch* Strove in Vain,
With *Gordian* Knots this *Proteus* to reftrain.

Her Claws, by *Sommers* clip'd increafe in Strength:
With Ink difcolour'd, and o'ergrown in Length.

Ramparts and *Dykes of Law*, too feeble Foes,
Refift th' Invafion, but in vain oppofe.

72 With *Creeping Guile* fhe Saps the Eafy Ground,
Or with *High Torrent* breaks th' Obftructing Mound.

Sydrac Salutes the *Fiend*, and bending low,
With diftant awe reveres her wrinkled Brow.

Then Tempting Gold difplays: *She* with Delight
Views the bright Scene, and dwells upon the Sight.

When

57. bubbled: duped.
72. saps: undermines.

140

CANTO V.

When thus the Sire——*Contention's* Mighty Queen !
Unqueftion'd You o'er *Kings* and *Peafants* Reign.
Thro' Thee, *Force* ufelefs is, and *Laws* are weak ;
Statutes, like *Cobwebs*, You at pleafure Break.
For Thee the *Hind* Sweats at his drudging Plough ;
For Thee his Flocks are fleec'd, his Meadows grow,
For thee he Yearly reaps his *Golden Fields* ;
To Thee his Rich *Autumnal* Labour Yields.
If from my Infant Years I've Thee ador'd,
And *Seas of Ink* on thy dread *Altars* pour'd,
Difdain not, *Mighty Goddefs* ! now to own
In his declining Years thy faithful Son.
Induftrious *Fautrefs* of *Vexation*, Hear,   90
And Anfwer an imploring *Prelate's* Pray'r.
For on the Ruins of his Bright Renown
An envious Rival has advanc'd his own :
The *Defk* Deftroying with a forceful Band ;   94
The *Defk*, late Re-erected by our Hand.
Exhauft thy Fatal Knowledge in this Caufe,   }
Revolve the Books, Create Eternal Flaws,   }
And with *Dædalean* Wiles confound the Laws.   }

                                                   Be

---

90. Fautress: feminine form of *fautor*, abettor, promoter.
94. Desk: Ozell's translation of *lutrin*.

The LUTRIN

Be to thy Darling Sons thofe Arts difplay'd
Which *puzzle* * *Themis* in the Rules fhe *made* !

----

* *The Goddefs of Juftice.*

When all seems lost, the treasurer uses a ritual blessing as an
offensive weapon, incidentally emphasing the formalistic quality of
the disputants' religion. The treasurer needed his whole hand to
subdue his foes; for Belinda, in the reduced scale of *The Rape of the
Lock*, one finger and a thumb suffices.

The *Prelate* faw their Fall with ghaftful Eyes,
And fent to Heav'n a Scream that pierc'd the Skies.
Struck back with Horror and Appal'd with Fear,
He curfes in his Heart the *God* of *War.*

      With

CANTO V.

With Silent Indignation he Retreats,

Yet ſtill the *Chanter* in his Mind defeats.

Then rallying his loſt Spirits, Makes a Stand,

And from his *Caſſock* Draws his Vengeful Hand.

Yes, ſaid the Mighty Chief, Tho' *Armies* fail,

Theſe *Bleſſing-giving Fingers* ſhall prevail.

Forward ſte moves, and upwards turns his Eyes,

Then Stretch'd his Fingers forth in Holy-Wiſe.

Kneeling in heaps the *Paſſengers* Receive

The *Benedictions* He prepars to Give

With politic deſign to turn the Rout

Upon his Foes, who durſt not *Stand* him Out.

The Zealous Vulgar force down All they Meet,

Nor will they Suffer One to keep his Feet.

Th' Out-witted Adverſe Hoſt, Confounded ſtare

At this unthought of Stratagem in War,

And dread the Storm approaching from afar.

Vainly the Trembling *Chanter* ſeeks for Aid

From his own Courage, or his Firm Brigade ;

By *Both* Forſaken, *He* too now muſt *Fly*,

Or *Fall* before his Haughty Enemy.

The Conſternated Troops themſelves Disband ;

Yet None Eſcape the ſwift-purſuing *Hand*.

F 4 Driv'n

The L U T R I N.

Driv'n on each others Backs, and fpur'd by **Fear** ;
Still Hangs the Conqu'ring *Finger* on their **Rear**.
Ev'rard, in Hopes to hide his threatn'd **Head**
247 From Holy Infult, to a Corner **Fled**.

The Watchful *Prelate* faw his clofe **Retreat**,
And ftrait March'd up, his Conqueft to **Compleat** ;
Then Turning to the Right, he wheel'd **around**,
And *Blefs'd* the frightn'd Champion to the **Ground**.
Thrice he Erects his Rebel Head in **Vain**,
The lengthen'd *Finger* forc'd him down **again**.
Oblig'd to Kneel, becaufe the *Mob*'s fo **near** ;
And what he owes to *Rev'rence* Pays to *Fear*.

_____

247. insult: in the archaic sense of attack or assault.

Samuel Garth, *The Dispensary*

In April 1698, the Royal College of Physicians of London opened a small dispensary — in modern terms an outpatient clinic — where poor patients were examined without charge and drugs provided at cost. This project had been planned for many years, but its completion had been delayed by the combined opposition of the London apothecaries, who feared that the dispensary might decrease their business, and of a sizable group in the college, called "apothecaries' physicians." Some time before the end of 1698, one of these apothecaries' physicians became involved in an undignified scuffle with several employees of the dispensary. This "trivial thing" provided Dr. Samuel Garth, a firm supporter of the dispensary and later a friend of Pope, with the inspiration for his poem, which in 1699 expanded the scuffle into an epic-scale military attack on the dispensary. It should be noted that the chief combatants are the rival factions of physicians; the apothecaries play a relatively small part. *The Dispensary* was very popular; it went into a fourth edition in 1700 and an eighth in 1718, not counting several piracies, and inspired a number of "keys". In style and diction, *The Dispensary* is perhaps less elegant than *Le Lutrin;* the gap between subject and style is narrower. Compared to *The Rape of the Lock*, Garth's poems is rather static and repetitious, consisting primarily of speeches and of journeys to the haunts of several different allegorical personages.

The following selections are taken from the sixth edition (1706), the latest to appear before *The Rape of the Lock*. Pope's copy of this edition, with his annotations, is now in the Huntington Library. The poem has recently been edited by Frank H. Ellis in the sixth volume of *Poems on Affairs of State* (Yale University Press, 1970), to which I am indebted for many notes. Garth's occasional brief notes have been incorporated into mine. I have followed Ellis' lead in filling the blanks which Garth usually left in the real names of some of his incidental satiric victims, but I have not often identified the main characters, since their real names mean little more to a modern reader than their fictitious ones.

Canto I

Apart from the general convention of the invocation, several motifs in *The Rape of the Lock* parallel parts of this canto. The laboratory is a workaday version of Belinda's dressing table, and the Den of Sloth has a function similar to that of the Cave of Spleen, though its nature is quite different. The Cave of Envy in canto 2 is closer in spirit to Spleen.

THE

Dispensary.

CANTO I.

Speak, Goddefs! fince 'tis Thou that beft canft tell,
How ancient Leagues to modern Difcord fell;
And why Phyficians were fo cautious grown
Of others Lives, and lavifh of their own;
How by a Journey to th' *Elyfian* Plain
Peace triumph'd, and old Time return'd again.

Not far from that moft celebrated Place,   7
Where angry ¹ Juftice fhews her awful Face;

B   Where

---

7. Place: the Old Bailey, London's Central Criminal Court.

The Dispensary.

Where little Villains muft fubmit to Fate,
That great Ones may enjoy the World in State;
There ftands a ² Dome, Majeftick to the Sight,
And fumptuous Arches bear its oval Height;
A golden Globe plac'd high with artful Skill,
Seems, to the diftant Sight, a gilded Pill:
This Pile was, by the Pious Patron's Aim,
Rais'd for a Ufe as Noble as its Frame:
Nor did the Learn'd Society decline
The Propagation of that great Defign;
In all her Mazes, Nature's Face they view'd,
And as fhe difappear'd, their Search purfu'd.
Wrapt in the Shades of Night the Goddefs lyes,
Yet to the Learn'd unveils her dark Difguife,
But fhuns the grofs Accefs of vulgar Eyes.
Now fhe unfolds the faint, and dawning Strife
Of infant Atoms kindling into Life:

And

---

11. Dome: the College of Physicians.
21. Goddess: i.e., Nature.

CANTO I.

How ductile Matter new Meanders takes,

And flender Trains of twifting Fibres makes.

And how the Vifcous feeks a clofer Tone,

By juft degrees to harden into Bone;

While the more Loofe flow from the vital Urn,   30

And in full Tides of Purple Streams return;

How lambent Flames from Life's bright Lamp arife,

And dart in Emanations through the Eyes;

How from each Sluice a gentle Torrent pours,

To flake a feav'rifh Heat with ambient Show'rs.

Whence, their Mechanick Pow'rs, the Spirits claim,

How great their Force, how delicate their Frame:

How the fame Nerves are fafhion'd to fuftain

The greateft Pleafure and the greateft Pain.

Why bileous Juice a Golden Light puts on,

And Floods of Chyle in Silver Currents run.   41

How the dim Speck of Entity began

To work its brittle Being up to Man.

B 2   To

---

30. vital Urn: the heart. This line and the next refer to the circulation of the blood.
41. Chyle: a milky fluid found in the small intestine.

The Dispensary.

To how minute an Origin we owe

45 Young *Ammon*, *Cæfar*, and the Great *Naffau*.

Why paler Looks impetuous Rage proclaim,

And why chill Virgins redden into Flame.

Why Envy oft transforms with wan Difguife,

And why gay Mirth fits fmiling in the Eyes.

50 All Ice why *Lucrece*, or *Sempronia*, Fire,

Why *S——* rages to furvive Defire.

Whence *Milo*'s Vigour at *Olympick*'s fhown,

Whence Tropes to *F——h*, or Impudence to *S——n*.

Why *Atticus* polite, *Brutus* fevere,

Why *Me——n* muddy, *M——gue* why clear.

Hence 'tis we wait the wond'rous Caufe to find,

How Body acts upon impaffive Mind.

How Fumes of Wine the thinking Part can fire,

Paft Hopes revive, and prefent Joys infpire:

Why our Complexions oft our Soul declare,

And how the Paffions in the Features are.

How

---

45. Ammon: Alexander the Great. Ammon was an Egyptian god identified by the Greeks with Zeus, from whom Alexander claimed to have been descended.
　　Nassau: William III, King of England.
50-55. The poem provides the essential information about the names mentioned in this passage.

CANTO I.

How Touch and Harmony arife between
Corporeal Subftances, and Things unfeen.
With mighty Truths, myfterious to defcry,
Which in the Womb of diftant Caufes lye.

But now thofe great Enquiries are no more,
And Faction skulks, where Learning fhone before;
The drooping Sciences neglected pine,
And *Pœan*'s Beams with fading Luftre fhine.   69
No Readers here with Hectick Looks are found,
Or Eyes in Rheum, thro' midnight-watching drown'd:
The lonely Edifice in Sweats complains
That nothing there but empty Silence reigns.

This Place fo fit for undifturb'd Repofe,
The God of Sloth for his *Afylum* chofe.
Upon a Couch of Down in thefe Abodes
Supine with folded Arms he thoughtlefs nods.

B 3

Indulging

69. Pæan: physician to the Olympian Gods.

The Dispensary.

Indulging Dreams his Godhead lull to Ease,
With Murmurs of soft Rills, and whisp'ring Trees.
The *Poppy* and each numming Plant dispense
Their drowzy Virtue, and dull Indolence.
No Passions interrupt his easie Reign,
No Problems puzzle his Lethargick Brain.
But dark Oblivion guards his peaceful Bed,
And lazy Fogs hang ling'ring o'er his Head.

As at full Length the pamper'd Monarch lay
Batt'ning in Ease, and slumb'ring Life away:
A spiteful Noise his downy Chains unties,
Hastes forward, and encreases as it flies.

90   First, some to cleave the stubborn ³ Flint engage,
'Till urg'd by Blows, it sparkles into Rage.
92 Some temper Lute, some spacious Vessels move;
These Furnaces erect, and Those approve.

Here

90ff. These lines describe the building of the dispensary.
92. Lute: a kind of clay used for cementing laboratory vessels. To temper it is to mix it
with water to the proper consistency.

CANTO I.

Here Phyals in nice Difcipline are fet,

There Gally-pots are rang'd in Alphabet. 95

In this place, Magazines of Pills you fpy;

In that, like Forage, Herbs in Bundles lye.

While lifted Peftles brandifh'd in the Air

Defcend in Peals, and Civil Wars declare.

Loud Stroaks, with pounding Spice, the Fabrick rend,

And Aromatick Clouds in Spires afcend.

So when the *Cyclops* o'er their Anvils fweat, 102

And their fwoln Sinews ecchoing Blows repeat;

From the *Vulcano's* grofs Eruptions rife,

And curling Sheets of Smoke obfcure the Skies.

The flumb'ring God amaz'd at this new Din,

Thrice ftrove to rife, and thrice funk down agen.

Liftlefs he ftretch'd, and gaping rubb'd his Eyes,

Then falter'd thus betwixt half Words and Sighs.

B 4

How

---

95. Gally-pot: gallipot, "a small earthen glazed pot, especially one used by apothecaries for ointments and medicines" (*OED*).
102. Cyclops: not the savage monsters that Odysseus encountered, but rather, as in the tradition followed by Hesiod, semidivine blacksmiths who forged thunderbolts for Zeus.

CANTO II

After complaining at length about his interrupted slumber, the God of Sloth sends his messenger, Phantom, to bring the news to the Cave of Envy.

THE

Dispensary.

CANTO II.

SOON as with gentle Sighs the Ev'ning Breeze
   Begun to whisper thro' the murm'ring Trees;
And Night to wrap in Shades the Mountains Heads,
While Winds lay hush'd in Subterranean Beds;
Officious *Phantom* did with speed prepare
To slide on tender Pinions through the Air.
Oft he attempts the Summit of a Rock,
And oft the Hollow of some blasted Oak;
At length approaching where bleak Envy lay,
The hissing of her Snakes proclaim'd the way

B₂-

The Dispensary.

Beneath the gloomy Covert of an Yew,
That taints the Grafs with fickly Sweats of Dew;
No verdant Beauty entertains the Sight,
14 But baneful Hemlock, and cold Aconite;
In a dark Grott the baleful Haggard lay,
Breathing black Vengeance, and infecting Day.
But how deform'd, and worn with fpightful Woes,
18 Rapacious *Verres*, late a Statefman, knows.
The cheerful Blood her meager Cheeks forfook,
And Bafilisks fate Brooding in her Look.
A bald and bloated Toad-ftool rais'd her Head;
The Plumes of boding Ravens were her Bed.
From her chapp'd Noftrils fcalding Torrents fall,
And her funk Eyes boil o'er in Floods of Gall.
Volcano's labour thus with inward Pains,
Whilft Seas of melted Oar lye wafte the Plains.

Around

---

14. Aconite: See note to *Le Lutrin*: 1:69, p. 134.
18. Verres: governor of Sicily (73-70 B.C.). Prosecuting him on behalf of the citizens of Sicily and therefore not an impartial witness, Cicero presented him as an extraordinarily corrupt and rapacious tyrant. Little other information about him has survived.

C A N T O II.

Around the Fiend in hideous Order fate
Foul bawling Infamy, and bold Debate:
Gruff Difcontent, thro' Ignorance mifs-led,
And clam'rous Faction at her Party's Head:
Reftlefs Sedition ftill diffembling Fear,
And fly Hypocrifie with Pious Leer.

Glouting with fullen Spight the Fury fhook   33
Her clotter'd Locks, and blafted with each Look.   34
Then tore with canker'd Teeth the pregnant Scrolls,
Where Fame the Acts of Demy-Gods enrolls.
And as the rent Records in pieces fell,
Each Scrap did fome Immortal Action tell.

---

33. glouting: frowning, scowling.
34. clotter'd: stuck together, matted.

Canto III

Assuming the appearance of Colon (not certainly identified), Envy flies off to inform Horoscope, an "apothecaries' physician" and the "sage" and "magus" of the following passage.

THE
Difpenfary.

C A N T O III.

ALL Night the Sage in Penfive Tumults lay,
    Complaining of the flow Approach of Day;
Oft turn'd him round, and ftrove to think no more
Of what fhrill *Colon* fpoke the Day before.
Cowflips and *Poppies* o'er his Eyes he fpread,
And *S——* Works he laid beneath his Head. 6
But thofe blefs'd Opiats ftill in vain he tries,
Sleep's gentle Image his Embraces flies.
Tumultuous Cares lay rolling in his Breaft,
And thus his anxious Thoughts the Sage expreft.
                                  Oft

---

6. Salmon: according to one key, a "Quack doctor, and indefatigable Scribbler." One of his works was an attack on the dispensary.

After a long soliloquy, Horoscope vows that the dispensary shall fall. The council that follows is based on part of the "great consult" of the fallen angels in *Paradise Lost* (2:50-298), with Diasenna, Colocynthis, and Ascaris playing the parts of Belial, Moloch, and Mammon respectively. Diasenna and colocynthis are strong cathartics, and the ascaris (plural, ascarides) is the roundworm, an intestinal parasite.

With that, a Glance from mild *Aurora*'s Eyes

Shoots thro' the Chryftal Kingdoms of the Skies;

The Savage Kind in Forefts ceafe to roam,

And Sots o'ercharg'd with naufeous Loads reel home.

Light's chearful Smiles o'er th'Azure Wafte are fpread,

·And Mifs from Inns o' Court bolts out unpaid.

The Sage tranfported at th'approaching Hour,

Imperioufly thrice thunder'd on the Floor;

Offici-

CANTO III.

Officious *Squirt* that Moment had accefs, 59
His Truft was great, his Vigilance no lefs.
To him thus *Horofcope*,

My kind Companion in this dire Affair,
Which is more light, fince you affume a Share;
Fly with what hafte you us'd to do of old,
When *Clyfter* was in danger to be cold: 65
With Expedition on the Beadle call,
To fummon all the Company to th' *Hall*.

Away the trufty Coadjutor flies,
Swift as from Phyal Steams of *Harts-horn* rife.
The *Magus* in the int'rim mumbles o'er
Vile Terms of Art to fome Infernal Pow'r,
And draws Myfterious Circles on the Floor.
But from the gloomy Vault no glaring Spright,
Afcends to blaft the tender Bloom of Light.

D 2   No

---

59. Squirt: (a) diarrhea; (b) a syringe, probably in this case one used to administer enemas.
65. Clyster: an enema, or the apparatus used in its administration.

The Dispensary.

No mystick Sounds from *Hell*'s detested Womb,
In dusky Exhalations upwards come.
And now to raise an Altar He decrees,
To that devouring Harpy call'd *Disease*.
Then Flow'rs in Canisters he hastes to bring,
The wither'd Product of a blighted Spring,
81 With cold *Solanum* from the *Pontick* Shore,
The Roots of *Mandrake* and Black *Ellebore*.
And on the Structure next he heaps a Load
Of *Saffafras* in Chips, and *Mastick* Wood.
Then from the Compter he takes down the File,
And with Prescriptions lights the solemn Pile.

Feebly the Flames on clumsie Wings aspire,
And smoth'ring Fogs of Smoke benight the Fire.
With Sorrow he beheld the sad Portent,
Then to the Hag these *Orizons* he sent.

Dis-

81-84. Beyond the general irony of a physician sacrificing medicines to Disease, the
particular drugs named do not seem to have any special significance.

CANTO III.

Disease! thou ever moſt propitious Pow'r,

Whoſe kind Indulgencies we taſte each Hour;

Thou well canſt boaſt thy num'rous Pedigree

Begot by Sloth, maintain'd by Luxury.

In gilded Palaces thy Prowefs reigns,

But flies the humble Sheds of Cottage Swains.

To You ſuch Might and Energy belong,

You nip the Blooming, and unnerve the Strong.

The Purple Conqueror in Chains you bind,

And are to us your Vaſſals only kind.

If, in return, all Diligence we pay

To fix your Empire, and confirm your Sway,

Far as the weekly Bills can reach around,   103

From *Kent-ſtreet* end to fam'd St. *Giles's-Pound;*   104

Behold this poor Libation with a Smile,

And let auſpicious Light break through the Pile.

---

103. Bills: the weekly "Bills of Mortality," or lists of deaths, published for London and the surrounding parishes since 1592.
104. These locations marked respectively the approximate southeast and northwest limits of greater London.

The Dispensary.

He spoke; and on the Pyramid he laid
Bay-Leaves and Vipers Hearts, and thus he said;
As *These* confume in this myfterious Fire,
So let the curs'd *Difpenfary* expire;
And as *Those* crackle in the Flames, and die,
So let its Veffels burft, and Glaffes fly.
113 But a finifter Cricket ftrait was heard,
The Altar fell, the Off'ring difappear'd.
As the fam'd Wight the Omen did regret,
Squirt brought the News the Company was met.

117   Nigh where *Fleet-Ditch* defcends in fable Streams,
To wafh his footy *Naiads* in the *Thames*;
119 There ftands a * Structure on a rifing Hill,
Where *Tyro*'s take their Freedom out to kill.
Some Pictures in thefe dreadful Shambles tell,
122 How, by the *Delian* God, the *Pithon* fell;

And

113. sinister Cricket: although the cricket is usually called "merry" and considered a sign of good fortune, its chirp can also foretell rain or death.
117. Fleet-Ditch: the largest and most malodorous of London's open sewers.
119. Structure: Apothecaries' Hall.
122. Apollo killed the monster Python with arrows as soon as it was engendered in the slime left behind by the deluge (Ovid, *Metamorphoses*, 1:416-51).

C A N T O III.

And how *Medea* did the *Philter* brew, 123

That cou'd in *Æfon*'s Veins young Force renew.

In healing Tears how *Myrrha* mourn'd her Fall, 125

And what befel the beauteous Criminal.

How *Mentha* and *Althea*, Nymphs no more, 127

Revive in facred Plants, and Health reftore.

How fanguine Swairs their am'rous Hours repent,

When Pleafure's paft, and Pains are permanent; 130

And how frail Nymphs, oft by Abortion, aim

To lofe a Subftance, to preferve a Name.

123-24. Medea renewed the youth of her father-in-law, Aeson, by replacing his blood with a spectacular witch's brew (*Metamorphoses*, 7:159-296).

125-26. Overcome by incestuous lust, Myrrha seduced her father. After repenting she was transformed into a myrrh-bearing tree from which Adonis was born (*Metamorphoses* 10:298-518).

127-28. Mentha is mint. Althaea, derived from a Greek word meaning "to heal,", is a genus of plants that includes the marsh mallow and the hollyhock. I have been unable to trace their careers as nymphs.

130. Pains: likely the result of venereal disease.

Diasenna counsels a negotiated peace, but Colocynthis, echoing
Sarpedon, urges

"Arm therefore, gallant Friends, 'tis Honour's Call,
Or let us boldly Fight, or bravely Fall."

(233-34)

One of the Ascarides then holds forth on the nature of honor, which
he views much as Thalestris does when she urges Belinda to avenge
the loss of her lock.

when Privilege and Right
Are once invaded, Honour bids us Fight.

But e'er we once engage in Honour's Caufe,

Firft know what Honour is, and whence it was.

Scorn'd

CANTO III.

Scorn'd by the Bafe, 'tis courted by the Brave,
The Heroe's Tyrant, and the Coward's Slave.
Born in the noifie Camp, it lives on Air;
And both exifts by Hope and by Defpair.
Angry when e'er a Moment's Eafe we gain,
And reconcil'd at our Returns of Pain.
It lives, when in Death's Arms the Heroe lies,
But when his Safety he confults, it dies.
Bigotted to this Idol, we difclaim
Reft, Health, and Eafe, for nothing but a Name.

CANTO IV

Frightened from Apothecaries' Hall by an explosion in the laboratory beneath the meeting room, the apothecaries and their supporters continue their discussion in a tavern, a scene several socioeconomic levels below Hampton Court, whither Pope's heroes and nymphs resort (3:9ff).

THE

Dispensary.

CANTO IV.

NOT far from that frequented Theater, [pair; 2
Where wand'ring Punks each Night at Five re-

Where Purple Emperors in Buskins tread,

And rule imaginary Worlds for Bread;

Where *Bently*, by Old Writers, wealthy grew, 5

And *Briscoe* lately was undone by New :

There triumphs a *Physician* of Renown,

To none, but such as rust in Health, unknown.

None e'er was plac'd more fitly to impart

His known Experience, and his healing Art.

E 2

When

---

2. Punks: prostitutes.
5-6. Bently, Briscoe: booksellers and publishers.

The Dispensary.

When *Bur*——*fs* deafens all the lift'ning Prefs
With Peals of moft Seraphick Emptinefs;
Or when Myfterious *F*——*n* mounts on high,
To preach his Parifh to a Lethargy:
15 This *Æfculapius* waits hard by, to eafe
The *Martyrs* of fuch Chriftian Cruelties.

Long has this happy Quarter of the Town,
For Lewdnefs, Wit, and Gallantry been known.
All Sorts meet here, of whatfoe'er Degree,
To blend and juftle into Harmony.
The Criticks each advent'rous Author fcan,
And praife or cenfure as They like the Man.
The Politicians of *Parnaffus* prate,
And Poets canvafs the Affairs of State;
25 The Cits ne'er talk of Trade and Stock, but tell
How *Virgil* writ, how bravely *Turnus* fell.

The

---

15. Æsculapius: son of Apollo and, like his father, a god of medicine.
25. Cit: i.e., citizen — a derogatory term for merchants and tradesmen, as opposed to the polite world.

C A N T O IV.

The Country-Dames drive to *Hippolito's*, 27
Firſt find a Spark, and after loſe a Noſe. 28
The Lawyer for Lac'd Coat the Robe does quit,
He grows a Mad-man, and then turns a Wit.
And in the Cloiſter penſive *Strephon* waits,
'Till *Chloe*'s Hackney comes, and then retreats;
And if th'ungenerous Nymph a Shaft lets fly
More fatally than from a ſparkling Eye,
Mirmillo, that fam'd *Opifer*, is nigh. 35

Apothecaries thither throng to Dine,
And want of Elbow-room's ſupply'd in Wine.
Cloy'd with Variety, they ſurfeit there,
Whilſt the wan Patients on thin Gruel fare.
'Twas here the Champions of the Party met,
Of their Heroick Enterprize to treat.

---

27. Hippolito's: a chocolate-house in Covent Garden.
28. Advanced syphilis can destroy the cartilage of the nose.
35. Mirmillo: the *"Physician* of Renown" of line 7. In Latin, a *myrmillo* is a kind of gladiator, i.e., someone who assures his own survival by killing others.
    Opifer: from the motto of the Company of Apothecaries, "Opiferque Per Orbem Dicor" ("I am called an assistant throughout the world").

171

After Horoscope has confessed his failure to invoke the aid of
Disease, a "Bard" interrupts. The bard is Sir Richard Blackmore,
leader of the apothecaries' physicians and author of several long, dull
epics, including *Prince Arthur*, in ten books (1695) and *King Arthur*,
in twelve books (1697). Lines 178-86 are self-quotations.

In vain your Magick Myfteries you ufe,

Such Sounds the *Sybil*'s facred Ears abufe.

Thefe Lines the pale Divinity fhall raife,

Such is the Pow'r of Sound, and Force of Lays.

(clafh,
Arms meet with Arms, Fauchions with Fauchions

And fparks of Fire ftruck out from Armour flafh.

Thick Clouds of Duft contending Warriors raife,

And hideous War o'er all the Region brays.

Some raging ran with huge Herculean *Clubs,*

Some maffy Balls of Brafs, fome mighty Tubs

Of Cynders bore.————

Naked and half-burnt Hills with hideous Wreck

Affright the Skies, and fry the Ocean's Back.

As he went rumbling on, the *Fury* ftrait

Crawl'd in, her Limbs cou'd fcarce fupport her Weight.

A

C A N T O IV.

A noifom Rag her penfive Temples bound,
And faintly her parch'd Lips thefe Accents found.

Mortal, how dar'ft thou with fuch Lines addrefs
My awful Seat, and trouble my Recefs?
In *Effex* Marfhy Hundreds is a Cell,   193
Where lazy Fogs, and drifling Vapours dwell:
Thither raw Damps on drooping Wings repair,
And fhiv'ring Quartans fhake the fickly Air.   196
There, when fatigu'd, fome filent Hours I pafs,
And fubftitute Phyficians in my place.
Then dare not, for the future, once rehearfe
The Diffonance of fuch unequal Verfe.
But in your Lines let Energy be found,
And learn to rife in Senfe, and fink in Sound.
Harfh Words, tho' pertinent, uncouth appear,
None pleafe the Fancy, who offend the Ear.

In

---

193. Hundreds: A "hundred" is a subdivision of a county or a shire; the Hundreds of Essex were notoriously damp and unhealthy.
196. Quartans: fevers that recur every fourth day.

After disparaging Blackmore's verse at greater length, Disease declares that the apothecaries should seek the favor of the goddess Fortune, and Horoscope gallantly flies off in search of her.

The Ev'ning now with Blushes warms the Air,

The Steer resigns the Yoke, the Hind his Care.

The Clouds aloft with golden Edgings glow,

And falling Dews refresh the Flow'rs below.

The Bat with footy Wings flits thro' the Grove,

The Reeds scarce rustle, nor the Aspine move,

And all the feather'd Folks forbear their Lays of love.

Thro' the transparent Region of the Skies,

Swift as a Wish the Missionary flies.

With Wonder he surveys the upper Air,

And the gay gilded Meteors sporting there.

How

C A N T O IV.

How lambent Jellies kind'ling in the Night, 252
Shoot thro' the *Æther* in a Trail of Light.

How rifing Steams in th'azure Fluid blend,
Or fleet in Clouds, or in foft Show'rs defcend;

Or if the ftubborn Rage of Cold prevail,
In Flakes they fly, or fall in moulded Hail.

How Hony Dews embalm the fragrant Morn,
And the fair Oak with lufcious Sweats adorn.

How Heat and Moifture mingle in a Mafs,
Or belch in Thunder, or in Light'ning blaze.

Why nimble Corufcations ftrike the Eye,
And bold *Tornado's* blufter in the Sky.

Why a prolifick *Aura* upwards tends,
Ferments, and in a living Show'r defcends.

How Vapours hanging on the tow'ring Hills
In Breezes figh, or weep in warbling Rills

Whence Infant Winds their tender Pinions try,
And River Gods their thirfty Urns fupply.

F 2   The

---

252. Jellies: meteors. A kind of jellylike alga sometimes found on the ground was thought to be the remains of a fallen meteor.

175

CANTO V

In the midst of a sleepless night, Mirmillo resolves to try to compose the quarrel, but the goddess Discord appears to him disguised as Querpo and reanimates his contentiousness. In the morning, "where Honour calls, he flies," and the battle gets under way. For bold Homer's gods, we have a combat between whales.

And now the Signal summons to the Fray;

Mock Falchions flash, and paltry Enfigns play.

Their

176

CANTO V.

Their Patron God his filver Bow-ftring twangs;
Tough Harnefs ruftles, and bold Armour clangs.
The piercing *Caufticks* ply their fpightful Pow'r;
Emeticks ranch, and keen *Catharticks* fcour. 217
The deadly Drugs in double Dofes fly;
And Peftles peal a martial Symphony.

Now from their levell'd *Syringes* they pour
The liquid Volly of a miffive Show'r.
Not Storms of Sleet, which o'er the *Baltick* drive,
Pufh'd on by *Northern* Gufts, fuch Horror give.
Like Spouts in *Southern* Seas the Deluge broke,
And Numbers funk beneath th'impetuous Stroke.

So when *Leviathans* difpute the Reign
And uncontroll'd Dominion of the Main;
From the rent Rocks whole *Coral* Groves are torn,
And Ifles of *Sea-weed* on the Waves are born.

Such

---

217. ranch: to tear, cut, scratch.

Such watry Stores from their spread Nostrils fly,
'Tis doubtful which is Sea, and which is Sky.

And now the stagg'ring *Braves*, led by Despair,
Advance, and to return the Charge, prepare.
Each seizes for his Shield a spacious *Scale*,
And the *Brass Weights* fly thick as Show'rs of Hail.
Whole Heaps of Warriors welter on the Ground,
With Gally-Pots, and broken Phials crown'd;
Whilst empty Jarrs the dire Defeat resound.

Thus when some Storm its Crystal Quarry rends,
And *Jove* in ratling Show'rs of *Ice* descends;
Mount *Athos* shakes the Forests on his Brow,
Whilst down his wounded Sides fresh Torrents flow,
And Leaves and Limbs of Trees o'er-spread the Vale
[below.

But

CANTO V.

But now, all Order loft, promifcuous Blows
Confus'dly fall; perplex'd the Battel grows.

A personification of Health appears on the scene, orders the physicians to cease fighting, and sends Celsus to the Elysian Fields in search of William Harvey, who discovered the circulation of the blood and was renowned as the greatest English physician. Only he can adjudicate the quarrel. Celsus enters the realm of Death, another forerunner of the Cave of Spleen, though it adds little to those we've already visited. He finally makes his way to "the silent Mansion of disastrous Love" where he suddenly encounters a former mistress who had killed herself. Her tirade provides one perspective on Belinda's predicament.

Olivia here in Solitude he found,

Her down-caſt Eyes fix'd on the ſilent Ground:

Her Dreſs neglected, and unbound her Hair,

She ſeem'd the mournful Image of Deſpair.

How

CANTO VI.

How lately did this celebrated *Thing*
Blaze in the Box, and fparkle in the Ring,   245
'Till the Green-ficknefs and Love's force betray'd   246
To Death's remorflefs Arms th'unhappy Maid.

All o'er confus'd the guilty Lover ftood,
The Light forfook his Eyes, his Cheeks the Blood;
An Icy Horrour fhiver'd in his Look,
As to the cold-complexion'd Nymph He fpoke:

Tell me, dear Shade, from whence fuch anxious Care,
Your Looks diforder'd, and your Bofom bare?
Why thus you languifh like a drooping Flow'r.
Crufh'd by the weight of fome unfriendly Show'r?
Your languid Looks, your late ill Conduct tell;
O that inftead of Trafh you'd taken Steel!   257

I Stabb'd

245. Box: a theater seat.
   Ring: a circular drive for carriages in Hyde Park, one of the favorite places in London for seeing and being seen.
246. Green-sickness: a kind of anemia thought to be characteristic of young unmarried women.
257. Trash: adulterated drugs.
   Steel: Steel filings were a common medicine at the time. There is perhaps also a suggestion that she should have stabbed herself.

The Dispensary.

Stabb'd with th'unkind Reproach, the Confcious
 [Maid
Thus to her late infulting Lover faid;
When Ladies liften not to loofe Defire,
You ftile our Modefty, our want of Fire.
Smile or Forbid, Encourage or Reprove,
You ftill find Reafons to believe we love:
Vainly you think a Liking we betray,
And never mean the peevifh Things we fay.

Cuftom, reply'd the Lover, is your Guide,
Difcretion is but Fear, and Honour, Pride.
To do nice Conduct Right, you Nature wrong;
Impulfes are but weak, where Reafon's ftrong.
Some want th'Affurance oft, but Few the Flame;
They like the Thing, That ftartle at the Name.
The lonely *Phœnix*, tho' profefs'd a Nun,
Warms into Love, and kindles at the Sun.

Thofe

C A N T O VI.

Thofe Tales of fpicy Urns and fragrant Fires,
Are but the Emblems of her fcorch'd Defires.

Then as he ftrove to clafp the fleeting *Fair*,
His empty Arms confefs'd th'impaffive Air.
From his Embrace th'unbody'd Spectre flies,
And as fhe mov'd, fhe chid him with her Eyes.

Celsus finally finds Harvey, who advises him to refer the case to
John Somers, Lord Chancellor of England and President of the Royal
Society, and the poem ends with a panegyric to William III.

PART III

Le Comte de Gabalis

As Pope acknowledges in his prefatory letter to Arabella, he borrowed the basic conception of his sylphs from the account of the Rosicrucian spirits contained in *Le Comte de Gabalis*, published in Paris in 1670 by the Abbé de Montfaucon de Villars. Thus he was able to observe the rule which required that epic machinery be based on established doctrines rather than being invented for the occasion. Two English translations, by Philip Ayres and A. Lovell, appeared in 1680; the following selections are taken from Ayres' version, which appears to have been the better known, since it was reissued in 1692 as part of a series of "Modern Novels." Shortly after *The Rape of the Lock* appeared in 1714, an enterprising predecessor of the present editor brought out still another translation, "very necessary for Readers of Mr. Pope's *Rape of the Lock*."

De Villars' little book presents an unnamed narrator who engages in a series of dialogues with the title character, a Rosicrucian initiate. The narrator remains skeptical throughout, arguing that the sylphs, if they exist at all, are really fallen angels, whereas the count insists that they are pure spirits who worship the true God. De Villars was ridiculing Rosicrucian and Cabalistic notions, but his irony is delicate enough to leave open the possibility that the book might be a serious treatise. Lovell took it as such, according to Emile Audra, and Pope's letter seems designed to lead Belinda to believe that it is a serious exposition capable of being mistaken for a novel. Had Pope read Lovell's version? Had he read Ayres or the original but missed the irony? Or was he playing a little joke on Arabella? Beyond this level of elegant badinage, the count's doctrine that the sylphs are serious rivals of human spouses, combined with the kind of appeal that Ariel addresses to Belinda, perhaps helps to constitute an oblique comment on the nature of Belinda's human relationships.

After exchanging several letters with the count, the narrator receives an unexpected visit from him:

186

of Gabalis.

let not thy self be puft up with Pride, that he sends to thee one of the Children of Wisdom, to Constitute thee a Fellow of their Society, and make thee Partaker of the Wonders of his Omnipotency.

This strange Manner of Salutation, did upon the suddain, surprize me; and I began, at first, to question, whether or no it might not be some Apparition: Neverthelefs, recovering my Spirits the best I could, and looking upon him as Civilly as the little Fear I was seized with, could permit me. What ever you be (said I to him) whose Complement favours not of this World, you do me a great Honor, in making me this Visit. But I befeech you, if you pleafe, before I Worship this *God* of the *Sages,* let me know, of what *God,* and what *Sages* you speak?

I was Astonished one Remarkable Day, when I saw a Man come in a most Excellent Mein; who, Saluting me gravely, said to me in the *French* Tongue, but in the Accent of a Forreigner: *Adore, my Son; Adore the most Glorious and Great* God *of the* Sages: *And let*

187

The Count

You are about to Learn, how to command Nature; *God* alone, shall be your Master; and the *Sages* only, shall be your Equals: The Supream, Intelligences shall esteem it a Glory, to obey your Desires: The *Devils* shall not dare to approach, where you are; Your Voyce shall make them tremble, in the most profound Caves of their Abyss. And all the Invisible People, who inhabit the Four Elements, shall account themselves Happy, to be the Ministers of your Pleasures. I Adore thee, O Great *God!* for having Crowned *Man* with so much Glory, and for having Established *him* the Soveraign Monarch over all the Works of thy Hands! Do you feel, my Son, (added he, turning himself towards me) Do you feel this Heroick Ambition, which is the certain Character of

2 *of Gabalis.*

of the Children of *wisdom?* Dare you desire, to Serve nothing but *God* only ; and to Rule over all Things, which is not of *God?* Have you comprehended, what it is to be a Man? And, Do you not detest the being of a Slave, since you were Born to be a Soveraign? And if you have these Noble Thoughts, as the Figure of your Nativity suffers me not to doubt ; consider *soberly*, if you can have the Courage, and Strength, to Renounce all Things, which may be an Obstacle to you, in the attaining that Greatness, to which you were Born? He stopt there, and beheld me stedfastly ; as attending my Answer, or as if he were reading my Heart.

How muchsoever the beginning of this Discourse had made me hope, that we should enter presently upon the Matter ; so much

much the more was I become desperate at what he had last said. The word *RENOUNCE*, so affrighted me, that I questioned, whether or no he was not about to propose to me, the Renouncing of my *Baptism*, or *Paradise*. So that, not knowing how to get out of these Streights: Renounce, (said I to him!) Why, Sir, need I Renounce any thing? Truly, (reply'd he) there is need enough; and so much need, that we must begin with that Point first: I know not whether or no you can resolve upon it; but I know very well, that *wisdom* does not inhabit a Body subject to Sin, no more, than it enters into a Soul, prepossessed with Error or Malice. The *sages* will never admit you into their Society, if you do not Renounce from this very present, a Thing which cannot stand in Compe-

Competition with Wisdom. You must (added he, stooping down, and whispering in my Ear) *You must Renounce all Carnal Commerce with Women.*

I could not forbear breaking out into a fit of Laughter at this pleasant Proposition. Well Sir, (cryed I!) you have quitted me for a very small Matter: I had thought, that you would have proposed to me some strange Renunciation; but since it is only *women*, I assure you, that Work is long since done. I am very Chaft (*God be thanked!*) Nevertheless, Sir, in regard that *Solomon* was Wiser than I, it may be, shall ever be, and that all his Wisdom could not hinder him from being Corrupted by them. I beseech you tell me, what Expedient you Gentlemen take, to keep you from this Sex? And, what Inconvenience there would be,

C

1

---

1. Solomon's corruption: CF. *Paradise Lost*, 1:444-46 (above, p. 116).

be, if in the *Philofophers Paradice*, every *Adam* had his *Eve*.

There you ask great Matters, (reply'd he, confulting with himfelf, if he fhould Anfwer my Queftion or not) but yet fince I fee, that you defert *Women* without any Trouble, · I fhall tell you one of the Reafons, which have obliged the *Sages* to impofe this Condition on their Difciples; and from thence you will know in what Ignorance all thofe Live, who are not of our Number.

When you fhall be enrolled amongft the Children of *Philofophy*, and that your Eyes fhall be Fortifyed by the ufe of our Sacred Medicine; you fhall immediatly difcover, that the *Elements* are inhabited by moft Perfect Creatures; from the Knowledge and Commerce of whom, the Sin of the Unfortunate *Adam*, has excluded all his too Unhappy Pofterity.

fterity. This immenfe Space, which is between the Earth, and the *Heavens*, has more Noble Inhabitants, than *Birds* and *Flyes*: This vaft Ocean has alfo other Troops, befides *Dolphins* and *Whales*: The Profoundity of the Earth, is not only for *Moles*; And the *Element* of *Fire*, (more Noble than the other Three) was not made to be Unprofitable and Voyd.

The *Air* is full of an innumerable Multitude of People, having Human Shape, fomewhat Fierce in appearance, but Tractable upon experience: Great Lovers of the Sciences, Subtil, Officious to the *Sages*, and Enemies to Sots and Ignorants. Their Wives, and their Daughters have a kind of Mafculine Beauty, fuch as we defcribe the *Amazons* to have. How Sir, (cryed I!) Would you perfwade me, that thefe

C 2   Fiends

---

2. Elements: i.e., the traditional four elements: earth, air, fire, and water.

The Count

Fiends you fpeak of, are Marryed.

Be not fo Fierce, my Son, (reply'd he) for fo fmall a Matter. Believe whatfoever I tell, you, to be Solid and true, *I am mak-ing known nothing to you*, but the Principles of the Antient *Cabal*; [3] and there needs nothing more to juftify them, than that you fhould believe your own Eyes: But receive with a Meek Spirit, the Light which *God* fends you by my Interpofition. Forget all that you may have heard touching thefe Matters, in the Schools of the Ignorants: whereat you will be difpleafed, when you fhall be convinced by Experience, and be obliged to difown, what formerly you had a good Opinion of to no purpofe.

Liften then to the End; and know, that the *Seas* and *Rivers* are Inhabited, as well as the *Air*: The

of Gabalis.

The Antient *Sages* have called thefe kind of People *Undians* or *Nymphs*. They have but few Males amongft them; but the Women are there in great Numbers: Their Beauty is marvel-lous; and the Daughters of Men have nothing in them, compara-ble to thefe.

The Earth is filled almoft to the Center with *Gnomes* or *Pharyes*; a People of fmall Stature; the Guardians of Treafures, of Mines, and of Precious Stones. They are Ingenious, Friends of Men, and eafie to be command-ed. They furnifh the Children of the *Sages* with as much Mo-ney, as they have need of; and never afk any other Reward of their Services, than the Glory of being Commanded. The *Gno-mides* or Wives of thefe *Gnomes* or *Pharyes*, are Little, but very

C 3   Hand-

---

3. Cabal: the Cabala, a system of esoteric knowledge derived ultimately from figurative Jewish interpretations of the Old Testament.

Handfom; and their Habit marvelloufly Curious.

As for the *Salamanders*, the Inhabitants of the Region of *Fire*: They ferve the *Ph'lofophers*, but they feek not for their Company with any great Eagernefs; and their Wives and Daughters will rarely be feen. They do wifely, (interrupted I) and for my fhare, I fhall excufe their Appearing to me. Why fo, (faid the *Count*?) Why, Sir, (reply'd I?) What Bufinefs can I have, to Converfe with fo ugly a Creature as a *Salamander*, be it either Male or Female? You are miftaken, (anfwered he) that is the *Idea*, which the ignorant Painters and Sculpters have given them: The Wives of the *Salamanders* are Fair; nay, rather more Fair, than all others, feeing they are of a purer Element. But I forbear to fpeak more of that, and fhall give but

but a flight Defcription of thefe People; becaufe you fhall fee them your felf, at your Leafure; and that very eafily too, if you have the Curiofity for it. You fhall fee their Habits, their Diet, their Manners, their Policy, and their Admirable Laws. You will be Charmed more, with the Beauty of their Wit, than that of their Body: Yet you cannot choofe, but be grieved for thefe poor Wretches, when they fhall tell you, That their *Soul* is Mortal; and that they have no Hope of enjoying Eternal Happynefs, and of the Supreme Being, which they acknowledge, and Religioufly adore. They will tell us, That being Compofed of the moft pure Parts of the *Elements*, which they inhabit; and not having in them any contrary Qualities, feeing they are made but of one *Element*, they Dye not but

C 4 after

---

4. So ugly a creature as a Salamander: The narrator is thinking not of spirits but of the variety of lizard known as the salamander, which, according to legend, could live in fire.

after many Ages: But Alas! What is such a Time, in respect of Eternity? They must Eternally resolve into their Nothing. This Consideration does sorely afflict them; and we have Trouble enough, to comfort them concerning it.

Our Fathers, the *Philosophers*, speaking to *God* Face to Face, complained to him of the Unhappyness of these People; and *God*, whose Mercy is without bounds, revealed to them, that it was not impossible to find out a Remedy for this Evil. He inspired them, that by the same Means as Man, by the Alliance which he Contracted with *God*, has been made Partakers of the Divinity: The *Sylphs*, the *Gnomes*, the *Nymphs*, and the *Salamanders*, by the Alliance which they might Contract with Man, might be made Partakers of Immortality.

lity. So a She-*Nymph*, or a *Sylphide* becomes Immortal, and capable of the Blessing to which we aspire, when they shall be so happy as to be married to a *Sage*; a *Gnome*, or a *Sylphe* ceases to be Mortal, from the moment that he Espouses one of our Daughters.

Hence arose the Error of the former Ages, of *Tertullian*, of *Justin Martyr*, of *Lactantius*, *Cyprian*, *Clemens Alexandrinus*, *Athenagoras* the Christian *Philosopher*; and generally, of all the Writers of that time They had learnt, that these *Elementary Demimen*, had endeavored a Commerce with Maids; and they have from thence imagined, that the Fall of the *Angels* had not happened, but for the Love which they were touched with after *Women*. Certain *Gnomes*, desirous of becoming Immortal, had a

C 5   mind

5

---

5. Tertullian . . . Athenagoras: early Christian theologians.

193

mind to gain the good Affecti-
ons of our. *Daughters*; and had
brought abundance of. Precious,
Stones, of which they are the
Natural Cuardians: And thefe
Authors, relying on the Book of
6　*Enoch*, which they mif-under-
ftood, thought that it was the
Attempt which thefe Amorous
Angels had offered to the Cha-
ftity of our Wives. In the Beginning, thefe *Children* of *Heaven* begat Famous *Gyants*, by
making themfelves beloved by
7　the Daı ghters of Men : · And the
8　ill Cabalifts, *Jofephus* and *Philo*,
(as all the *Jews* are ignorant)
and after them all the other *Authors*, which I have juft now na-
9,10　med, as well as *Origen* and *Macrobius*, have faid, that they were
Angels; and have not known,
that tl ey were the *Sylphes*, and
other Peofle of the *Elements*;
that under the Name of the *Children*.

dren of *Elohim*, are diftinguifh-
ed from the *Children* of Men.
Likewife, that which the *Sage*
Saint *Auguftine*, has had the Modefty to leave · undetermined,
touching the Purfuits which thofe
called *Faunes*. or *Satyrs*, made
after the *Africans* of his time, is
cleared by that which I have
now alledged, of the Defire which
all thefe *Elementary* Inhabitants
have, of Allying themfelves to
Men; as the only means to attain to the Immortality which
they have not.

No, no ! Our *Sages* have never Err'd fo, as to attribute the
Fall of the firft *Angels*, to their
Love of *women*, no more than
they have put Men under the
Power of the *Devil*; by imputing all the Adventures of the
Nymphs and *Sylphs* to him, of
which the *Hiftorians* fpeak fo
largely. There was nothing Criminal

---

6. Book of Enoch: part of the Old Testament apochrypha. Enoch, who was taken to
God without dying (Genesis 5:24), recounts visions and esoteric knowledge.

7. Gyants . . . Men: Genesis 6:1-4; cf. Pope's note to *The Rape of the Lock*, 1:145,
quoted below, p. 204.

8. Josephus and Philo: Flavius Josephus (37/38-c. 100) was a Jewish military leader,
historian, and scriptural interpreter. Philo Judaeus (c. 20 B.C.-after A.D. 40) wrote
voluminous allegorical interpretations of the Old Testament.

9. Origen: another early Christian writer, fond of allegorizing the Bible.

10. Macrobius: a Roman writer best known for a book on the interpretation of dreams.

11. Elohim: one of the Hebrew terms for God.

12. him: i.e., the Devil.

minal in all that. They were
the *Sylphs*, which endeavoured
to become Immortal. Their Innocent Purfuits, far enough from
being able to fcandalize the *Philofophers*, have appeared fo Juft
to us, that we are all refolved by
common Confent, utterly to Renounce *Women*; and intirely to
give our felves to the Immor-
talizing of the *Nymphs* and
Sylphs.

Good Lord, (cryed I!) What
do I hear? Was there ever fuch
marvellous F—— Yes, my Son,
(interrupted the *Count*) Admire
the marvellous Felicity of the
Sages! Inftead of *Women*, whofe
fading Beauty pafs away in a
fhort time, and are followed
with horrible Wrinkles and Ug-
lynefs, the *Philofophers* enjoy Beauties which never wax old, and
whom they have the glory to
make Immortal. Guefs at the
Love

Love and Acknowledgment of
thefe invifible Miftreffes; and
with what Ardor they ftrive to
pleafe the Charitable *Philofopher*,
who Labours to Immortalize
them.

Ah! Sir, (cryed I once again)
I Renounce——. Yes, my Son,
(purfued he, without giving me
the Leafure to finifh) Renounce
the fading Pleafures, which are
to be had with *Women*; the Fair-
eft amongft them all, is Loath-
fom, in refpeft of the Homelieft
Sylphide: No Difpleafure ever
follows our *Sage* Embraces. Miferable Ignorants! How fhould
you complain, that ye have not
the Power to taft of the *Phylofo-
phick* Pleafures!

13. Felicity: the narrator had presumably intended to say Fancy, Folly, or something of
the sort.

195

Children of sylphs versus children of women:

What do you mean by the Children of Sin? Sir (interrupted I.)

They are (my Son, continued he) They are all thofe Children who are born after the ordinary way; Children conceived by the Will of the Flefh, not by the Will of God; Children of Wrath, and of the Curfe; In a word, Children of Man and Woman. You have a mind to interrupt me. I perceive, what you would fay to me. 'Tis true, (my Child) You muft know that it was never

ver the Will of God, that Man and Woman fhould have Children as they have. The defign of the moft prudent Artift was far more noble, he intended to have peopled the World, after a different manner than it is. If *the* miferable *Adam*, had not foolifhly difobeyed the order which he had from God, not to touch *Eve* ; and that he had been contented with the other Fruits of the Garden of pleafure, with all the Beautys of the *Nymphs* and *sylphides* : The World had not fuffered the fhame of feeing it felf peopled with Men fo imperfect, that they may pafs for Monfters, where the Children of Phylofophers are prefent.

How Sir (faid I to him) you think, fo far as I perceive, that the Sin of *Adam* was fomething elfe than eating of the Apple ? Why, my Son (replied the Count) are

are you of the Number of thofe, who have the fimplicity, to take the Hiftory of the Apple, in the litteral fence ? Alas! you muft know, that the Holy Tongue ufes innocent Metaphors, to remove from us, the unfeemly Ideas of an action, which has been caufe of all the miferies of mankind. For fo, when *Saloman* faid, *I will get upon the* Palm, *and I will gather the Fruits thereof* ; He had another Appetite than eating Dates. This Tongue which the Angels confecrate, and whereof they make ufe, to fing their Hymns to the Living God ; has not a term to exprefs that, which it names figuratively an Apple or Date. But the *Sage* unriddles thefe chaft figures, when he fees that the Pallat and Mouth of *Eve* efcape unpunifhed, and that fhe brings forth with pain, he knew that it was not the Pallat that had been criminal ;

---

14. not to touch Eve: Early theologians usually assigned the cause of the sin of Adam and Eve to either pride or lust; Milton shares the former, and more common, opinion; the count maintains the latter.

15. that: if.

16. I . . . thereof: Song of Solomon, 7:8, in the Vulgate and versions derived from it. The Authorized Version reads "take hold of the boughs thereof."

minal; and difcovering what the firft Sin was, by the care which the firft Sinners took to cover with leaves certain parts of their Bodies; He concluded that God would not have had men multiply by this beaftly way. O *A-dam!* thou fhouldeft not have begot men, but fuch as fhould have been like thy felf, or elfe *Heroes* or *Gyants.*

Alas! what expedient (interrupted I) can there be for reparation of one or other of thefe marvellous generations. Obey God (replyed he) Touch none but the *Nymphs*, the *Gnomes*, the *Sylphides*, or the *Salamanders.* So fhould we fee *Heroes* born, and the *Univerfe* fill'd with marvellous People, repleat with ftrength and wifdome.

The count condemns the false teachings that have made the sylphs seem repulsive and thus made it very difficult for them to find earthly lovers:

The Count of Gabalis.

She thinks not but with Horror, on this Commerce; and trembles at the very Aspect of a *Sylphe?* Where is the Man, who flyes not from the Sight of them, if he pretends but never so little to be a virtuous honest Man? How rarely do we find a Man of worth, who desires their Familiarity? Nor are there any but Debauched Persons, or Covetous, or Ambitious, or Impostors, who seek for this Honour; which yet they shall never attain to, I assure you: For, *The Fear of the Lord, is the Beginning of Wisdom.*

What then (said I) shall become of all these Airy People, since all such as are Honest, are so set against them? Well, (said he) *The Arme of* God *is not shortned;* and the *Devil* shall not draw to himself, all the Advantages, he hopes for, from the Ignorance and Error, which he has vented to their prejudice: For besides the *Philosophers,* who are a great number, and remedy it the best they can, by utterly Renouncing *Women;* God has permitted all these People, to use all Innocent Arts, which they can contrive, to converse with Men, without their Knowledge. What do you tell me, Sir? (cryed I) I tell you Truth, (pursued he) Do you believe, that a *Dog* may have Children by a Woman? No, (answered I.) Nor a *Munky?* (added he) Neither, (replyed I.) Nor a *Bear?* (continued he) Neither *Dog,* nor *Munkey,* nor *Bear,* (said I to him.) For that is impossible, without all doubt: 'Tis against Nature, against Reason, and against Common Sense. Very good, (said the *Count*) But are not the Kings of the *Goths,* descended from a *Bear,* and a *Swedish* Princess? 'Tis true, (said I) the

199

the Hiſtory ſayes it. And were not the *Piguſians*, and *Syonians* of *India*, (reply'd he) Born from a *Dog*, and a *Woman*? I have read that too, (ſaid I to him.) And had not that *Portugeſs* Woman, (continued he) who was expoſed in a Deſart *Iſland*, Children by a great *Munkey*? Our Divines, Sir, (ſaid I) anſwer to that, That the *Devil*, taking the Shape of theſe Beaſts —— You are going to alledge again, (interrupted the *Count*) the Nonſenſical Imaginations of your Authors. Pray, comprehend once for all, that the *Sylphes*, ſeeing themſelves taken for *Devils*, when they appear in Human Shape, to diminiſh this Averſion, which is had againſt them, take the Shapes of theſe Beaſts; and ſo addreſs themſelves to the wanton Frailty of *Women*; who are affrighted at a Lovely *Sylphide*, but not at a *Dog*, or *Munkey*.

Munkey. I could tell you many Tales of your little *Bolognian Dogs*, and certain pretty *Ladyes* in the World : But I have a greater Secret to teach you.

Know, my Son, that many a one thinks himſelf the Son of a *Man*, who is the Son of a *Sylphe*. Another thinks, that he is in Bed with his *wife*; and without ever knowing it, he Immortalized a *Sylphe*. This *woman* ſuppoſes, that ſhe is Embracing her *Huſband*; and ſhe is Hugging betwixt her Arms, a *Salamander* : And that *Girle* durſt ſwear when ſhe awakes, that ſhe is a *Virgin*; that has had in her Sleep, an Honour that ſhe little dreamt on. So the *Devil*, and the *Ignorants*, are equally abuſed.

The count's final argument is based on visible manifestations of the sylphs at various times in the past.

The Famous Cabalift *Zede-chias*, was moved in his Spirit, in the Reign of your King *Pe-pin*, to Convince the World, that the *Elements* are Inhabited by all thefe People, whofe Nature I have been defcribing to you. The Expedient to bring all this about, was in this manner; He advifed the *Sylphs*, to fhew themfelves in the Air to all the World. They did it with great Magnifi-cence: Thefe Creatures appear-ing in the Air, in Human Shape; Sometimes ' ranged in Battle,

I 3   March-

Marching in good Order, or standing to their Arms, or Encamped under most Majestick Pavillions: At other times, on Airy Ships of an Admirable Structure, whose Flying Navy was tost about at the Will of the *Zephirus*'s. Well, and what was the Issue of all this? Do you think, that this Ignorant Age fell into a Consultation, about the Nature of these Marvellous Spectacles? The People presently believed, that they were *Sorcerers*, who had gotten a Power in the Air, there to exercise their Conjurations, and to make it Hail upon their Corn-Fields. The Learned Men, the Divines, and the Lawyers, were presently of the same Opinion with the Rabble. The Emperors also believed; and this Ridiculous *Chymæra* got such Credit amongst All, that the Wise *Charlemaine*, and after him *Lewis* the *Debonaire* inflicted grievous

vous Torments on all those pretended *Tyrants* of the *Air*. See this in the *First Chapter of the Capitularies* of these two Emperors.

The *Sylphs*, seeing the People, the *Pedants*, and the Crowned Heads also, thus taking up Arms against them, resolved to make them lose this Evil Opinion, which they had of their Innocent Fleet; and to manifest themselves wholly and clearly to Men in all Places; to let them see their Beautiful Wives, their Common-Wealth, and their Government; and then to come down into the Earth, in divers Parts of the World. They did, as they had projected; and the People who saw these Men descend, remove thither from all Places, already possessed with an Opinion, that they were *Sorcerers*, who had left their Companions, to throw Poyson upon their Fruits,

PART IV

Miscellaneous

The Bible

The Bible usually appears in *The Rape of the Lock* filtered through *Paradise Lost*, but Pope occasionally alludes to it directly, especially in Ariel's speech to Belinda in canto 1. Ariel is fond of the language of Psalm 91; he assumes the protective role there assigned to the Lord, giving his sylphs charge over Belinda and guarding her from "the Glance by Day, the Whisper in the Dark" as the Lord guards the psalmist from "the terror by night" and "the arrow that flieth by day." (An anonymous paraphrase of this psalm, probably by Pope himself, appeared in 1717. Two lines of it, based on verse 11, are closer than the psalm itself to the language of Ariel's speech:

> I see protecting Myriads round thee fly,
> And all the bright *Militia* of the sky.)

The most important of the many "Virgins visited by Angel-Pow'rs" is of course Mary, to whom Gabriel announced that she was to be the mother of Jesus. Ariel's antithesis between "Learned Pride" and "Maids and Children" is a parody of Matthew 11:25.

Elsewhere, the sun that shines on all alike, as does Belinda, perhaps derives from Matthew 5:45. Pope alludes rather mysteriously to the passage from Genesis in a note to 1:145: *"Antient Traditions of the* Rabbi's *relate, that several of the fallen Angels became amorous of Women, and particularize some; among the rest Asael, who lay with Naamah, the wife of Noah, or of Ham; and who continuing impenitent, still presides over the Women's Toilets. Bereshi Rabbi in Genes, 6.2."* See also *Le Comte de Gabalis*, p. 194.

The Authorized (King James) version is cited here for convenience, though Pope and his Catholic readers would probably have been more familiar with the Rheims-Douay version and perhaps also with the Latin Vulgate.

GENESIS

And it came to pass, when men began to multiply on the face of the earth, and daughters were born unto them, that the sons of God saw the daughters of men that they were fair; and they took them wives of all which they chose. And the Lord said, My spirit shall not always strive with man, for that he also is flesh: yet his days shall be an hundred and twenty years. There were giants in the earth in those days; and also after that, when the sons of God came in unto the daughters of men, and they bare children to them, the same became mighty men which were of old, men of renown. (6:1-4)

PSALM 91

1 He that dwelleth in the secret place of the most High shall abide under the shadow of the Almighty.

2 I will say of the Lord, He is my refuge and my fortress: my God; in him will I trust.

3 Surely he shall deliver thee from the snare of the fowler, and from the noisome pestilence.

4 He shall cover thee with his feathers, and under his wings thou shalt trust: his truth shall be thy shield and buckler.

5 Thou shalt not be afraid for the terror by night; nor for the arrow that flieth by day;

6 Nor for the pestilence that walketh in darkness; nor for the destruction that wasteth at noonday.

7 A thousand shall fall at thy side, and ten thousand at thy right hand; but it shall not come nigh thee.

8 Only with thine eyes shalt thou behold and see the reward of the wicked.

9 Because thou hast made the Lord, which is my refuge, even the most High, thy habitation;

10 There shall no evil befall thee, neither shall any plague come nigh thy dwelling.

11 For he shall give his angels charge over thee, to keep thee in all thy ways.

12 They shall bear thee up in their hands, lest thou dash thy foot against a stone. . . .

The Gospel According to St. Matthew

He [God] maketh his sun to rise on the evil and on the good, and sendeth rain on the just and on the unjust. (5:45)

At that time Jesus answered and said, I thank thee, O Father, Lord of heaven and earth, because thou hast hid these things from the wise and prudent, and hast revealed them unto babes. (11:25)

The Gospel According to St. Luke

And in the sixth month the angel Gabriel was sent from God unto a city of Galilee, named Nazareth, to a virgin espoused to a man whose name was Joseph, of the house of David; and the virgin's name was Mary. And the angel came in unto her, and said, Hail, thou that art highly favoured, the Lord is with thee: blessed art thou among women. And when she saw him, she was troubled at his saying, and cast in her mind what manner of salutation this should be. And the angel said unto her, Fear not, Mary: for thou hast found favour with God. And, behold, thou shalt conceive in thy womb, and bring forth a son, and shalt call his name JESUS. He shall be great, and shall be called the Son of the Highest: and the Lord God shall give unto him the throne of his father David: and he shall reign over the house of Jacob forever; and of his kingdom there shall be no end.

Then said Mary unto the angel, How shall this be, seeing I know not a man?

And the angel answered and said unto her, The Holy Ghost shall come upon thee, and the power of the Highest shall over-shadow thee: therefore also that holy thing which shall be born of thee shall be called the Son of God.

(1:26-35)

Catullus, "The Lock of Berenice" (*Poems*, 66)

The following version of Catullus' poem appeared in 1707 as part of an anonymous translation called *The Adventures of Catullus, and History of His Amours with Lesbia . . . Done from the French*. It is included here, despite considerable flatness and obscurity, because it may have given Pope a hint or two and because it could not have been influenced, like some later translations, by *The Rape of the Lock*. The poem is narrated by the lock itself, after its transformation to a constellation. Unlike Belinda, Berenice had sacrificed her own hair as a thanksgiving-offering to the gods after her husband Ptolemy returned safely from the wars. Most of Pope's direct allusions are concentrated at the end of the *Rape of the Lock*, 5:129ff.

> *Conon* the nice Observer of the Skies,
> That knows how Planets set, and how they rise;
> How Suns are darken'd and eclips'd their light,
> And why the Stars are sometimes hid from sight,
> How *Luna* smitten with *Endymion*'s Charms   5
> Under Mount Latmus takes him in her Arms;°
> That *Conon*, in Astronomy so read,
> Saw me amidst those Luminaries spread,
> My Rays, that was a Lock on *Berenice*'s Head.
> A Lock she to the Gods devoted gave,   10
> On Terms that they her *Ptolemy* wou'd save,
> . . . .

5-6. So handsome was Endymion that the moon (Luna) fell in love with him and came down from the sky every night to embrace him. Note the contrast between her action and the fate of the lock.

What Offerings did you° not bequeath and vow   41
To Heav'n, wou'd Heav'n his quick Return allow!
Send him to your Embrace with Laurels crown'd!
And *Egypt*'s Realms with conquer'd *Asia* bound!
The Gods have done their Part, and in return,   45
I to the Gods to Answer yours am Born.°   46
O Queen, unwillingly from Earth I fled,
Be you my Witness, and your sacred Head!
Heav'ns Vengeance light on those that falsly swear;
But who can with all conquering Steel compare?   50
Steel levell'd high Mount *Athos* with the Ground   51
Where *Thessaly*'s Inhabitants are found;
When *Persian* Ships o'er *Euxine* Seas prevail'd,
And where the Mountain stood, Great *Xerxes* sail'd.°
How shall poor *HAIRS* not these Disasters feel,   55
When such things own the force of unresistless Steel?
Grant *Jove*, this Mineral henceforth may cease,
May be destroy'd with all its direful Race,
And with it may *he* perish that at first
Taught it the Veins of crusted Earth to burst.   60
My favourite Sister *Locks* behind me left,
Mourn'd my departure, and bewail'd your Gifts;
When *Pegasus* with hasty *Pinnions* flew,
Offering his Services to me, for you;
And wing'd me through the vast expanded Skie,   65
That I in *Cytherea*'s° Lap might lye.   66
Venus her self this Messenger had sent,
Venus, that to *Egyptians* gives content;
And for this end that *Ariadne*'s Crown
Shou'd not amidst the Stars be only known,   70
But that I likewise shou'd devoted Shine,
And to the Planets add another Sign.
Puff'd by the Goddess Breath into a Star,
I touch'd the *Maid*, the *Lyon*, and the *Bear*,   74
As I before Bootes° urge my Way,   75
Who late in Ocean drowns his sloathful Ray.
But tho I *set*, as other Signs at Night,
Thetys at Morn restores me to the Light:
O *Nemesis*, thy leave that I reveal
A Truth, no Fear shall force me to conceal;   80
A Truth, shall spight of all the Stars appear
Tho' they for it in Pieces shou'd me tear.
I'm not so *joyful* for this Heav'nly State,

---

41. you: The lock is now addressing Berenice.
46. born: carried.
51-54. As part of his preparations for the invasion of Greece in 480 B.C. Xerxes, king of
Persia, had a canal cut across the peninsula connecting Mt. Athos to the mainland.
66. Cytherea: Venus.
74-75. Maid . . . Bootes: constellations.

208

That I'm above the reach of *Chance* and *Fate*,
As discontented that I still must be,   85
Absent from my Dear *Queen*, and *she* from *me*.
Upon whose Head, e'er since her Zone° unty'd,   87
Spoke her no more a Virgin but a Bride;
Ten thousand Ointments all their Sweets display'd,
Tho' she ne'er us'd those Ointments when a Maid.   90
Now, all ye New made Brides, whom Love has join'd,
To whom soft *Hymen*° Husbands has consign'd,   92
Never unlace, or let your Breasts be loose,
With Bodies prostrate to your Consort's use;
Before each Box of Ointment duly pays   95
Part of its Sweets to my propitious Rays.
Your Box, and only yours whose Love is chast;
Let theirs, whose Flame's impure on Earth be cast.
For I'll from Hands unclean no Gift receive
To *Stars Adult'rous* let *Adulterers* give.   100
But O ye *Brides*, this Counsel will you take,
Let *Love* your Habitations ne'er forsake;
Let *Concord* your Abodes eternal Grace,
Let one continued *Hony-moon* take Place,
And your whole course of Life be Love's perpetual Race.   105
And you, O Queen, when with uplifted Eyes
You offer up a bloodless Sacrifice;
When with bright Tapers you at *Venus* Shrine,
Implore the Blessings of her Powers Divine.
Remember, Oh! remember, that you pay   110
Large Gifts for my Return; not only *pray*,
But *Bribe*, that I with you may ever stay.
Why do the *Stars* obstruct my swift descent?
Why am I not to my lov'd Mistress sent?
O that I might again resume my Place!   115
O that once more her Royal Temples Grace!
Inverted then might Nature's Course appear,
Were I no *Constellation*, but her Hair.

---

87. Zone: girdle, sash.
92. Hymen: a god of marriage.

Livy, *History of Rome*

Toward the end of the poem, the lock's ascent to heaven is compared to that of Romulus, and the poet, the only person who saw what happened to the lock, to Proclus. Livy implies strongly that Romulus' ascension was a political fiction concocted to restore political unity among the Romans, and the stellification of the lock is of course a poetical fiction devised for a similar end. This translation, by Aubrey de Sélincourt, was published by Penguin Books in 1960.

Such, then, were the deeds of Romulus, and they will never grow old. One day while he was reviewing his troops on the Campus Martius near the marsh of Capra, a storm burst, with violent thunder. A cloud enveloped him, so thick that it hid him from the eyes of everyone present; and from that moment he was never seen again upon earth.

The troops, who had been alarmed by the sudden storm, soon recovered when it passed over and the sun came out again. Then they saw that the throne was empty, and, ready though they were to believe the senators, who had been standing at the king's side and now declared that he had been carried up on high by a whirlwind, they none the less felt like children bereft of a father and for a long time stood in sorrowful silence. Then a few voices began to proclaim Romulus's divinity; the cry was taken up, and at last every man present hailed him as a god and son of a god, and prayed to him to be for ever gracious and to protect his children. However, even on this great occasion there were, I believe, a few dissentients who secretly maintained that the king had been torn to pieces by the senators. At all events the story got about, though in veiled terms; but it was not important, as awe, and admiration for Romulus's greatness, set the seal upon the other version of his end, which was, moreover, given further credit by the timely action of a certain Julius Proculus, a man, we are told, honoured for his wise counsel on weighty matters. The loss of the king had left the people in an uneasy mood and suspicious of the senators, and Proculus, aware of the prevalent temper, conceived the shrewd idea of addressing the Assembly. "Romulus," he declared, "the father of our City, descended from heaven at dawn this morning and appeared to me. In awe and reverence I stood before him, praying for permission to look upon his face without sin. 'Go,' he said, 'and tell the Romans that by heaven's will my Rome shall be capital of the world. Let them learn to be soldiers. Let them know, and teach their children, that no power on earth can stand against Roman arms.' Having spoken these words, he was taken up again into the sky."

Proculus's story had a most remarkable effect; the army and commons, cruelly distressed at the loss of their king, were much comforted once they were assured of his immortality.

(1:16)

Ovid, *Metamorphoses*

Although perhaps less often acknowledged than the more sage and serious Virgil, Ovid had a more extensive influence on English poetry through the eighteenth century than any other classical author, and he also provided a fertile field for translators, from schoolboys to poets laureate. The *Metamorphoses* consists primarily of a string of independent mythological tales, but the scope of the poem — from the beginning of the world to Ovid's own time — the philosophy of change and process that underlies it, and its protean hospitality to allegorical interpretations of all kinds led some readers to grant it a status close to that of the epic. The latest complete poetic translation before *The Rape of the Lock* was that of George Sandys; the annotated version appeared in 1632 and was often reprinted before the Restoration. Dryden translated many episodes throughout his career. In 1717 two complete collaborative versions appeared, one edited by George Sewell, the other by Pope's friend Dr. Samuel Garth.

Echo and Narcissus (Book 3)

This tale is the archetypal literary treatment of self-love, and Narcissus the ancestor of all the mirror gazers of Western literature. Sandys' version is given here, because it was available to Pope's readers and, more important, because the traditional moral allegory that Sandys expounded forms part of the background against which Pope places Belinda. Such allegories were beginning to seem quaint and old-fashioned in Pope's day, but they were not yet dead. Samuel Garth was modern enough not to include any in his edition, but in his preface he defended allegorical interpretation in principle and specifically recommended Sandys "to those, that are curious in this figurative learning."

The line numbers that follow are supplied by the present editor. The "He" in line 4 is Tiresias, the blind prophet.

The lovely Nymph (who not unfruitfull prov'd)
Brought forth a boy, even then to be belov'd,
Narcissus nam'd. Enquiring if old age
Should crowne his Youth; He, in obscure presage,
Made this reply: Except° himselfe he knowe.   5
Long, they no credit on his words bestowe:
Yet did the event the prophecie approve,
In his strange ruine and new kinde of love.
Now, he to fifteene added had a yeare:
Now in his looks both boy and man appeare.   10
Many a love-sick Youth did him desire;
And many a Maid his beauty set on fire:
Yet, in his tender age his pride was such,
That neither youth nor Mayden might him touch.
　　The vocall Nymph,° this lovely Boy did spy   15
(She could not proffer speech, nor not reply)
When busie in persuit of salvage spoyles,
He drave the Deere into his corded toyles.
Eccho was then a body, not a Voyce:
Yet then, as now, of words she wanted choyce;   20
But only could reiterate the close
Of every speech. This *Juno* did impose.
For, often when she might have taken *Jove*,
Compressing there the Nymphs, who weakely strove;
Her° long discourses made the Goddesse° stay,   25
Untill the Nymphs had time to run-away.
Which when perceiv'd; shee said, For this abuse
Thy tongue henceforth shall bee of little use.
Those threats are deeds: she yet ingeminates°   29
The last of sounds, and what she hears relates.   30
　　Narcissus seene, intending thus the chace;
She forth-with glowes, and with a noyselesse pace
His steps persues; the more she did persew,
More hot (as neerer to her fire) she grew:
And might be likened to a sulph'rous match;   35
Which instantly th' approached flame doth catch.
How oft would shee have woo'd him with sweete words!
But, Nature no such liberty affords:
Begin she could not, yet full readily
To his expected speech she would reply.   40
The Boy, from his companions parted, said;
Is any nigh? I, *Eccho* answere made.
He, round about him gazed (much appall'd)

---

5. except: unless.
15. vocall Nymph: Echo.
25. Her: Echo's; Goddesse: Juno.
29. ingeminates: repeats.

And cry'd out, Come. She him, who called, call'd.
Then looking back; and seeing none appear'd,   45
Why shunst thou mee? The selfe-same voyce he heard,
Deceived by the Image of his words;
Then let us joyne, said he: no sound accords
More to her wish: her faculties combine
In deare consent; who answer'd, *Let us joyne!*   50
Flattering her selfe, out of the woods she sprung;
And would about his struggling neck have hung.
Thrust back; he said, Life shall this breast forsake,
Ere thou, light Nymph, on me thy pleasure take.
On me thy pleasure take, the Nymph replyes   55
To that disdainefull Boy, who from her flyes.
Despis'd; the wood her sad retreat receaves;
Who covers her ashamed face with leaves;
And sculks in desert caves. Love still possest
Her soule; through griefe of her repulse, increast.°   60
Her wretched body pines with sleeplesse care:
Her skinne contracts: her blood converts to ayre.
Nothing was left her now but voyce and bones:
The voyce remaynes; the other turne to stones.
Conceal'd in Woods, in Mountaines never found,   65
Yet heard in all: and is but a Sound.
   Thus her, thus other Nymphs, in mountaynes born,
And sedgy brooks, the Boy had kild with scorn.
Thus many a Youth he had afore deceiv'd:
When one thus praid, with hands to heav'n upheav'd;   70
So may he love himselfe, and so despaire!
Rhamnusia° condescends to his just pray'r.   72
   A Spring there was, whose silver Waters were,
As smooth as any mirror, nor lesse cleare:
Which neither Heards-men, tame, nor salvage Beast,   75
Nor wandring Fowle, nor scattered leaves molest;
Girt round with grasse, by neighbouring moysture fed,
And Woods, against the Sunnes invasion spred.
He, tyr'd with heat and hunting, with the Place
And Spring delighted, lyes upon his face.   80
Quenching his thirst, another thirst doth rise;
Rays'd by the forme which in that glasse he spyes.
The hope of nothing doth his powers invade:
And for a body he mistakes a shade.
Himselfe, himselfe distracts: who pores thereon   85
So fixedly, as if of *Parian* stone.
Beholds his eyes, two starres! his dangling haire
Which with unshorn *Apollo's* might compare!
His fingers worthy *Bacchus!* his smooth chin!
His Ivory neck! his heavenly face! where-in   90

---

60. increast: "Love" is the implied subject.

72. Rhamnusia: Nemesis, Fate conceived of as an agent of punishment for impiety; see Sandys' commentary below.

The linked Deities their Graces fix!
Where Roses with unsullied Lillies mix!
Admireth all; for which, to be admir'd:
And unconsiderately himselfe desir'd.
The prayses, which he gives, his beautie claym'd.   95
Who seeks, is sought: th' Inflamer is inflam'd.
How often would he kisse the flattering spring!
How oft with downe-thrust arms sought he to cling
About that loved neck! Those cous'ning° lips   99
Delude his hopes; and from himselfe he slips.   100
Not knowing what, with what he sees he fryes:
And th' error that deceives, incites his eyes.
O Foole! that striv'st to catch a flying shade!
Thou seek'st what's no-where: Turn aside, 'twill fade.
Thy formes reflection doth thy sight delude: 105
Which is with nothing of its owne indu'd.
With thee it comes; with thee it staies; and so
'Twould goe away, hadst thou the powre to goe.
Nor sleep, nor hunger could thy lover rayse:
Who, lay'd along, on that false forme doth gaze   110
With lookes, which looking never could suffice;
And ruinates himselfe with his owne eyes.
At length, a little lifting up his head;
    You Woods, that round about your branches spred,
Was ever so unfortunate a Lover!   115
You know, to many you have beene a cover;
From your first growth to this long distant day
Have you knowne any, thus to pine away!
I like, and see: but yet I cannot find
The lik't, and seene. O Love, with error blind!   120
What grieves me more; no Sea, no Mountayne steep,
No wayes, no walls, our joyes a-sunder keep:
Whom but a little water doth divide;
And he himselfe desires to be injoy'd.
As oft as I kisse the flood decline,   125
So oft his lips ascend, to close with mine.
You'ld thinke we toucht: so small a thing doth part
Our equall loves! Come forth, what ere thou art.
Sweet Boy, a simple Boy beguile not so:
From him that seeks thee, whither would'st thou go?   130
My age nor beauty merit thy disdaine:
And me the Nymphs have often lov'd in vaine.
Yet in thy friendly shewes my poore hopes live;
Still striving to receive the hand I give:
Thou smil'st my smiles: when I a teare let fall,   135
Thou shedd'st an other; and consent'st in all.
And, lo, thy sweetly-moving lips appeare
To utter words, that come not to our eare.
Ah, He is I! now, now I plainly see:

---

99. cous'ning: cozening, cheating.

214

Nor is't my shaddow that bewitcheth me.   140
Love of my selfe me burnes; (o too too sure!)
And suffer in those flames which I procure.
Shall I be woo'd, or wooe? What shall I crave?
Since what I covet, I already have.
Too much hath made me poore! O, you divine   145
And favoring Powres, me from my selfe dis-joyne!
Of what I love, I would be dispossest:
This, in a Lover, is a strange request!
Now, strength through griefe decayes: short is the time
I have to live; extinguisht in my prime.   150
Nor grieves it me to part with well-mist breath;
For griefe will find a perfect cure in death:
Would he I love might longer life injoy!
Now, two ill-fated Lovers, in one, die.
    This said; againe upon his Image gaz'd;   155
Teares on the troubled water circles rais'd:
The motion much obscur'd the fleeting shade.
With that, he cry'd (perceiving it to vade),°   158
O, whither wilt thou! stay: nor cruell prove,
In leaving me, who infinitely love.   160
Yet let me see, what cannot be possest;
And, with that emptie food, my fury feast.
Complaining thus, himselfe he disarrayes;
And to remoreselesse hands his brest displays:
The blowes that solid snowe with crimson stripe;°   165
Like Apples party-red,° or Grapes scarce ripe.   166
But, in the water when the same appeare,
He could no longer such a sorrow beare.
As Virgin wax dissolves with fervent heat;
Or morning frost, whereon the Sunne-beames beat: 170
So thawes he with the ardor of desire;
And, by degrees consumes in unseene fire.
His meagre cheeks now lost their red and white;
That life; that favour lost, which did delight.
Nor those divine proportions now remaine,   175
So much by *Eccho* lately lov'd in vaine.
Which when she saw; although she angry were,
And still in minde her late repulse did beare;
As often as the miserable cry'd,
Alas! Alas, the wofull Nymph reply'd.   180
And ever when he struck his sounding brest,
Like° sounds of mutuall sufferance exprest.   182
His last words were, still hanging o're his shade;
Ah, Boy, belov'd in vaine! so *Eccho* said.
Farewell. Farewell, sigh't she. Then downe he lyes: 185
Deaths cold hand shuts his self-admiring eyes:

---

158. vade: to fate, disappear.
165. stripe: a verb; the subject is "blowes."
166. party: parti-colored, variegated.
182. like: similar. The subject of "exprest" is the nymph (line 180).

Which now eternally their gazes fix
Upon the Waters of infernall *Styx*.°   188
The wofull *Naiades*° lament the dead;   189
And their clipt hair upon their brother spred.   190
The wofull *Dryades*° pertake their woes: 191
With both, sad *Eccho* joynes at every close.
The funerall Pyle prepar'd, a Herse they brought
To fetch his body, which they vainely sought.
In stead whereof a yellow flowre was found,   195
With tufts of white about the button crown'd.

The morall:
Narcissus, a youth; that is, the soule of a rash and ignorant man;
beholds not his owne face, nor considers of his proper essence or virtue,
but pursues his shadow in the fountaine, and strives to imbrace it; that
is, admireth bodily beauty, fraile and like the fluent water; which is no
other then the shadow of the soule: for the mind doth not truly affect
the body, but its owne similitude in a bodily forme. Such *Narcissus*,
who ignorantly affecting one thing, pursues another; nor can ever
satisfie his longings. Therefore he resolves into tears and perisheth:
that is, the soule so alienated from it selfe, and doting on the body, is
tortured with miserable perturbations; and dyes, as it were, infected
with that poyson: so that now it rather appeareth a mortall body then
an immortall soule. This fable likewise presents the condition of those,
who adorned by the bounty of nature, or inriched by the industry of
others, without merit, or honour of their owne acquisition, are
transported with selfe-love, and perish, as it were, with that madnesse.
Who likely sequester themselves from publique converse and civill
affaires, as subject to neglects and disgraces, which might too much
trouble and deject them: admitting but of a few to accompany their
solitarinesse; those being such as only applaud and admire them,
assenting to what they say, like as many *Ecchos*. Thus depraved, puft
up with uncessant flattery, and strangly intoxicated with selfe admiration; at length they contract such a wounderfull sloth, as stupifies their
sences, and deprives them of all their vigour and alacrity. *Narcissus* is
therefore converted to a flower of his name, which signifies stupid:
flourishing onely in the Spring, like these who are hopefull in the first
of youth, but after fall from expectance & opinion: the flower, as they,
altogether unprofitable, being sacred to *Pluto*[1] and the *Eumenides*,[2] for
what bore of it selfe no fruite, but past and was forgotten, like the way of
a ship in the sea, was consecrated of old to the infernall Deities. But a
fearfull example we have of the danger of selfe-love in the fall of the
Angells; who intermitting the beatificall vision, by reflecting upon
themselves, and admiration of their owne excellency, forgot their
dependance upon their creator. Our *Narcissus*, now a flowre, instructs
us that wee should not flourish too soone or be wise too timely, nor
overlove, or admire our selves: which although hatefull in all ages, in
youth is intollerable. And therefore *Nemesis* is introduced to revenge
such pride and insolency; and to make his vices his owne destruction.

---

188. Styx: the main river of the underworld.
189. Naiades: water nymphs.
191. Dryades: wood nymphs.

1. Pluto: god of the underworld.
2. Eumenides: the Furies, winged female agents of vengeance.

Of the Pythagorean Philosophy (Book 15)

Ovid climaxes his long series of wondrous transformations by making explicit his intuition of the constant process of change that underlies the entire natural world. A similar intuition lies behind *The Rape of the Lock*: from the origins of the sylphs to Belinda's makeup, from the tortoise and elephant transformed to combs to the bodies changed to various forms by spleen, from the ravages of smallpox to the slow deterioration of aging, from scores of other details to the final transformation of Belinda's lock into a star, it is one of the most radically metamorphic poems ever written. Dryden's translation appeared in *Fables Ancient and Modern* (1700), and was included in Garth's edition of the *Metamorphoses*.

Then, Death, so call'd, is but old Matter dress'd
In some new Figure, and a vary'd Vest:
Thus all Things are but alter'd, nothing dies;
And here and there th' unbodied Spirit flies,   240
By Time, or Force, or Sickness dispossest,
And lodges, where it lights, in Man or Beast;
Or hunts without, till ready Limbs it find,
And actuates those according to their kind;
From Tenement to Tenement is toss'd;   245
The Soul is still the same, the Figure only lost:
And, as the soften'd Wax new Seals receives,
This Face assumes, and that Impression leaves;
Now call'd by one, now by another Name;
The Form is only chang'd, the Wax is still the same: 250
So Death, so call'd, can but the Form deface,
Th' immortal Soul flies out in empty space;
To seek her Fortune in some other Place.
Then let not Piety be put to flight,

To please the tast of Glutton-Appetite;   255
But suffer inmate Souls secure to dwell,
Lest from their Seats your Parents you expel;
With rabid Hunger feed upon your kind,
Or from a Beast dislodge a Brother's Mind.
And since, like *Tiphys* parting from the Shore,   260
In ample Seas I sail, and Depths untry'd before,
This let me further add, that Nature knows
No stedfast Station, but, or Ebbs, or Flows:
Ever in motion; she destroys her old,
And casts new Figures in another Mold.   265
Ev'n Times are in perpetual Flux; and run
Like Rivers from their Fountain rowling on;
For Time no more than Streams, is at a stay:
The flying Hour is ever on her way;
And as the Fountain still supplies her store,   270
The Wave behind impels the Wave before;
Thus in successive Course the Minutes run,
And urge their Predecessor Minutes on,
Still moving, ever new: For former Things
Are set aside, like abdicated Kings: 275
And every moment alters what is done,
And innovates some Act till then unknown.
    Darkness we see emerges into Light,
And shining Suns descend to Sable Night;
Ev'n Heav'n it self receives another die,   280
When weari'd Animals in Slumbers lie,
Of Midnight Ease: Another when the gray
Of Morn preludes the Splendor of the Day.
The disk of *Phoebus*° when he climbs on high,   284
Appears at first but as a bloodshot Eye;   285
And when his Chariot downward drives to Bed,
His Ball is with the same Suffusion red;
But mounted high in his Meridian Race
All bright he shines, and with a better Face:
For there, pure Particles of Æther flow,   290
Far from th' Infection of the World below.
    Nor equal Light th' unequal Moon adorns,
Or in her wexing or her waning Horns.
For ev'ry Day she wanes, her Face is less,
But gath'ring into Globe, she fattens at increase.   295
    Perceiv'st thou not the process of the Year,   ⎫
How the four Seasons in four Forms appear,   ⎬
Resembling human Life in ev'ry Shape they wear?   ⎭
Spring first, like Infancy, shoots out her Head,   ⎫
With milky Juice requiring to be fed: ⎬   300
Helpless, tho' fresh, and wanting to be led.   ⎭
The green Stem grows in Stature and in Size,
But only feeds with hope the Farmer's Eyes;

---

284. disk of Phoebus: the sun.

218

Then laughs the childish Year with Flourets crown'd,
And lavishly perfumes the Fields around,   305
But no substantial Nourishment receives,
Infirm the Stalks, unsolid are the Leaves.
    Proceeding onward whence the Year began
The Summer grows adult, and ripens into Man.
This Season, as in Men, is most repleat,   310
With kindly Moisture, and prolifick Heat.
Autumn succeeds, a sober tepid Age,
Not froze with Fear, nor boiling into Rage;
More than mature, and tending to decay,
When our brown Locks repine to mix with odious Grey.   315
    Last Winter creeps along with tardy pace,
Sour is his Front, and furrow'd is his Face;
His Scalp if not dishonour'd quite of Hair,
The ragged Fleece is thin, and thin is worse than bare.
    Ev'n our own Bodies daily change receive,   320
Some part of what was theirs before, they leave;
Nor are to Day what Yesterday they were;
Nor the whole same to Morrow will appear.
     . . . .

    So *Helen*° wept when her too faithful Glass   354
Reflected to her Eyes the ruins of her Face: 355
Wondring what Charms her Ravishers cou'd spy,
To force her twice, or ev'n but once enjoy!
    Thy Teeth, devouring Time, thine, envious Age,
On Things below still exercise your Rage:
With venom'd Grinders you corrupt your Meat,   360
And then at lingring Meals, the Morsels eat.
    Nor those, which Elements we call, abide,
Nor to this Figure, nor to that are ty'd:
For this eternal World is said of Old
But four prolifick Principles to hold,   365
Four different Bodies; two to Heaven ascend,
And other two down to the Center tend:
Fire first with Wings expanded mounts on high,
Pure, void of weight, and dwells in upper Sky;
Then Air, because unclogg'd in empty space   370
Flies after Fire, and claims the second Place:
But weighty Water as her Nature guides,
Lies on the lap of Earth; and Mother Earth subsides.
    All Things are mix'd of these, which all contain,
And into these are all resolv'd again: 375
Earth rarifies to Dew; expanded more,
The subtil Dew in Air begins to soar;
Spreads as she flies, and weary of her Name
Extenuates° still, and changes into Flame;   379
Thus having by degrees Perfection won,   380

---

354. Helen: Helen of Troy, over whom the Trojan War was fought.
379. Extenuates: becomes thinner.

Restless they soon untwist the Web they spun,
And Fire begins to lose her radiant Hue,
Mix'd with gross Air, and Air descends to Dew:
And Dew condensing, does her Form forego,
And sinks, a heavy lump of Earth below.   385
    Thus are their Figures never at a stand,
But chang'd by Nature's innovating Hand;
All Things are alter'd, nothing is destroy'd,
The shifted Scene, for some new Show employ'd.
    Then to be born, is to begin to be   390
Some other Thing we were not formerly:
And what we call to Die, is not t'appear,
Or be the Thing that formerly we were.
Those very Elements which we partake,
Alive, when Dead some other Bodies make: 395
Translated° grow, have Sense, or can Discourse,   396
But Death on deathless Substance has no force.
    That Forms are chang'd I grant; that nothing can
Continue in the Figure it began:
The Golden Age, to Silver was debas'd: 400
To Copper that; our Mettal came at last.
    The Face of Places, and their Forms decay;
And that is solid Earth, that once was Sea:
Seas in their turn retreating from the Shore,
Make solid Land, what Ocean was before;   405
And far from Strands are Shells of Fishes found,
And rusty Anchors fix'd on Mountain-Ground:
And what were Fields before, now wash'd and worn
By falling Floods from high, to Valleys turn,
And crumbling still descend to level Lands;   410
And Lakes, and trembling Bogs are barren Sands:
And the parch'd Desart floats in Streams unknown;
Wondring to drink of Waters not her own.

---

396. translated: transported.

Juvenal, *Satire 6*

Ever since its publication in the second century, this work has been one of the great fountainheads of antifeminine satire, most of which has shared its harsh and uncompromising tone. It is thus a benchmark by which Pope's subtlety and balance can be measured. Juvenal's ladies clearly prefer lapdogs to husbands; Pope's appear to hold them in equal esteem. Dryden's translantion, excerpted here, appeared in 1692.

For, if she hasts abroad, to take the Ayr,
Or goes to *Isis* Church, (the Bawdy, House of Pray'r,)
She hurries all her Handmaids to the Task;
Her Head, alone, will twenty Dressers ask.   630
Psecas, the chief, with Breast and Shoulders bare,
Trembling, considers every Sacred Hair;
If any Stragler from his Rank be found,
A pinch must, for the Mortal Sin, compound.
Psecas is not in Fault: But, in the Glass,   635
The Dame's Offended at her own ill Face.
That Maid is Banish'd; and another Girl
More dextrous, manages the Comb, and Curl:
The rest are summon'd, on a point so nice;
And first, the Grave Old Woman gives Advice.   640
The next is call'd, and so the turn goes round,
As each for Age, or Wisdom, is Renown'd:
Such Counsel, such delib'rate care they take,
As if her Life and Honour lay at stake.
. . . .
They Read th' Example of a Pious Wife,   850
Redeeming, with her own, her Husband's Life;
Yet, if the Laws did that Exchange afford,
Wou'd save their Lapdog sooner than their Lord.

221

Ludovico Ariosto, *Orlando Furioso*

This lengthy amalgamation of classical heroism, medieval chivalry, and modern humor appeared in 1516 and, with additions, in 1532. Spenser's *Faerie Queene* shows its influence in many places. Sir John Harington's translation was published in 1591. In the following selection from book 34, based on the folio edition of 1634, Duke Astolso, in search of Ariosto's lost wits, is being guided around the moon by St. John the Evangelist. Pope cites the passage as a source for the "Lunar Sphere," 5:114ff.

72

. . . .

But to be short, at last his guide him brings
Unto a goodly valley, where he sees
A mighty mass of things strangely confus'd,
Things that on earth were lost, or were abus'd.

73

A store-house strange, that what on earth is lost,
By fault, by time, by fortune there is found,
And like a merchandize is there ingrost,°   3
In stranger sort than I can well expound;
Nor speak I sole of wealth, or things of cost,
In which blind fortunes power doth most abound,
But ev'n of things quite out of fortunes power,
Which wilfully we wast each day and houre.

73.3. ingrost: engrossed, collected together.

74

The precious time that fooles mis-spend in play,
The vaine attempts that never take effect,
The vowes that sinners make, and never pay,
The counsels wise that carelesse men neglect,
The fond desires that lead us oft astray,
The praises that with pride the heart infect,
And all we lose with folly and mis-spending,
May there be found unto this place ascending.

75

Now as *Astolso* by those regions past,
He asked many questions of his guide,
And as he on one side his eye did cast,
A wondrous hill of bladders he espi'd;
And he was told they had been in time past,
The pompous crowns and scepters full of pride,
Of monarchs of *Assyria* and of *Greece*,
Of which now scantly° there is left a peece.   8

76

He saw great store of baited hooks with gold,
And those were gifts that foolish men preferd
To give to Princes covetous and old,
With fondest hope of future vaine reward;
Then were there ropes all in sweet garlands rold,
And those were all false flatteries he herd,
Then heard he crickets songs, like to the verses
The servant in his masters praise reherses.

77

There did he see fond loves, that men pursue,
To look like golden gives° with stones all set,   2
Then things like Eagles Talents° he did view,   3
Those offices that favourites do get:
Then saw he bellowes large that much wind blew,
Large promises that Lords make, and forget,
Unto their *Ganimeds*° in flowre of youth,   7
But after nought but beggery ensu'th.

75.8. scantly: scarcely.
77.2. gives: gyves; fetters or shackles.
   3. talents: talons?
   7. Ganimeds: young favorites. Ganymede was a youth carried off to Olympus by
Zeus because of his beauty and made cupbearer to the gods.

78

He saw great Cities seated in faire places,
That overthrowne quite topsie turvie stood,
He ask'd and learn'd, the cause of their defaces
Was treason, that doth never turne to good:
He saw foule serpents with faire womens faces,
Of coyners° and of theeves the cursed brood, 6
He saw fine glasses all in peeces broken,
Of service lost in Court, a wofull token.

79

Of mingled broth he saw a mighty masse
That to no use all spilt on ground did lie,
He ask'd his teacher, and he heard it was
The fruitlesse almes that men give when they die:
Then by a faire green mountaine he did passe,
That once smelt sweet, but now it stinks perdye,° 6
This was that gift° (be't said without offence) 7
That *Constantine* gave *Silvester* long since.

80

Of bird-lime° rods he saw no little store, 1
And these (O Ladies faire) your beauties be,
I do omit ten thousand things and more
Like unto these, that there the Duke did see:
For all that here is lost, there evermore
Is kept, and thither in a trice doth flee,
Howbeit more nor lesse there was no folly,
For still that here with us remaineth wholly.

81

He saw some of his own lost time and deeds,
But yet he knew them not to be his own,
They seem'd to him disguis'd in so strange weeds,° 3
Till his instructor made them better known:
But last, the thing which no man thinks he needs,
Yet each man needeth most, to him was shown,
By name mans wit, which here we leese° so fast, 7
As that one substance all the others past.° 8

82

It seem'd to be a body moist and soft,
And apt to mount by ev'ry exhalation,

78.6. coyners: counterfeiters.
79.6. perdye: "by God," i.e., here, greatly.
7-8. gift: the "Donation of Constantine," a medieval forgery in which Constantine, the first Christian Roman emperor, purportedly ceded dominion over most of the western world to Pope Sylvester I. It was used during the middle ages to support the papacy's claim to temporal power, and was exposed as a forgery in the fifteenth century.
80.1. bird-lime: a sticky substance spread on twigs to capture birds.
81.3. weeds: garments.
  7. leese: lose.
  8. past: i.e., surpassed in quantity.

224

And when it hither mounted was aloft,
It there was kept in pots of such a fashion,
As we call jarrs, where oyle is kept in oft:
The Duke beheld (with no small admiration)
The jarrs of wit, amongst which one had writ
Upon the side thereof, *Orlandos* wit.

83

This vessell bigger was than all the rest,
And ev'ry vessel had ingrav'n with art
His name that erst° the wit therein possest: 3
There of his own the Duke did find a part,
And much he mus'd, and much himself he blest,
To see some names of men of great desert,°   6
That think they have great store of wit, and boast it,
When here it plaine appear'd they quite had lost it.

84

Some lose their wit with love, some with ambition,
Some running to the sea, great wealth to get,
Some following Lords, and men of high condition,
And some in faire jewels rich and costly set:
One hath desire to prove a rare Magician,
And some with Poetrie their wit forget,
Another thinks to be an Alcumist,
Till all be spent; and he his number mist.

85

Astolso takes his own before he goes,
For so th' *Evangelist* doth him permit;
He set the vessels mouth but to his nose,
And to his place he snuft up all his wit:
Long after wise he liv'd, as *Turpin*° showes,   5
Untill one fault he after did commit:
By name the love of one faire Northerne lasse,
Sent up his wit into the place it was.

86

The vessell where *Orlandos* wit was clos'd,
Astolso took, and thence with him did beare;
It was far heavier than he had suppos'd,
So great a quantity of wit was there;
But yet ere back their journey they dispos'd,
The holy Prophet brought *Astolso*, where
A pallace (seldome seen by mortall man)
Was plac'd, by which a thick dark river ran.

83.3. erst: formerly.
    6. desert: reward; cf. the phrase "just deserts."
85.5. Turpin: one version of the Orlando story was attributed to an Archbishop
Turpin.

Shakespeare, *Romeo and Juliet*

Early in the play (act 1, scene 4), Mercutio teases Romeo about his infatuation for Rosaline, his first love. The speech is the most famous literary use of native English fairy lore, which combined with more exotic strains to produce Pope's sylphs.

> Oh then, I see Queen Mab hath been with you.
> She is the fairies' midwife, and she comes
> In shape no bigger than an agate stone   55
> On the forefinger of an alderman,
> Drawn with a team of little atomies
> Athwart men's noses as they lie asleep —
> Her wagon spokes made of long spinners'° legs;   59
> The cover, of the wings of grasshoppers;   60
> Her traces,° of the smallest spider's web;   61
> Her collars, of the moonshine's watery beams;
> Her whip, of cricket's bone; the lash, of film;
> Her wagoner, a small gray-coated gnat
> Not half so big as a round little worm°   65
> Pricked from the lazy finger of a maid.
> Her chariot is an empty hazelnut,
> Made by the joiner° squirrel or old grub,   68
> Time out o' mind the fairies' coachmakers.
> And in this state she gallops night by night   70
> Through lovers' brains, and then they dream of love . . .

---

59. spinners: spiders.
61. traces: the part of the harness which connects the animal's collar to the vehicle being pulled.
65. worm: According to legend, minute worms grew in the fingers of lazy servants.
68. joiner: carpenter.

John Dryden, *The Flower and the Leaf* (1700)

This is a modernization of a medieval poem ascribed in Dryden's
time to Chaucer. The narrator, a woman, has gone for a stroll in the
woods and observed a tournament between two bands of fairy
knights. Like Pope's sylphs, these fairies were once human beings.

This when I saw, inquisitive to know
The secret Moral of the Mystique Show,   460
I started from my Shade in hopes to find
Some Nymph to satisfy my longing Mind:
And as my fair Adventure fell, I found
A Lady all in White with Lawrel crown'd
Who clos'd the Rear, and softly pac'd along,   465
Repeating to her self the former Song.
With due respect my Body I inclin'd,
As to some Being of Superiour Kind,
And made my Court, according to the Day,
Wishing her Queen and Her a happy *May*.   470
Great Thanks my Daughter, with a gracious Bow
She said; and I who much desir'd to know
Of whence she was, yet fearful how to break
My mind, adventur'd humbly thus to speak.
Madam, Might I presume and not offend,   475
So may the Stars and shining Moon attend
Your Nightly Sports, as you vouchsafe to tell, ⎫
What Nymphs they were who mortal Forms excel, ⎬
And what the Knights who fought in listed Fields so well. ⎭
    To this the Dame reply'd, Fair Daughter know   480
That what you saw, was all a Fairy Show:
And all those airy Shapes you now behold
Were humane Bodies once, and cloath'd with earthly Mold:
Our Souls not yet prepar'd for upper Light,

Till Doomsday wander in the Shades of Night;   485
This only Holiday of all the Year,
We priviledg'd in Sun-shine may appear:
With Songs and Dance we celebrate the Day,
And with due Honours usher in the *May*.
At other Times we reign by Night alone,   490
And posting through the Skies pursue the Moon:
But when the Morn arises, none are found;
For cruel *Demogorgon* walks the round,
And if he finds a Fairy lag in Light,
He drives the Wretch before; and lashes into Night.   495
    All Courteous are by Kind; and ever proud
With friendly Offices to help the Good.
In every Land we have a larger Space
Than what is known to you of mortal Race:
Where we with Green adorn our Fairy Bow'rs,   500
And ev'n this Grove unseen before, is ours.
Know farther; Ev'ry Lady cloath'd in White,
And, crown'd with Oak and Lawrel ev'ry Knight,
Are Servants to the Leaf, by Liveries known
Of Innocence; and I my self am one.   505
Saw you not Her so graceful to behold
In white Attire, and crown'd with Radiant Gold:
The Soveraign Lady of our Land is She,
Diana call'd, the Queen of Chastity:
And, for the spotless Name of Maid she bears,   510
That *Agnus castus*° in her Hand appears: 511
And all her Train with leavy Chaplets crown'd
Were for unblam'd Virginity renown'd:
But those the chief and highest in Command
Who bear those holy Branches in their Hand: 515
The Knights adorn'd with Lawrel-Crowns, are they
Whom Death nor Danger ever cou'd dismay,   }
Victorious Names, who made the World obey:
Who while they liv'd, in Deeds of Arms excell'd,
And after Death for Deities were held.   520
But those who wear the Woodbine on their Brow
Were Knights of Love, who never broke their Vow:
Firm to their plighted Faith, and ever free
From Fears and fickle Chance, and Jealousy.
The Lords and Ladies, who the Woodbine bear,   525
As true as *Tristram*, and *Isotta* were.

---

511. *Agnus castus:* a species of tree thought to preserve chastity.

PART V

Restoration Comedy

Among the important but hard to assess influences on *The Rape of the Lock* is "Restoration Comedy," the works of Wycherley, Etherege, Dryden, Congreve, and their satellites. Relevant features of these plays include their piercing analyses of relations between the sexes in general and of marriage in particular, the relentless pursuit of sexual gratification that obsesses a large proportion of the characters, and an outspoken, blunt treatment of sexual themes which was nevertheless combined with an insistence on elegant conversation and witty repartee. Their relation to Pope's own age was problematical. The aging Wycherley and the young Pope were friends; the wits in whose circle Pope was beginning to move around 1712 were in some senses the heirs of those who had written and criticized the plays; the elegant society depicted in *The Rape of the Lock* probably looked to Congreve for a standard of well-bred wit. Yet new standards of decorum, or hypocrisy, were making the sexual licence and frank language of these plays less and less acceptable.

The selections given here, from Wycherley's *Country Wife* and Congreve's *Way of the World*, emphasize respectively sex and repartee. Horner, Wycherley's hero, has spread around town a false rumor that a recent bout of venereal disease has left him impotent. The purpose of this trick is to convince husbands that their wives are safe in his company; he can thus at once seduce the wives, expose their hypocrisy, and deceive the husbands who mistakenly feel pity mingled with contempt towards him. In the famous "china scene" his conquests visit him in such quick succession that he has all he can do to satisfy them without blowing his cover. The sardonic treatment of honor and hypocrisy find echoes in Pope's poem, and the inescapable double entendres involving china probably contributed something to Pope's much more delicate and muted use of the same image.

Millamant ("mille amants," a thousand lovers) and Mirabell, heroine and hero of *The Way of the World*, are probably the gayest of the gay couples that frolic through these plays, though their gaiety doesn't prevent them from ruthlessly analyzing their motives. Yet, like Belinda, they often seem trapped and stifled by the very conventions they so assiduously uphold, by a reluctance to acknowledge genuine emotion. Millamant is first described from the outside, by Mirabell, as he tries to account for the attraction she exercises on him. In act 2 she emerges on stage, like Belinda the center of all attention, but much more articulate. (Witwoud is Congreve's masterly rendition of a stock Restoration character, the kind of man who aspires to wit and elegance only to fall overboard into foppery and affectation.) Act 4 contains the celebrated "proviso scene," a foretaste of the kind of life Belinda may be trying to escape from.

⌒

The Country Wife

ACT IV, SCENE III. *The Scene changes to* HORNER's *lodging*

[Enter] QUACK and HORNER

QUACK Well, sir, how fadges[1] the new design? Have you not the luck of all your brother projectors,[2] to deceive only yourself at last?

HORNER. No, good domine doctor, I deceive you, it seems, and others too; for the grave matrons, and old, rigid husbands think me as unfit for love as they are; but their wives, sisters, and daughters know, some of 'em, better things already.

QUACK. Already!

HORNER. Already, I say. Last night I was drunk with half a dozen of your civil persons, as you call 'em, and people of honor, and so was made free of their society and dressing rooms for ever hereafter; and am already come to the privileges of sleeping upon their pallets, warming smocks, tying shoes and garters, and the like, doctor, already, already, doctor.

QUACK. You have made use of your time, sir.

HORNER. I tell thee, I am now no more interruption to 'em when they sing, or talk bawdy, than a little squab[3] French page who speaks no English.

QUACK. But do civil persons and women of honor drink, and sing bawdy songs?

---

1. fadges: succeeds.
2. projectors: planners, schemers.
3. squab: short, plump.

231

HORNER. Oh, amongst friends, amongst friends. For your bigots in honor are just like those in religion; they fear the eye of the world more than the eye of Heaven, and think there is no virtue but railing at vice, and no sin but giving scandal. They rail at a poor little kept player, and keep themselves some young modest pulpit comedian[4] to be privy to their sins in their closets, not to tell 'em of them in their chapels.

QUACK. Nay, the truth on't is, priests, amongst the women now, have quite got the better of us lay-confessors, physicians.

HORNER. And they are rather their patients, but —

Enter MY LADY FIDGET, *looking about her*

Now we talk of women of honor, here comes one. Step behind the screen there, and but observe if I have not particular privileges with the women of reputation already, doctor, already. (QUACK *retires*)

LADY FIDGET. Well, Horner, am not I a woman of honor? You see, I'm as good as my word.

HORNER. And you shall see, madam, I'll not be behindhand with you in honor; and I'll be as good as my word too, if you please but to withdraw into the next room.

LADY FIDGET. But first, my dear sir, you must promise to have a care of my dear honor.

HORNER. If you talk a word more of your honor, you'll make me incapable to wrong it. To talk of honor in the mysteries of love, is like talking of Heaven or the Deity in an operation of witchcraft just when you are employing the devil; it makes the charm impotent.

LADY FIDGET. Nay, fy! let us not be smutty. But you talk of mysteries and bewitching to me; I don't understand you.

HORNER. I tell you, madam, the word money in a mistress's mouth, at such a nick of time, is not a more disheartening sound to a younger brother, than that of honor to an eager lover like myself.

LADY FIDGET. But you can't blame a lady of my reputation to be chary.[5]

HORNER. Chary! I have been chary of it already, by the report I have caused of myself.

LADY FIDGET. Ay, but if you should ever let other women know that dear secret, it would come out. Nay, you must have a great care of your conduct; for my acquaintance are so censorious (oh, 'tis a wicked, censorious world, Mr. Horner!), I say, are so censorious and detracting that perhaps they'll talk to the prejudice of my honor, though you should not let them know the dear secret.

HORNER. Nay, madam, rather than they shall prejudice your honor, I'll prejudice theirs; and, to serve you, I'll lie with 'em all, make the secret their own, and then they'll keep it. I am a Machiavel in love, madam.

---

4. pulpit comedian: i.e., a clergyman.
5. chary: cautious.

LADY FIDGET. Oh, no, sir, not that way.

HORNER. Nay, the devil take me if censorious women are to be silenced any other way.

LADY FIDGET. A secret is better kept, I hope, by a single person than a multitude; therefore pray do not trust anybody else with it, dear, dear Mr. Horner.   (*Embracing him*)

Enter SIR JASPER FIDGET

SIR JASPER FIDGET. How now!

LADY FIDGET. (*Aside*) Oh my husband! — prevented — and what's almost as bad, found with my arms about another man — that will appear too much — what shall I say? — Sir Jasper, come hither. I am trying if Mr. Horner were ticklish, and he's as ticklish as can be. I love to torment the confounded toad; let you and I tickle him.

SIR JASPER FIDGET. No, your ladyship will tickle him better without me, I suppose. But is this your buying china? I thought you had been at the china-house.

HORNER. (*Aside*) China-house; that's my cue. I must take it. — A pox! can't you keep your impertinent wives at home? Some men are troubled with the husbands, but I with the wives; but I'd have you to know, since I cannot be your journeyman by night, I will not be your drudge by day, to squire your wife about, and be your man of straw, or scarecrow only to pies and jays, that would be nibbling at your forbidden fruit; I shall be shortly the hackney[6] gentleman usher of the town.

SIR JASPER FIDGET. (*Aside*) He! he! he! poor fellow, he's in the right on't, faith. To squire women about for other folks is as ungrateful an employment as to tell money for other folks. — He! he! he! be'n't angry, Horner.

LADY FIDGET. No, 'tis I have more reason to be angry, who am left by you to go abroad indecently alone; or, what is more indecent, to pin myself upon such ill-bred people of your acquaintance as this is.

SIR JASPER FIDGET. Nay, prithee, what has he done?

LADY FIDGET. Nay, he has done nothing.

SIR JASPER FIDGET. But what d'ye take ill, if he has done nothing?

LADY FIDGET. Ha! ha! ha! faith, I can't but laugh, however; why, d'ye think the unmannerly toad would come down to me to the coach? I was fain to come up to fetch him, or go without him, which I was resolved not to do: for he knows china very well, and has himself very good, but will not let me see it lest I should beg some; but I will find it out, and have what I came for yet.

Exit LADY FIDGET, *followed by* HORNER *to the door*

HORNER. (*Apart to* LADY FIDGET.) Lock the door, madam. So, she has got into my chamber and locked me out. Oh the impertinency of

---

6. hackney: i.e., for public hire, like a hackney-coach.

233

womankind! Well, Sir Jasper, plain-dealing is a jewel; if ever you suffer your wife to trouble me again here she shall carry you home a pair of horns,[7] by my lord mayor she shall; though I cannot furnish you myself, you are sure, yet I'll find a way.

SIR JASPER FIDGET. Ha! ha! he! — (*Aside*) At my first coming in, and finding her arms about him, tickling him it seems, I was half jealous, but now I see my folly. — He! he! he! poor Horner.

HORNER. Nay, though you laugh now, 'twill be my turn ere long. Oh, women, more impertinent, more cunning, and more mischievous than their monkeys, and to me almost as ugly! — Now is she throwing my things about and rifling all I have; but I'll get in to her the back way, and so rifle her for it.

SIR JASPER FIDGET. Ha! ha! ha! poor angry Horner.

HORNER. Stay here a little. I'll ferret her out to you presently, I warrant.

Exit at t'other door
(SIR JASPER calls *through the door to his wife;*
she answers from within)

SIR JASPER FIDGET. Wife! my Lady Fidget! wife! he is coming in to you the back way.

LADY FIDGET. Let him come and welcome, which way he will.

SIR JASPER FIDGET. He'll catch you, and use you roughly, and be too strong for you.

LADY FIDGET. Don't you trouble yourself, let him if he can.

QUACK. (*Behind*) This indeed I could not have believed from him, not any but my own eyes.

Enter MRS. SQUEAMISH[8]

MRS. SQUEAMISH. Where's this woman-hater, this toad, this ugly, greasy, dirty sloven?

SIR JASPER FIDGET. [*Aside*] So, the women all will have him ugly; methinks he is a comely person, but his wants make his form contemptible to 'em; and 'tis e'en as my wife said yesterday, talking of him, that a proper handsome eunuch was as ridiculous a thing as a gigantic coward.

MRS. SQUEAMISH. Sir Jasper, your servant. Where is the odious beast?

SIR JASPER FIDGET. He's within in his chamber, with my wife; she's playing the wag with him.

MRS. SQUEAMISH. Is she so? and he's a clownish beast, he'll give her no quarter, he'll play the wag with her again, let me tell you. Come, let's go help her. — What, the door's locked?

---

7. carry home a pair of horns: i.e., become a cuckold. In folklore men whose wives were unfaithful grew horns on their foreheads; cf. *The Rape of the Lock* 4:71.

8. Mrs. Squeamish: At this time "Mrs." was used of both married and unmarried women.

234

SIR JASPER FIDGET. Ay, my wife locked it.

MRS. SQUEAMISH. Did she so? Let us break it open then.

SIR JASPER FIDGET. No, no; he'll do her no hurt.

MRS. SQUEAMISH. No. — (*Aside*) But is there no other way to get in to 'em? Whither goes this? I will disturb 'em.

Exit MRS. SQUEAMISH *at another door*

Enter OLD LADY SQUEAMISH

OLD LADY SQUEAMISH. Where is this harlotry, this impudent baggage, this rambling tomrigg?[9] O Sir Jasper, I'm glad to see you here; did you not see my vile grandchild come in hither just now?

SIR JASPER FIDGET. Yes.

OLD LADY SQUEAMISH. Ay, but where is she then? where is she? Lord, Sir Jasper, I have e'en rattled myself to pieces in pursuit of her. But can you tell what she makes here? They say below, no woman lodges here.

SIR JASPER FIDGET. No.

OLD LADY SQUEAMISH. No! what does she here then? Say, if it be not a woman's lodging, what makes she here? But are you sure no woman lodges here?

SIR JASPER FIDGET. No, nor no man neither; this is Mr. Horner's lodging.

OLD LADY SQUEAMISH. Is it so, are you sure?

SIR JASPER FIDGET. Yes, yes.

OLD LADY SQUEAMISH. So, then there's no hurt in't, I hope. But where is he?

SIR JASPER FIDGET. He's in the next room with my wife.

OLD LADY SQUEAMISH. Nay, if you trust him with your wife, I may with my Biddy. They say he's a merry harmless man now, e'en as harmless a man as ever came out of Italy with a good voice,[10] and as pretty, harmless company for a lady as a snake without his teeth.

SIR JASPER FIDGET. Ay, ay, poor man.

Enter MRS. SQUEAMISH

MRS. SQUEAMISH. I can't find 'em. — Oh, are you here, grandmother? I followed, you must know, my Lady Fidget hither; 'tis the prettiest lodging, and I have been staring on the prettiest pictures —

Enter LADY FIDGET *with a piece of china in her hand,*
and HORNER *following*

LADY FIDGET. And I have been toiling and moiling for the prettiest piece of china, my dear.

HORNER. Nay, she has been too hard for me, do what I could.

---

9. tomrigg: tomboy.

10. harmless ... voice: Many Italian male singers had been castrated young to preserve their soprano voices.

MRS. SQUEAMISH. O Lord, I'll have some china too. Good Mr. Horner, don't think to give other people china, and me none; come in with me too.

HORNER. Upon my honor, I have none left now.

MRS. SQUEAMISH. Nay, nay, I have known you deny your china before now, but you shan't put me off so. Come.

HORNER. This lady had the last there.

LADY FIDGET. Yes, indeed, madam, to my certain knowledge, he has no more left.

MRS. SQUEAMISH. Oh, but it may be he may have some you could not find.

LADY FIDGET. What, d'ye think if he had had any left, I would not have had it too? for we women of quality never think we have china enough.

HORNER. Do not take it ill, I cannot make china for you all, but I will have a roll-waggon[11] for you too, another time.

MRS. SQUEAMISH. Thank you, dear toad.

LADY FIDGET. (*To* HORNER *aside*) What do you mean by that promise?

HORNER. (*Apart to* LADY FIDGET) Alas, she has an innocent, literal understanding.

OLD LADY SQUEAMISH. Poor Mr. Horner! he has enough to do to please you all, I see.

HORNER. Ay, madam, you see how they use me.

OLD LADY SQUEAMISH. Poor gentleman, I pity you.

HORNER. I thank you, madam. I could never find pity but from such reverend ladies as you are; the young ones will never spare a man.

MRS. SQUEAMISH. Come, come, beast, and go dine with us; for we shall want a man at ombre after dinner.

HORNER. That's all their use of me, madam, you see.

MRS. SQUEAMISH. Come, sloven, I'll lead you, to be sure of you.
(*Pulls him by the cravat*)

OLD LADY SQUEAMISH. Alas, poor man, how she tugs him! Kiss, kiss her; that's the way to make such women quiet.

HORNER. No, madam, that remedy is worse than the torment; they know I dare suffer anything rather than do it.

OLD LADY SQUEAMISH. Prithee kiss her, and I'll give you her picture in little, that you admired so last night; prithee do.

HORNER. Well, nothing but that could bribe me. I love a woman only in effigy and good painting, as much as I hate them. I'll do't, for I could adore the devil well painted. (*Kisses* MRS. SQUEAMISH)

MRS. SQUEAMISH. Foh, you filthy toad! nay, now I've done jesting.

OLD LADY SQUEAMISH. Ha! ha! ha! I told you so.

MRS. SQUEAMISH. Foh! a kiss of his —

SIR JASPER FIDGET. Has no more hurt in't than one of my spaniel's.

MRS. SQUEAMISH. Nor no more good neither.

QUACK. (*Behind*) I will now believe anything he tells me.

---

11. roll-waggon: probably a kind of vase with a cylindrical body. See note in Gerald Weales' edition of Wycherley's *Complete Plays* (Anchor, 1966), p. 369.

Enter PINCHWIFE

LADY FIDGET. O Lord, here's a man! Sir Jasper, my mask, my mask! I would not be seen here for the world.

SIR JASPER FIDGET. What, not when I am with you?

LADY FIDGET. No, no, my honor — let's be gone.

MRS. SQUEAMISH. O grandmother, let us be gone; make haste, make haste, I know not how he may censure us.

LADY FIDGET. Be found in the lodging of anything like a man! — Away.

Exeunt SIR JASPER FIDGET, LADY FIDGET, OLD LADY SQUEAMISH, MRS. SQUEAMISH

⌐

The Way of the World

ACT I

FAINALL. Joy of your success, Mirabell; you look pleased.

MIRABELL. Aye; I have been engaged in a matter of some sort of mirth, which is not yet ripe for discovery. I am glad this is not a cabal night. I wonder, Fainall, that you, who are married and of consequence should be discreet, will suffer your wife to be of such a party.

FAINALL. Faith, I am not jealous. Besides, most who are engaged are women and relations; and for the men, they are of a kind too contemptible to give scandal.

MIRABELL. I am of another opinion. The greater the coxcomb, always the more the scandal; for a woman who is not a fool, can have but one reason for associating with a man who is one.

FAINALL. Are you jealous as often as you see Witwoud entertained by Millamant?

MIRABELL. Of her understanding I am, if not of her person.

FAINALL. You do her wrong; for, to give her her due, she has wit.

MIRABELL. She has beauty enough to make any man think so; and complaisance enough not to contradict him who shall tell her so.

FAINALL. For a passionate lover, methinks you are a man somewhat too discerning in the failings of your mistress.

MIRABELL. And for a discerning man, somewhat too passionate a lover; for I like her with all her faults — nay, like her for her faults. Her follies are so natural, or so artful, that they become her; and those affectations which in another woman would be odious, serve but to make her more agreeable. I'll tell thee, Fainall, she once used me with that insolence, that in revenge I took her to pieces, sifted her, and separated her failings; I studied 'em, and got 'em by rote. The catalogue was so large that I was not without hopes one day or other to hate her heartily; to which end I so used myself to think of 'em that at length, contrary to my design and expectation, they gave me every hour less and less disturbance, till in a few days it became habitual to me to remember 'em without being displeased. They are now grown as familiar to me as my own frailties, and, in all probability, in a little time longer I shall like 'em as well.

FAINALL. Marry her, marry her! Be half as well acquainted with her charms as you are with her defects, and my life on't, you are your own man again.

MIRABELL. Say you so?

FAINALL. Aye, aye, I have experience: I have a wife, and so forth.

ACT II

MIRABELL. Here she comes, i'faith, full sail, with her fan spread and her streamers out, and a shoal of fools for tenders. Ha, no, I cry her mercy!

MRS. FAINALL. I see but one poor empty sculler, and he tows her woman after him.

MIRABELL. [*To* MRS. MILLAMANT] You seem to be unattended, madam. You used to have the *beau monde*¹ throng after you, and a flock of gay fine perukes hovering round you.

WITWOUD. Like moths about a candle. — I had like to have lost my comparison for want of breath.

MRS. MILLAMANT. Oh, I have denied myself airs to-day. I have walked as fast through the crowd —

WITWOUD. As a favorite just disgraced, and with as few followers.

MRS. MILLAMANT. Dear Mr. Witwoud, truce with your similitudes; for I'm as sick of 'em —

WITWOUD. As a physician of a good air. — I cannot help it, madam, though 'tis against myself.

MRS. MILLAMANT. Yet again! Mincing, stand between me and his wit.

WITWOUD. Do, Mrs. Mincing, like a screen before a great fire. — I confess I do blaze to-day; I am too bright.

MRS. FAINALL. But, dear Millamant, why were you so long?

MRS. MILLAMANT. Long! Lord, have I not made violent haste? I have asked every living thing I met for you; I have inquired after you as after a new fashion.

WITWOUD. Madam, truce with your similitudes. — No, you met her husband, and did not ask him for her.

MRS. MILLAMANT. By your leave, Witwoud, that were like inquiring after an old fashion, to ask a husband for his wife.

WITWOUD. Hum, a hit! a hit! a palpable hit! I confess it.

MRS. FAINALL. You were dressed before I came abroad.

MRS. MILLAMANT. Aye, that's true. — Oh, but then I had — Mincing, what had I? Why was I so long?

MINCING. O mem, your la'ship stayed to peruse a pecquet² of letters.

----

1. beau monde: the fashionable world.
2. pecquet: packet. Mincing combines affectation with mispronunciation.

MRS. MILLAMANT. Oh, aye, letters — I had letters — I am persecuted with letters — I hate letters. — Nobody knows how to write letters — and yet one has 'em, one does not know why. They serve one to pin up one's hair.

WITWOUD. Is that the way? Pray, madam, do you pin up your hair with all your letters? I find I must keep copies.

MRS. MILLAMANT. Only with those in verse, Mr. Witwoud; I never pin up my hair with prose. I think I tried once, Mincing.

MINCING. O mem, I shall never forget it.

MRS. MILLAMANT. Aye, poor Mincing tift and tift³ all the morning.

MINCING. Till I had the cremp in my fingers, I'll vow, mem; and all to no purpose. But when your la'ship pins it up with poetry, it sits so pleasant the next day as anything, and is so pure and so crips.

WITWOUD. Indeed, so "crips"?

MINCING. You're such a critic, Mr. Witwoud.

MRS. MILLAMANT. Mirabell, did you take exceptions last night? Oh, aye, and went away. Now I think on't I'm angry — No, now I think on't I'm pleased — for I believe I gave you some pain.

MIRABELL. Does that please you?

MRS. MILLAMANT. Infinitely; I love to give pain.

MIRABELL. You would affect a cruelty which is not in your nature; your true vanity is in the power of pleasing.

MRS. MILLAMANT. Oh, I ask your pardon for that — one's cruelty is one's power; and when one parts with one's cruelty, one parts with one's power; and when one has parted with that, I fancy one's old and ugly.

MIRABELL. Aye, aye, suffer your cruelty to ruin the object of your power, to destroy your lover — and then how vain, how lost a thing you'll be! Nay, 'tis true: you are no longer handsome when you've lost your lover; your beauty dies upon the instant, for beauty is the lover's gift. 'Tis he bestows your charms — your glass is all a cheat. The ugly and the old, whom the looking glass mortifies, yet after commendation can be flattered by it and discover beauties in it; for that reflects our praises, rather than your face.

MRS. MILLAMANT. Oh, the vanity of these men! Fainall, d'ye hear him? If they did not commend us, we were not handsome! Now you must know they could not commend one, if one was not handsome. Beauty the lover's gift! — Lord, what is a lover, that it can give? Why, one makes lovers as fast as one pleases, and they live as long as one pleases, and they die as soon as one pleases: and then, if one pleases, one makes more.

WITWOUD. Very pretty. Why, you make no more of making of lovers, madam, than of making so many card-matches.

---

3. tift: arranged (the hair).

MRS. MILLAMANT. One no more owes one's beauty to a lover, than one's wit to an echo. They can but reflect what we look and say — vain empty things if we are silent or unseen, and want a being.

MIRABELL. Yet to those two vain empty things you owe two the greatest pleasures of your life.

MRS. MILLAMANT. How so?

MIRABELL. To your lover you owe the pleasure of hearing yourselves praised, and to an echo the pleasure of hearing yourselves talk.

WITWOUD. But I know a lady that loves talking so incessantly, she won't give an echo fair play; she has that everlasting rotation of tongue, that an echo must wait till she dies before it can catch her last words.

MRS. MILLAMANT. Oh, fiction! — Fainall, let us leave these men.

MIRABELL. (*Aside to* MRS. FAINALL) Draw off Witwoud.

MRS. FAINALL. Immediately. — [*Aloud*] I have a word or two for Mr. Witwoud.

Exeunt WITWOUD *and* MRS. FAINALL

MIRABELL. [*To* MRS. MILLAMANT] I would beg a little private audience too. — You had the tyranny to deny me last night, though you knew I came to impart a secret to you that concerned my love.

MRS. MILLAMANT. You saw I was engaged.

MIRABELL. Unkind! You had the leisure to entertain a herd of fools — things who visit you from their excessive idleness, bestowing on your easiness that time which is the encumbrance of their lives. How can you find delight in such society? It is impossible they should admire you; they are not capable — or if they were, it should be to you as a mortification, for sure to please a fool is some degree of folly.

MRS. MILLAMANT. I please myself. Besides, sometimes to converse with fools is for my health.

MIRABELL. Your health! Is there a worse disease than the conversation of fools?

MRS. MILLAMANT. Yes, the vapors; fools are physic for it, next to asafoetida.

MIRABELL. You are not in a course of fools?

MRS. MILLAMANT. Mirabell, if you persist in this offensive freedom, you'll displease me. I think I must resolve, after all, not to have you. We shan't agree.

MIRABELL. Not in our physic, it may be.

MRS. MILLAMANT. And yet our distemper, in all likelihood, will be the same; for we shall be sick of one another. I shan't endure to be reprimanded nor instructed; 'tis so dull to act always by advice, and so tedious to be told of one's faults — I can't bear it. Well, I won't have you, Mirabell, — I'm resolved — I think — you may go. — Ha, ha, ha! What would you give that you could help loving me?

MIRABELL. I would give something that you did not know I could not help it.

240

MRS. MILLAMANT. Come, don't look grave, then. Well, what do you say to me?

MIRABELL. I say that a man may as soon make a friend by his wit, or a fortune by his honesty, as win a woman with plain dealing and sincerity.

MRS. MILLAMANT. Sententious Mirabell! Prithee, don't look with that violent and inflexible wise face, like Solomon at the dividing of the child in an old tapestry hanging.

MIRABELL. You are merry, madam, but I would persuade you for a moment to be serious.

MRS. MILLAMANT. What, with that face? No, if you keep your countenance, 'tis impossible I should hold mine. Well, after all, there is something very moving in a lovesick face. Ha, ha, ha! — Well, I won't laugh; don't be peevish — Heigho! now I'll be melancholy — as melancholy as a watch-light.[4] Well, Mirabell, if ever you will win me, woo me now. — Nay, if you are so tedious, fare you well; I see they are walking away.

MIRABELL. Can you not find in the variety of your disposition one moment —

MRS. MILLAMANT. To hear you tell me Foible's married, and your plot like to speed? No.

MIRABELL. But how came you to know it?

MRS. MILLAMANT. Without the help of the devil, you can't imagine — unless she should tell me herself. Which of the two it may have been I will leave you to consider; and when you have done thinking of that, think of me.

[*Exit* MRS. MILLAMANT]

MIRABELL. I have something more — Gone! — Think of you? To think of a whirlwind, though 'twere in a whirlwind, were a case of more steady contemplation — a very tranquility of mind and mansion. A fellow that lives in a windmill, has not a more whimsical dwelling than the heart of a man that is lodged in a woman. There is no point of the compass to which they cannot turn, and by which they are not turned; and by one as well as another. For motion, not method, is their occupation. To know this, and yet continue to be in love, is to be made wise from the dictates of reason, and yet persevere to play the fool by the force of instinct. —

ACT IV

Enter MRS. MILLAMANT *and* MRS. FAINALL

FOIBLE. Madam, I stayed here to tell your ladyship that Mr. Mirabell has waited this half-hour for an opportunity to talk with you — though my lady's orders were to leave you and Sir Wilfull together. Shall I tell Mr. Mirabell that you are at leisure?

_____
4. watch-light: a night-light in a sickroom.

MRS. MILLAMANT. No. What would the dear man have? I am thoughtful, and would amuse myself. Bid him come another time.

(Repeating, and walking about)

There never yet was woman made
Nor shall, but to be cursed.

That's hard!

MRS. FAINALL. You are very fond of Sir John Suckling to-day, Millamant, and the poets.

MRS. MILLAMANT. He? Aye, and filthy verses — so I am.

FOIBLE. Sir Wilfull is coming, madam. Shall I send Mr. Mirabell away?

MRS. MILLAMANT. Aye, if you please, Foible, send him away, or send him hither — just as you will, dear Foible. I think I'll see him — shall I? Aye, let the wretch come.

[Exit FOIBLE]
(Repeating)

Thyrsis, a youth of the inspired train.

Dear Fainall, entertain Sir Wilfull — thou hast philosophy to undergo a fool. Thou art married and hast patience. I would confer with my own thoughts.

[Enter Sir Wilfull]

. . . .

MRS. MILLAMANT. If it is of no great importance, Sir Wilfull, you will oblige me to leave me; I have just now a little business —

SIR WILFULL. Enough, enough, cousin; yes, yes, all a case. — When you're disposed, when you're disposed. Now's as well as another time, and another time as well as now. All's one for that — Yes, yes, if your concerns call you, there's no haste; it will keep cold, as they say. Cousin, your servant. — I think this door's locked.

MRS. MILLAMANT. You may go this way, sir.

SIR WILFULL. Your servant; then with your leave I'll return to my company.

MRS. MILLAMANT. Aye, aye; ha, ha, ha!
Like Phoebus sung the no less amorous boy.

Exit

Enter MIRABELL

MIRABELL. "Like Daphne she, as lovely and as coy." Do you lock yourself up from me to make my search more curious, or is this pretty artifice contrived to signify that here the chase must end, and my pursuit be crowned? For you can fly no further.

MRS. MILLAMANT. Vanity! No — I'll fly and be followed to the last moment. Though I am upon the very verge of matrimony, I expect you should solicit me as much as if I were wavering at the grate of a monastery, with one foot over the threshold. I'll be solicited to the very last — nay, and afterwards.

MIRABELL. What, after the last?

MRS. MILLAMANT. Oh, I should think I was poor and had nothing to bestow, if I were reduced to an inglorious ease and freed from the agreeable fatigues of solicitation.

MIRABELL. But do not know that when favors are conferred upon instant [5] and tedious solicitation, that they diminish in their value, and that both the giver loses the grace, and the receiver lessens his pleasure?

MRS. MILLAMANT. It may be in things of common application; but never, sure, in love. Oh, I hate a lover that can dare to think he draws a moment's air, independent of the bounty of his mistress. There is not so impudent a thing in nature as the saucy look of an assured man, confident of success. The pedantic arrogance of a very husband has not so pragmatical an air. Ah! I'll never marry unless I am first made sure of my will and pleasure.

MIRABELL. Would you have 'em both before marriage? or will you be contented with the first now, and stay for the other till after grace?

MRS. MILLAMANT. Ah! don't be impertinent. — My dear liberty, shall I leave thee? my faithful solitude, my darling contemplation, must I bid you then adieu? Ay-h adieu — my morning thoughts, agreeable wakings, indolent slumbers, all ye *douceurs,* ye *sommeils du matin,* [6] *adieu.* — I can't do't, 'tis more than impossible. — Positively, Mirabell, I'll lie abed in a morning as long as I please.

MIRABELL. Then I'll get up in a morning as early as I please.

MRS. MILLAMANT. Ah? Idle creature, get up when you will — and d'ye hear, I won't be called names after I'm married; positively, I won't be called names.

MIRABELL. Names!

MRS. MILLAMANT. Aye, as wife, spouse, my dear, joy, jewel, love, sweetheart, and the rest of that nauseous cant, in which men and their wives are so fulsomely familiar — I shall never bear that. Good Mirabell, don't let us be familiar or fond, nor kiss before folks, like my Lady Fadler and Sir Francis; nor go to Hyde Park together the first Sunday in a new chariot, to provoke eyes and whispers, and then never be seen there together again, as if we were proud of one another the first week, and ashamed of one another ever after. Let us never visit together, nor go to a play together; but let us be very strange and well-bred. Let us be as strange as if we had been married a great while, and as well-bred as if we were not married at all.

MIRABELL. Have you any more conditions to offer? Hitherto your demands are pretty reasonable.

---

5. instant: insistent.
6. doucers: sweetnesses; sommeils du matin: morning slumbers.

MRS. MILLAMANT. Trifles — as liberty to pay and receive visits to and from whom I please; to write and receive letters, without interrogatories or wry faces on your part; to wear what I please, and choose conversation with regard only to my own taste; to have no obligation upon me to converse with wits that I don't like, because they are your acquaintance; or to be intimate with fools, because they may be your relations. Come to dinner when I please; dine in my dressing-room when I'm out of humor, without giving a reason. To have my closet inviolate; to be sole empress of my tea-table, which you must never presume to approach without first asking leave. And lastly, wherever I am, you shall always knock at the door before you come in. These articles subscribed, if I continue to endure you a little longer, I may by degrees dwindle into a wife.

MIRABELL. Your bill of fare is something advanced in this latter account. Well, have I liberty to offer conditions — that when you are dwindled into a wife, I may not be beyond measure enlarged into a husband?

MRS. MILLAMANT. You have free leave. Propose your utmost; speak and spare not.

MIRABELL. I thank you. — *Imprimis* then, I covenant that your acquaintance be general; that you admit no sworn confidante or intimate of your own sex — no she-friend to screen her affairs under your countenance, and tempt you to make trial of a mutual secrecy. No decoy-duck to wheedle you a fop-scrambling to the play in a mask, then bring you home in a pretended fright, when you think you shall be found out, and rail at me for missing the play and disappointing the frolic which you had, to pick me up and prove my constancy.

MRS. MILLAMANT. Detestable *imprimis*. I go to the play in a mask!

MIRABELL. *Item*, I article that you continue to like your own face as long as I shall; and while it passes current with me, that you endeavor not to new-coin it. To which end, together with all vizards for the day, I prohibit all masks for the night, made of oiled-skins and I know not what — hog's bones, hare's gall, pig-water, and the marrow of a roasted cat. In short, I forbid all commerce with the gentle-woman in what-d'ye-call-it Court. *Item*, I shut my doors against all gawds with baskets, and pennyworths of muslin, china, fans, atlases,[7] etc. — *Item*, when you shall be breeding —

MRS. MILLAMANT. Ah! name it not.

MIRABELL. Which may be presumed, with a blessing on our endeavors —

MRS. MILLAMANT. Odious endeavors!

MIRABELL. I denounce against all strait[8] lacing, squeezing for a shape, till you mould my boy's head like a sugar-loaf, and instead of

---

7. atlas: a kind of satin.
8. strait: narrow, tight.

a man-child, make me father to a crooked billet.[9] Lastly, to the dominion of the tea-table I submit — but with proviso, that you exceed not in your province, but restrain yourself to native and simple tea-table drinks, as tea, chocolate, and coffee; as likewise to genuine and authorized tea-table talk — such as mending of fashions, spoiling reputations, railing at absent friends, and so forth — but that on no account you encroach upon the men's prerogative, and presume to drink healths, or toast fellows; for prevention of which I banish all foreign forces, all auxiliaries to the tea-table, as orange-brandy, all aniseed, cinnamon, citron, and Barbadoes waters, together with ratafia, and the most noble spirit of clary,[10] but for cowslip wine, poppy water, and all dormitives, those I allow. These provisos admitted, in other things I may prove a tractable and complying husband.

MRS. MILLAMANT. O horrid provisos! filthy strong-waters! I toast fellows! odious men! I hate your odious provisos.

MIRABELL. Then we're agreed. Shall I kiss your hand upon the contract? And here comes one to be a witness to the sealing of the deed.

Enter MRS. FAINALL

MRS. MILLAMANT. Fainall, what shall I do? Shall I have him? I think I must have him.

MRS. FAINALL. Aye, aye, take him, take him; what should you do?

MRS. MILLAMANT. Well then — I'll take my death, I'm in a horrid fright. — Fainall, I shall never say it — well — I think — I'll endure you.

MRS. FAINALL. Fie! fie! Have him, have him, and tell him so in plain terms; for I am sure you have a mind to him.

MRS. MILLAMANT. Are you? I think I have — and the horrid man looks as if he thought so too. Well, you ridiculous thing you, I'll have you — I won't be kissed, nor I won't be thanked — here, kiss my hand though. — So, hold your tongue now; don't say a word.

MRS. FAINALL. Mirabell, there's a necessity for your obedience; you have neither time to talk nor stay. My mother is coming, and in my conscience if she should see you, would fall into fits, and maybe not recover time enough to return to Sir Rowland, who, as Foible tells me, is in a fair way to succeed. Therefore spare your ecstasies for another occasion, and slip down the backstairs, where Foible waits to consult you.

MRS. MILLAMANT. Aye, go, go. In the meantime I suppose you have said something to please me.

MIRABELL. I am all obedience.

[*Exit* MIRABELL]

---

9. billet: stick of firewood.
10. orange-brandy . . . clary: varieties of strong alcoholic drinks.

PART VI

Periodical Essays

Richard Steele developed the definitive form of the periodical essay in his immensely popular *Tatler*, which appeared three times a week from 12 April 1709 to 2 January 1711, for a total of 271 issues. After the venture was under way Joseph Addison became a frequent contributor, and after the demise of the *Tatler* the two men collaborated to found the *Spectator*, the most popular of all the essay periodicals and the most important for *The Rape of the Lock*. The first series appeared daily except Sunday from 1 March 1711 to 6 December 1712 (555 issues in all). A host of imitators appeared and disappeared throughout the rest of the century.

Pope owed a great deal to the *Spectator* and *Tatler*. They helped to encourage the habit of reading among the middle classes and especially among women, whose readership they wooed persistently and persuasively and over whose intellectual development they hovered solicitously. If Pope had not been able to count on a large feminine audience for his poem, its tone would have been quite different. The periodicals also made women's foibles the object of much of their rather bland and gentle satire. *The Rape of the Lock* assimilated some of this material and often adopted the "Spectator tone," but the common sense approach of Addison and Steele also provided a contrast to Pope's far more imaginative and mythic presentation of Belinda and her companions. By striving to popularize the learning of the day, including literary criticism, the *Spectator* enabled more readers to appreciate Pope's sophisticated wit. Its most important critical enterprise was Addison's series of eighteen papers on *Paradise Lost*, six on general topics and one on each of the twelve books. Sales of *Paradise Lost* immediately increased, and even those who knew the poem only as quoted by Addison would have been able to grasp some of Pope's allusions. Moreover, Pope's allusions to *Paradise Lost* often bring into play the ethical implications that Addison had found in the poem. Finally, as early as 1714 the *Spectator* had already achieved the status of a modern classic, as worthy as the ancients of being alluded to in its own right. For the twentieth-century reader, the *Spectator* and *Tatler* also provide the best means of getting acquainted with the social setting of *The Rape of the Lock*.

The Tatler no. 113. 29 December 1709 (Steele?)

A complete inventory of Sir Plume's or the Baron's personal effects might have produced a list much like the following of the frivolous and fashionable objects that they and their companions cherish so dearly. As the petition from Mrs. Cross-stitch shows, wide hoopskirts like Belinda's had long been a recognized object of satire.

The TATLER.

By *Isaac Bickerstaff* Esq;

Ecce iterum Crispinus ! Juv.

From *Tuesday December* 27. to *Thursday December* 29. 1709.

Haymarket, December 23.

Whereas the Gentleman that behaved himself in a very disobedient and obstinate Manner at his late Tryal in *Sheer-Lane* on the 20th Instant, and was carried off dead upon the taking away of his Snuff-Box, remains still unburied; the Company of Upholders not knowing otherwise how they should be paid, have taken his Goods in Execution to defray the Charge of his Funeral. His said Effects are to be exposed to Sale by Auction at their Office in the *Haymarket* on the 4th of *January* next, and are as follow:

A very rich Tweezer-Case, containing Twelve Instruments for the Use of each Hour in the Day.

Four Pounds of scented Snuff, with Three gilt Snuff-Boxes; one of them with an invisible Hinge, and a Looking-glass in the Lid.

Two more of Ivory, with the Portraitures on their Lids of Two Ladies of the Town; the Originals to be seen every Night in the Side-Boxes of the Playhouse.

A Sword with a Steel Diamond Hilt, never drawn but once, at *May-Fair*.

Six clean Packs of Cards, a Quart of Orange-Flower-Water, a Pair of *French* Scissors, a Toothpick Case, and an Eye-brow Brush.

A large Glass-Case, containing the Linnen and Clothes of the Deceased; among which are, Two embroidered Suits, a Pocket Perspective, a Dozen Pair of Red-heeled Shoes, Three Pair of Red Silk Stockings, and an Amber-headed Cane.

The strong Box of the Deceased, wherein were found, Five Billet-doux, a *Bath* Shilling, a crooked Sixpence, a Silk Garter, a Lock of Hair, and Three broken Fans.

A Press for Books, containing on the Upper Shelf, Three Bottles of Diet-Drink.

Two Boxes of Pills.

A Syringe, and other Mathematical Instruments.

On the Second Shelf are several Miscellaneous Works; as,

Lampoons.

Plays.

Taylors Bills.

And an *Almanack* for the Year Seventeen Hundred.

On the Third Shelf,

A Bundle of Letters unopened, indorsed, (in the Hand of the Deceased) *Letters from the Old Gentleman.*

Lessons for the Flute.

Toland's Christianity not Mysterious. And a Paper fill'd with Patterns of several fashionable Stuffs.

On the Lowest Shelf,

One Shoe.

A Pair of Snuffers.

A *French* Grammar.

A Mourning Hatband: And half a Bottle of Usquebaugh.

There will be added to these Goods, to make a compleat Auction, a Collection of Gold Snuff-Boxes and Clouded Canes, which are to continue in Fashion for Three Months after the Sale.

The Whole are to be set up and prized by *Charles Bubbleboy*, who is to open the Auction with a Speech.

I find that I am so very unhappy, that while I am busie in correcting the Folly and Vice of one Sex, several Exorbitances break out in the other. I have not throughly examined their new-fashioned Petticoats, but shall set aside one Day in the next Week for that Purpose. The following Petition on this Subject was presented to me this Morning.

The Humble Petition of William Jingle, *Coach-maker and Chair-maker of the Liberty of* Westminster.

To *Isaac Bickerstaff* Esq; Censor of *Great Britain.*

SHEWETH,

'That upon the late Invention of Mrs. *Catherine Cross-Stitch*, Mantoe-maker, the Petticoats of Ladies were too wide for entring into any Coach or Chair which was in Use before the said Invention.

'That for the Service of the said Ladies, your Petitioner has built a round Chair, in the Form of a Lanthorn, Six Yards and half in Circumference, with a Stool in the Centre of it; the said Vehicle being so contrived, as to receive the Passenger by opening in two in the Middle, and closing mathematically when she is seated.

'That

' That your Petitioner has alfo invented a Coach
' for the Reception of one Lady only, who is to
' be let in at the Top.
' That the faid Coach has been tryed by a Lady's
' Woman in one of thefe full Petticoats, who was
' let down from a Balcony, and drawn up again
' by Pullies, to the great Satisfaction of her Lady,
' and all who beheld her.
' Your Petitioner therefore moft humbly prays,
' That for the Encouragement of Ingenuity and
' ufeful Inventions, he may be heard before you
' pafs Sentence upon the Petticoats aforefaid.

No. 121. 17 January 1710 (Addison)

This essay testifies to the exaggerated affection that other young
ladies besides Belinda bestowed on lapdogs and parrots. By assigning
a cause to this disorder ("lack of the proper objects of love, as
husbands or children") and by humorously amplifying its effects
until a quarrel threatens to lead to a criminal prosecution, Addison
helps Pope's readers realize that such misplaced love may be more
than an innocent foible.

1. upholders: undertakers, funeral directors.
2. perspective: magnifying glass or telescope.
3. garter . . . fans: cf. the trophies that Pope's Baron sacrifices on his altar.
4. old gentleman: i.e., the father of the deceased.
5. Toland's . . . Mysterious: a deist attack on revelation and organized religion.
6. stuffs: fabrics.
7. snuffers: candle-snuffers.
8. usquebaugh: whisky.
9. lantern: a cupola built at the top of a dome to provide light or ventilation.

The TATLER.

By *Isaac Bickerstaff* Esq; Addison

―――*Similis tibi, Cynthia, vel tibi, cujus*
Turbavit nitidos extinctus Passer Ocellos. Juv.

From *Saturday January* 14. to *Tuesday January* 17. 1709.

From my own Apartment, January 16.

I Was recollecting the Remainder of my Vision, when my Maid came to me, and told me, there was a Gentlewoman below who seemed to be in great Trouble, and pressed very much to see me. When it lay in my Power to remove the Distress of an unhappy Person, I thought I should very ill employ my Time in attending Matters of Speculation, and therefore desired the Lady would walk in. When she entered, I saw her Eyes full of Tears. However, her Grief was not so great as to make her omit Rules; for she was very long and exact in her Civilities, which gave me Time to view and consider her. Her Clothes were very rich, but tarnished; and her Words very fine, but ill applied. These Distinctions made me without Hesitation (tho' I had never seen her before) ask her, If her Lady had any Commands for me? She then began to weep afresh, and with many broken Sighs told me, That their Family was in very great Affliction― I beseeched her to compose herself, for that I might possibly be capable of assisting them― She then cast her Eye upon my little Dog, and was again transported with too much Passion to proceed; but with much ado, she at last gave me to understand, That *Cupid*, her Lady's Lap-Dog, was dangerously ill, and in so bad a Condition, that her Lady neither saw Company, nor went abroad, for which Reason she did not come her self to consult me; that as I had mentioned with great Affection my own Dog, (here she courtsied, and looking first at the Cur, and then on me, said, indeed I had Reason, for he was very pretty) her Lady sent to me rather than to any other Doctor, and hoped I would not laugh at her Sorrow, but send her my Advice. I must confess, I had some Indignation to find my self treated like something below a Farrier; yet well knowing, that the best, as well as most tender Way, of dealing with a Woman, is to fall in with her Humours, and by that Means to let her see the Absurdity of them. I proceeded accordingly: Pray Madam, said I, can you give me any methodical Account of this Illness, and how *Cupid* was first taken? Sir (said she) we have a little ignorant Country Girl who is kept to tend him: She was recommended to our Family by one that my Lady once saw but once, at a Visit; and you know, Persons of Quality are always inclined to Strangers; for I could have helped her to a Cousin of my own, but― Good Madam (said I) you neglect the Account of the sick Body, while you are complaining of this Girl. No, no, Sir (said she) begging your Pardon: But it is the general Fault of Physicians, they are so in haste, that they never hear out the Case. I say, this silly Girl, after washing *Cupid*, let him stand half an Hour in the Window without his Collar, where he catched Cold, and in an Hour after began to bark very hoarse. He had however a pretty good Night, and we hoped the Danger was over; but for these Two Nights last past, neither he nor my Lady have slept a Wink. Has he (said I) taken any Thing? No (said she) but my Lady says, he shall take any Thing that you prescribe; provided you do not make Use of Jesuits Powder, or the Cold Bath. Poor *Cupid* (continued she) has always been Phtisical, and as he lies under something like a Chin-Cough, we are afraid it will end in a Consumption. I then asked her, if she had brought any of his Water to show me. Upon this, she stared me in the Face, and said, I am afraid, Mr. *Bickerstaff*, you are not serious; but if you have any Receipt that is proper on this Occasion, pray let us have it; for my Mistress is not to be comforted. Upon this, I paused a little without returning any Answer, and after some short Silence, I proceeded in the following Manner: I have considered the Nature of the Distemper, and the Constitution of the Patient, and by the best Observation that I can make on both, I think it is safest to put him into a Course of Kitchin Physick. In the mean time, to remove his Hoarseness, it will be the most natural Way to make *Cupid* his own Druggist; for which Reason, I shall prescribe to him, Three Mornings successively, as much Powder as will lie on a Groat, of that noble Remedy which the Apothecaries call *Album Græcum*. Upon hearing this Advice, the young Woman smiled, as if she knew how ridiculous an Errand she had been employed in; and indeed I found by the Sequel of her Discourse, That she was an arch Baggage, and of a Character that is frequent enough in Persons of her Employment, who are so used to conform themselves in every Thing to the Humours and Passions of their Mistresses, that they sacrifice Superiority of Sense to Superiority of Condition, and are insensibly betrayed into the Passions and Prejudices of those whom they serve, without giving themselves Leave to consider, that they are extravagant and ridiculous. However I thought it very natural, when her Eyes were thus open, to see her give a new Turn to her Discourse, and from sympathizing with her Mistress in her Follies, to fall a Railing at her. You cannot imagine, said she, Mr. *Bickerstaff*, what a Life she makes us lead for the Sake of this little ugly Cur: If he dies, we are the most unhappy Family in Town. She chanced to lose a Parrot last Year, which, to tell you truly, brought me into her Service; for she turned off her Woman upon it, who
had

had lived with her Ten Years, becaufe fhe neglected to give him Water, tho' every one of the Family fays, fhe was as innocent of the Bird's Death, as the Babe that is unborn. Nay, fhe told me this very Morning, That if *Cupid* fhould die, fhe would fend the poor innocent Wench I was telling you of, to *Bridewell*, and have the Milk-Woman tried for her Life at the *Old-Baly*, for putting Water into his Milk. In fhort, fhe talks like any diftracted Creature.

—Since it is fo, young Woman (faid I) I will by no means let you offend her by ftaying on this Meffage longer than is abfolutely neceffary, and fo forced her out.

While I am ftudying to cure thofe Evils and Diftreffes that are neceffary or natural to human Life, I find my Task growing upon me, fince by thefe accidental Cares, and acquired Calamities (if I may fo call them) my Patients contract Diftempers to which their Conftitution is of it felf a Stranger. But this is an Evil I have for many Years remarked in the Fair Sex; and as they are by Nature very much formed for Affection and Dalliance, I have obferved, That when by too obftinate a Cruelty, or any other means, they have difappointed themfelves of the proper Objects of Love, as Husbands, or Children, fuch Virgins have exactly at fuch a Year grown fond of Lap-dogs, Parrots, or other Animals. I know at this Time a celebrated Toaft, whom I allow to be one of the moft agreeable of her Sex, that in the Prefence of her Admirers, will give a Torrent of Kiffes to her Cat, any one of which a Chriftian would be glad of. I do not at the fame Time deny, but there are as great Enormities of this kind committed by our Sex as theirs. A *Roman* Emperor had fo very great an Efteem for an Horfe of his, that he had Thoughts of making him a Conful; and feveral Moderns of that Rank of Men whom we call Country 'Squires, won't fcruple to kifs their Hounds before all the World, and declare in the Prefence of their Wives, that they had rather falute a Favourite of the Pack, than the fineft Woman in *England*.

---

1. farrier: a horse-shoer, and by extension a veterinary.
2. Jesuit's powder: powdered bark of the Cinchona tree, a source of quinine; used to treat fevers.
3. phthisical: suffering from, or susceptible to, diseases of the lungs, especially tuberculosis.
4. water: urine.
5. receipt: recipe, prescription.
6. Album Græcum: "dried dung of dogs or hyenas sometimes used in dressing leather" (*Webster III*).
7. Bridewell: a London prison.
8. Old Bailey: London's central criminal court.
9. Roman emperor: Caligula.

The Spectator, no. 8. 9 March 1711 (Addison)

This letter to the editor comes from a member of the Society for the Reformation of Manners, which had been formed in 1690 to discourage drunkenness, swearing, and sabbath-breaking. It spells out the dangers to female purity that lurk in "Midnight Masquerades" and that the sylphs protect young virgins from, if Ariel's speech in the dream vision in canto 1 can be believed.

---

1. Hempen Manufacturer: Beating hemp was a common task of prisoners, especially prostitutes.
2. Counter: a prison attached to a city court.
3. obnoxious: vulnerable.

The SPECTATOR.

At Venus *obscuro gradientes aere sepsit,*
Et multo Nebulæ circum Dea fudit amictu,
Cernere ne quis eos ——.　　　　Virg.

Friday, March 9. 1711.

' which has of late been very frequently held in one
' of the most conspicuous Parts of the Town, and
' which I hear will be continued with Additions and
' Improvements. As all the Persons who compose
' this lawless Assembly are masqued, we dare not
' attack any of them in *our Way*, lest we should send
' a Woman of Quality to *Bridewell* or a Peer of
' *Great-Britain* to the *Counter*: Besides, that their
' Numbers are so very great, that I am afraid they
' would be able to rout our whole Fraternity, tho'
' we were accompanied with all our Guard of Con-
' stables. Both these Reasons which secure them
' from our Authority, make them obnoxious to
' yours; As both their Disguise and their Numbers
' will give no particular Person Reason to think
' himself affronted by you.
' If we are rightly inform'd, the Rules that are
' observed by this new Society are wonderfully con-
' triv'd for the Advancement of Cuckoldom. The
' Women either come by themselves or are intro-
' duced by Friends, who are obliged to quit them
' upon their first Entrance, to the Conversation of
' any Body that addresses himself to them. There
' are several Rooms where the Parties may retire,
' and, if they please, show their Faces by Consent.
' Whispers, Squeezes, Nods, and Embraces, are the
' innocent Freedoms of the Place. In short, the
' whole Design of this libidinous Assembly seems to
' terminate in Assignations and Intrigues; and I
' hope you will take effectual Methods by your
' publick Advice and Admonitions, to prevent such
' a promiscuous Multitude of both Sexes from meet-
' ing together in so clandestine a Manner.

' I am no less acquainted with the particular
' Quarters and Regions of this great Town, than
' with the different Parts and Distributions of the
' whole Nation. I can describe every Parish by its
' Impieties, and can tell you in which of our Streets
' Lewdness prevails, which Gaming has taken
' the Possession of, and where Drunkenness has got
' the better of them both. When I am disposed
' to raise a Fine for the Poor, I know the Lanes and
' Allies that are inhabited by common Swearers.
' When I would encourage the Hospital of *Bride-*
' *well* and improve the Hempen Manufacture, I am
' very well acquainted with all the Haunts and Re-
' sorts of Female Night-walkers.
' After this short Account of my self, I must let you
' know, that the Design of this Paper is to give you
' Information of a certain irregular Assembly which
' I think falls very properly under your Observation,
' especially since the Persons it is composed of are
' Criminals too considerable for the Animadversions
' of our Society. I mean, Sir, the Midnight Masque,

　　I am,

　　　Your humble Servant,

　　　　And Fellow-Labourer,

　　　　　T. B.

255

No. 10. 12 March 1711 (Addison)

This issue shows the double attitude toward women alluded to above in the general introduction to the periodical essays. Like a long tradition of antifeminine satirists, Mr. Spectator believed that women needed improvement; unlike many of his predecessors, he also believed that they were capable of it and that many of their faults were the product of social and economic conditions over which they had much less control than men. Thus the periodicals not only gave Pope some hints for his satire but also helped educate his female readers to appreciate his wit.

The SPECTATOR.

Non aliter quam qui adverso vix flumine lembum
Remigiis jubigit : si brachia forte remisit,
Atque illum in præceps prono rapit alveus amni. Vir

Monday, March 12. 1711.

It was said of *Socrates*, that he brought Philosophy down from Heaven, to inhabit among Men; and I shall be ambitious to have it said of me, that I have brought Philosophy out of Closets and Libraries, Schools and Colleges, to dwell in Clubs and Assemblies, at Tea-Tables, and in Coffee-Houses.

I would therefore in a very particular Manner recommend these my Speculations to all well regulated Families, that set apart an Hour in every Morning for Tea and Bread and Butter; and would earnestly advise them for their Good to order this Paper to be punctually served up, and to be looked upon as a Part of the Tea Equipage.

But there are none to whom this Paper will be more useful, than to the female World. I have often thought there has not been sufficient Pains taken in finding out proper Employments and Diversions for the Fair ones. Their Amusements seem contrived for them rather as they are Women, than as they are reasonable Creatures; and are more adapted to the Sex, than to the Species. The Toilet is their great Scene of Business, and the right adjusting of their Hair the principal Employment of their Lives. The sorting of a Suit of Ribbons, is reckon'd a very good Morning's Work; and if they make an Excursion to a Mercer's or a Toy-shop, so great a Fatigue makes them unfit for any thing else all the Day after. Their more serious Occupations are Sowing and Embroidery, and their greatest Drudgery the Preparation of Jellies and Sweetmeats. This, I say, is the State of ordinary Women; tho' I know there are Multitudes of those of a more elevated Life and Conversation, that move in an exalted Sphere of Knowledge and Virtue, that join all the Beauties of the Mind to the Ornaments of Dress, and inspire a kind of Awe and Respect, as well as Love, into their Male-Beholders. I hope to encrease the Number of these by publishing this daily Paper, which I shall always endeavour to make an innocent if not an improving Entertainment, and by that Means at least divert the Minds of my female Readers from greater Trifles. At the same Time, as I would fain give some finishing Touches to those which are already the most beautiful Pieces in humane Nature, I shall endeavour to point out all those Imperfections that are the Blemishes, as well as those Virtues which are the Embellishments, of the Sex. In the mean while I hope these my gentle Readers, who have so much Time on their Hands, will not grudge throwing away a Quarter of an Hour in a Day on this Paper, since they may do it without any Hindrance to Business.

NᵁᴹB. LXIX.

The SPECTATOR.

Hic fegetes, illic veniunt felicius uvæ:
Arborei fætus alibi, atque injuffa virefcunt
Gramina. Nonne vides, croceos ut Tmolus odores,
India mittit ebur, molles fua thura Sabæi?
At Chalybes nudi ferrum, virofaque Pontus
Caftorea, Eliadum palmas Epirus equarum?
Continuo has leges æternaque fædera certis
Impofuit Natura locis————Vir.

Saturday, May 19. 1711.

Nature feems to have taken a particular Care to diffeminate her Bleffings among the different Regions of the World, with an Eye to this mutual Intercourfe and Traffick among Mankind, that the Natives of the feveral Parts of the Globe might have a kind of Dependance upon one another, and be united together by their common Intereft. Almoft every Degree produces fomething peculiar to it. The Food often grows in one Country, and the Sauce in another. The Fruits of *Portugal* are corrected by the Products of *Barbadoes* : The Infufion of a *China* Plant fweetned with the Pith of an *Indian* Cane: The *Philippick* Iflands give a Flavour to our *European* Bowls. The fingle Drefs of a Woman of Quality is often the Product of an hundred Climates. The Muff and the Fan come together from the different Ends of the Earth. The Scarf is fent from the Torrid Zone, and the Tippet from beneath the Pole. The Brocade Petticoat rifes out of the Mines of *Peru,* and the Diamond Necklace out of the Bowels of *Indoftan.*

No. 73. 24 May 1711 (Addison)

Like "divine" and "angel," "idol" is one of many religious terms which also form part of the vocabularly of routine social compliment: "Each Maid cry'd, charming! and each Youth, divine!" (Pope's *Dunciad*, 4:410). Addison shows here that the full sense of the religious term may subvert the gallant use, that what is intended as idle flattery may from another perspective conceal profound criticism of a serious perversion of values. Thus far this essay would constitute an oblique commentary on Belinda's coquetry and on her image worship at the dressing table. But Addison's appeal to Milton's catalogue of pagan deities (see above, p. 114) gives this passage a significance for *The Rape of the Lock* which is somewhat different from that of Pope's direct allusion to it. Pope's allusion implies that the sylphs are the idols, Addison's that Belinda and her fellow-coquettes are. But the two perspectives are really one, since the sylphs are projections of woman's nature.

The SPECTATOR.

——— *O Dea certè!* Virg.

Thurſday, May 24. 1711.

The Paſſion for Praiſe, which is ſo very vehement in the fair Sex, produces excellent Effects in Women of Senſe, who deſire to be admired for that only which deſerves Admiration: and I think we may obſerve, without a Compliment to them, that many of them do not only live in a more uniform

Courſe of Virtue, but with an infinitely greater Regard to their Honour, than what we find in the Generality of our own Sex. How many Inſtances have we of Chaſtity, Fidelity, Devotion? How many Ladies diſtinguiſh themſelves by the Education of their Children, Care of their Families, and Love of their Husbands, which are the great Qualities and Atchievements of Womankind: As the making of War, the carrying on of Traffick, the Adminiſtration of Juſtice, are thoſe by which Men grow famous, and get themſelves a Name.

But as this Paſſion for Admiration, when it works according to Reaſon, improves the beautiful Part of our Species in every thing that is Laudable; ſo nothing is more Deſtructive to them when it is governed by Vanity and Folly. What I have therefore here to ſay, only regards the vain Part of the Sex, whom for certain Reaſons, which the Reader will hereafter ſee at large, I ſhall diſtinguiſh by the Name of *Idols*. An *Idol* is wholly taken up in the Adorning of her Perſon. You ſee in every Poſture of her Body, Air of her Face, and Motion of her Head, that it is her Buſineſs and Employment to gain Adorers. For this Reaſon your *Idols* appear in all publick Places and Aſſemblies, in order to ſeduce Men to their Worſhip. The Playhouſe is very frequently filled with *Idols*; ſeveral of them are carried in Proceſſion every Evening about the Ring, and ſeveral of them ſet up their Worſhip even in Churches. They are to be accoſted in the Language proper to the Deity. Life and Death are in their Power: Joys of Heaven and Pains of Hell are at their diſpoſal: Paradiſe is in their Arms, and Eternity in every Moment that you are preſent with them. Raptures, Tranſports and Extaſies are the Rewards which they confer: Sighs and Tears, Prayers and broken Hearts are the Offerings that are paid to them. Their Smiles make Men happy; their Frowns drive them to Deſpair. I ſhall only add under this Head, that *Ovid*'s Book of the Art of Love is a kind of Heathen Ritual, which contains all the Forms of Worſhip that are made uſe of to an *Idol*.

It would be as difficult a Task to reckon up theſe different kinds of *Idols*, as *Milton*'s was to number thoſe that were known in *Canaan*, and the Lands adjoining. Moſt of them are Worſhipped, like *Moloch love* in *fires* and Flames. Some of them, like *Baal*, love to fee their Votaries cut and flashed, and shedding their Blood for them. Some of them, like the

1 *Idol* in the *Apocrypha*, must have Treats and Collations prepared for them every Night. It has indeed been known, that some of them have been used by their incensed Worshippers like the *Chinese Idols*, who are Whipped and Scourged when they refuse to comply with the Prayers that are offered to them.

I must here observe, that those Idolaters who devote themselves to the *Idols* I am here speaking of, differ very much from all other kinds of Idolaters. For as others fall out because they Worship different *Idols*, these Idolaters quarrel because they Worship the same.

The Intention therefore of the *Idol* is quite contrary to the Wishes of the Idolater ; as the one desires to confine the *Idol* to himself, the whole Business and Ambition of the other is to multiply Adorers. This Humour of an *Idol* is prettily described

2 in a Tale of *Chaucer*: He represents one of them sitting at a Table with three of her Votaries about her, who are all of them courting her Favour, and paying their Adorations : She smiled upon one, drank to another, and trod upon the other's Foot which was under the Table. Now which of these three, says the old Bard, do you think was the Favourite ? In troth, says he, not one of all the three

The Behaviour of this old *Idol* in *Chaucer*, puts me in mind of the Beautiful *Clarinda*, one of the greatest *Idols* among the Moderns. She is Worshipped once a Week by Candle-light in the midst of a large Congregation generally called an Assembly. Some of the gayest Youths in the Nation endeavour to plant themselves in her Eye, while she sits in form with multitudes of Tapers burning about her. To encourage the Zeal of her Idolaters, she bestows a Mark of her Favour upon every one of them before they go out of her Presence. She asks a Question of one, tells a Story to another, glances an Ogle upon a third, takes a Pinch of Snuff from the fourth, lets her Fan drop by accident to give the fifth an occasion of taking it up. In short, every one goes away satisfied with his Success, and encouraged to renew his Devotions on the same Canonical Hour that Day Sevennight.

An *Idol* may be Undeified by many accidental Causes. Marriage in particular is a kind of Counter-*Apotheosis*, or a Deification inverted. When a Man becomes familiar with his Goddess, she quickly sinks into a Woman.

Old Age is likewise a great Decayer of your *Idol*: The truth of it is, there is not a more unhappy Being than a Superannuated *Idol*, especially when she has contracted such Airs and Behaviour as are only Graceful when her Worshippers are about her.

Considering therefore that in these and many other Cases the *Woman* generally outlives the *Idol*, I must return to the Moral of this Paper, and desire my fair Readers to give a proper Direction to their Passion for being admired: In order to which, they must endeavour to make themselves the Objects of a reasonable and lasting Admiration. This is not to be hoped for from Beauty, or Dress, or Fashion, but from those inward Ornaments that are not to be defaced by Time or Sickness, and that appear most amiable to those who are most acquainted with them.

---

1. The Idol in the Apochrypha: See "Bel and the Dragon," a chapter in the apochryphal portion of the Book of Daniel.
2. Tale of Chaucer: *The Remedie of Love,* written around 1520 but attributed to Chaucer in the eighteenth century.

No. 79. 31 May 1711 (Steele)

This passage may have been the inspiration for Belinda's celebrated "Puffs, Powders, Patches, Bibles, Billet-doux." Whether it was or not, it embodies the same technique: implying by juxtaposition that religious practice is totally subordinated to vanity and folly and simultaneously using the religious perspective to condemn the vanity.

The SPECTATOR.

Oderunt peccare boni virtutis amore. Hor.

Thurſday, May 31. 1711.

Mr. Spectator,

' I Write this to acquaint you, that very many La-
' dies, as well as my ſelf, ſpend many Hours
' more than we uſed at the Glaſs, for want of the
' Female Library of which you promiſed us a Cata-
' logue. I hope, Sir, in the Choice of Authors for
' us, you will have a particular Regard to Books of
' Devotion. What they are, and how many,
' muſt be your chief Care; for upon the Propriety of
' ſuch Writings depends a great deal. I have known
' thoſe among us who think, if they every M⬤n-
' ing

' ing and Evening ſpend an Hour in their Cloſet,
' and read over ſo many Prayers in Six or Seven
' Books of Devotion, all equally nonſenſical, with
' a ſort of Warmth, (that might as well be raiſed
1 ' by a Glaſs of Wine, or a Drachm of Citron) they
' may all the reſt of their time go on in whatever
' their particular Faſſion leads them to. The Beau-
' teous *Philautia,* who is (in your Language) an
' *Idol,* is one of theſe Votaries; ſhe has a very pret-
2 ' ty furniſhed Cloſet, to which ſhe retires at her
' appointed Hours: This is her Dreſſing-room, as
' well as Chappel; ſhe has conſtantly before her a
' large Looking-glaſs, and upon the Table, accord-
' ing to a very Witty Author,

Together lye her Prayer-Book and Paint,
At once t'improve the Sinner and the Saint.

' It muſt be a good Scene, if one could be pre-
' ſent at it, to ſee this *Idol* by turns lift up her Eyes
' to Heav'n and ſteal Glances at her own Dear
' Perſon. It cannot but be a pleaſant Conflict be-
' tween Vanity and Humiliation.

---

1. Citron: citron-water, brandy flavoured with citron or lemon peel.
2. closet: den, private room.

No. 89. 12 June 1711 (Addison)

This discourse can serve generally as a comment on Belinda's coquetry and more specifically as a gloss on Clarissa's speech in canto 5, though unlike some of Addison's other attacks on coquetry it remains closer to social badinage than to fundamental criticism. Milton's Eve appears here as a model to follow rather than as a fellow-victim of vanity.

---

1. Demurrage: delay, hesitation, objection.
2. following Passage: Adam is recounting the creation of Eve from his own point of view, beginning with his dream.
3. turn: good action.

The SPECTATOR.

—————Petite hinc Juvenesque senesque
Finem animo certum, miserisque viatica canis.
Cras hoc fiet. Idem cras fiet. Quid? quasi magnum
Nempe diem donas; sed cum lux altera venit,
Jam cras hesternum consumpsimus; ecce aliud cras
Egerit hos annos, & semper paulum erit ultra.
Nam quamvis prope te, quamvis temone sub uno
Vertentem sese frustra sectabere canthum. Per.

Tuesday, June 12. 1711.

In order to banish an Evil out of the World, that does not only produce great Uneasiness to private Persons, but has also a very bad Influence on the Publick, I shall endeavour to show the Folly of *Demurrage*, from two or three Reflections, which I earnestly recommend to the Thoughts of my Fair Readers.

First of all I would have them seriously think on the Shortness of their Time. Life is not long enough for a Coquet to play all her Tricks in. A timorous Woman drops into her Grave before she has done deliberating. Were the Age of Man the same that it was before the Flood, a Lady might sacrifice half a Century to a Scruple, and be two or three Ages in demurring. Had she Nine Hundred Years good, she might hold out to the Conversion of the *Jews*, before she thought fit to be prevailed upon. But, alas! she ought to play her Part in haste, when she considers that she

is suddenly to quit the Stage, and make room for others.

In the second Place, I would desire my Female Readers to consider, that as the Term of Life is short, that of Beauty is much shorter. The finest Skin wrinkles in a few Years, and loses the Strength of its Colouring so soon, that we have scarce time to admire it. I might embellish this Subject with Roses and Rain-bows, and several other ingenious Conceits, which I may possibly reserve for another Opportunity.

There is a third Consideration, which I would likewise recommend to a Demurrer, and that is the great Danger of her falling in Love when she is about Threescore, if she cannot satisfie her Doubts before that time. There is a kind of latter Spring, that sometimes gets into the Blood of an old Woman, and turns her into a very odd sort of an Animal. I would therefore have the Demurrer consider what a strange Figure she will make, if she chances to get over all Difficulties, and comes to a final Resolution in that unseasonable part of her Life.

I would not however be understood, by any thing I have here said, to discourage that natural Modesty in the Sex, which renders a Retreat from the first Approaches of a Lover both fashionable and graceful: All that I intend is to advise them, when they are prompted by Reason and Inclination, to demurr

only out of Form, and so far as Decency requires. A Virtuous Woman should reject the first Offer of Marriage, as a good Man does that of a Bishoprick; but I would advise neither the one nor the other to persist in refusing what they secretly approve. I would, in this Particular, propose the Example of *Eve* to all her Daughters, as *Milton* has represented her in the following Passage, which I cannot forbear transcribing entire, tho' only the twelve last Lines are to my present Purpose.

The Rib he form'd and fashion'd with his hands:
Under his forming hands a Creature grew,
Manlike, but diff'rent Sex, so lovely fair,
That what seem'd fair in all the World, seem'd now
Mean, or in her summ'd up, in her contain'd
And in her looks, which from that time infus'd
Sweetness into my heart, unfelt before,
And into all things from her Air inspir'd
The spirit of love and amorous delight.
She disappear'd, and left me dark, I wak'd
To find her, or for ever to deplore
Her Loss, and other pleasures to abjure:
When out of hope, behold her, not far off,
Such as I saw her in my Dream, adorn'd
With what all Earth or Heaven could bestow
To make her amiable: On she came,
Led by her Heav'nly Maker, though unseen,
And guided by his Voice, nor uninform'd
Of nuptial Sanctity and marriage Rites:
Grace was in all her Steps, Heav'n in her Eye,
In every Gesture dignity and love.
I overjoy'd could not forbear aloud.
This turn hath made amends; thou hast fulfill'd
Thy words, Creator bounteous and benign,
Giver of all things fair, but fairest this
Of all thy gifts, nor enviest. I now see
Bone of my Bone, Flesh of my Flesh, my Self
She heard me thus, and tho' divinely brought,
Innocence and Virgin Modesty,
Her virtue and the conscience of her worth,
That would be woo'd, and not unsought be won,

Not obvious, not obtrusive, but retir'd,
The more desirable, or to say all,
Nature her self, though pure of sinful thought,
Wrought in her so, that seeing me, she fled;
I follow'd her, she what was Honour knew,
And with obsequious Majesty approv'd
My pleaded reason. To the Nuptial Bowr
I led her blushing like the Morn:——

No. 127. 26 July 1711 (Addison)

Again the extravagances of the hoop-petticoat appear as an object of gentle satire. The sexual innuendoes (the old folklore that jennets are impregnated by wind, the use of the hoop to keep men at a distance or, contrariwise, to conceal pregnancies) are rather daring for the *Spectator* but quite similar to the tone of *The Rape of the Lock*.

---

1. jennit: jennet, a kind of small Spanish horse.
2. Love in a Tub: The reference is to Sir George Etherege's comedy, *The Comical Revenge; or, Love in a Tub* (1664).
3. Blazing Star: a comet.
4. coming into the World: i.e., one function of the hoop-petticoat may be to conceal pregnancies.

The SPECTATOR.

—————*Quantum eſt in rebus Inane?* Perſ.

Thurſday, July 26. 1711.

Mr. SPECTATOR,

'YOU have diverted the Town almoſt a whole
' Month at the Expence of the Country, it
' is now high time that you ſhould give the Coun-
' try their Revenge. Since your withdrawing from
' this Place, the fair Sex are run into great Extra-
' vagancies. Their Petticoats, which began to heave
' and ſwell before you left us, are now blown up
' into a moſt enormous Concave, and riſe every
' Day more and more: In a Word, Sir, ſince our
' Women know themſelves to be out of the Eye
' of the SPECTATOR, they will be kept within
' no Compaſs. You praiſed them a little too ſoon,
' for the Modeſty of their Head-dreſſes; For as the
' Humour of a Sick Perſon is often driven
' out of one Limb into another, their Super-
' fluity of Ornaments, inſtead of being entirely
' Baniſhed, ſeems only fallen from their Heads
' upon their lower Parts. What they have loſt in
' Height they make up in Breadth, and contrary to
' all Rules of Architecture widen the Foundations
' at the ſame time that they ſhorten the Superſtru-
1 ' cture. Were they, like *Spaniſh* Jennits, to impreg-
' nate by the Wind, they could not have thought
' on a more proper invention. But as we do not
' yet hear any particular Uſe in this Petticoat, or
' that it contains any thing more than what was
' ſuppoſed to be in thoſe of a Scantier Make, we
' are wonderfully at a loſs about it.

' The Women give out, in Defence of theſe
' wide Bottoms, that they are Airy, and very pro-
' per for the Seaſon; but this I look upon to be
' only a Pretence, and a piece of Art, for it is well
' known we have not had a more moderate Sum-
' mer theſe many Years, ſo that it is certain the
' Heat they complain of cannot be in the Weather:
' Beſides, I would fain ask theſe tender-conſtitution'd
' Ladies, why they ſhould require more Cooling
' than their Mothers before them.
' I find ſeveral Speculative Perſons are of Opi-
' nion that our Sex has of late Years been very Sau-
' cy, and that the Hoop-Petticoat is made uſe of
' to keep us at a diſtance. It is moſt certain that
' a Woman's Honour cannot be better entrenched
' than after this manner, in Circle within Circle, a-
' midſt ſuch a Variety of Outworks and Lines of
' Circumvallation. A Female who is thus inveſt-
' ed in Whale-Bone is ſufficiently ſecured againſt
' the Approaches of an ill-bred Fellow, and might
' as well think of Sir *George Etheridge*'s way of
' making Love in a Tub, as in the midſt of ſo 2
' many Hoops.
' Among theſe various Conjectures, there are
' Men of Superſtitious Tempers, who look upon
' the Hoop-Petticoat as a kind of Prodigy. Some
' will have it that it portends the Downfall of the
' *French* King, and obſerve that the Farthingale
' appeared in *England* a little before the Ruin of
' the *Spaniſh* Monarchy. Others are of Opinion
' that it foretells Battel and Bloodſhed, and believe
' it of the ſame Prognoſtication as the Tail of a
' Blazing Star. For my part, I am apt to think 3
' it is a Sign that Multitudes are coming into the
' World, rather than going out of it. 4

No. 325. 13 March 1712 (Eustace Budgell)

The epigraph from Ovid's tale of Narcissus, the original narcissist (see p. 211) provides this essay's first variation on the theme of mirrors. The function of the mirror in Will Honeycomb's tale is quite different: it serves as a means of communication, enabling two individuals to break out of their shells and relate to each other. Eve at the fountainside shares both tendencies: enthralled at first by her own beauty, she is soon led to recognize the existence and value of another. Belinda, as suggested in the general introduction, is primarily a narcissist, an Eve who rejects all her potential Adams.

> What could, fond youth, this helpless passion move?
> What kindle in thee this unpity'd love?
> Thy own warm blush within the water glows,
> With thee the colour'd shadow comes and goes,
> Its empty being on thyself relies;
> Step thou aside, and the frail charmer dies.

The SPECTATOR.

— Quid fruſtra Simulacra fugacia captas ?
Quod petis, eſt nuſquam : quod amas averteris perdes.
Iſta repercuſſæ quam cernis imaginis umbra eſt,
Nil habet iſta ſui ; tecum venitque, manetque,
Tecum diſcedet ſi tu diſcedere poſſis. Ovid.

Thurſday, March 13. 1712.

WILL. HONEYCOMB diverted us laſt Night with an Account of a young Fellow's firſt diſcovering his Paſſion to his Miſtreſs. The young Lady was one, it ſeems, who had long before conceived a favourable Opinion of him, and was ſtill in Hopes that he would ſome time or other make his Advances. As he was one Day talking with her in Company of her two ſiſters, the Converſation happening to turn upon Love, each of the young Ladies was, by way of Railery, recommending a Wife to him ; when, to the no ſmall Surprize of her who languiſhed for him in ſecret, he told them with a more than ordinary Seriouſneſs, That his Heart had been long engaged to one whoſe Name he thought himſelf obliged in Honour to conceal ; but that he could ſhew her Picture in the Lid of his Snuff-Box. The young Lady, who found her ſelf the moſt ſenſibly touched by this Confeſſion, took the firſt Opportunity that offered of ſnatching his Box out of his Hand. He ſeemed deſirous of recovering it, but finding her reſolved to look into the Lid, begged her, that if ſhe ſhould happen to know the Perſon ſhe would not reveal her Name. Upon carrying it to the Window ſhe was very agreeably ſurprized to find there was nothing within the Lid but a little looking Glaſs ; in which, after ſhe had viewed her own Face, with more Pleaſure than ſhe had ever done before, ſhe returned the Box with a Smile, telling him, She could not but admire at his Choice.

WILL. fancying that his Story took, immediately fell into a Diſſertation on the Uſefulneſs of Looking-Glaſſes, and applying himſelf to me, asked if there were any Looking-Glaſſes in the Times of the Greeks and Romans ; for that he had often obſerved in the Tranſlations of Poems out of thoſe Languages, that People generally talked of ſeeing themſelves in Wells, Fountains, Lakes and Rivers : Nay, ſays he, I remember Mr. Dryden in his Ovid tells us of a ſwingeing Fellow called Polypheme, that made uſe of the Sea for his Looking-Glaſs, and could never dreſs himſelf to Advantage but in a Calm.

My Friend WILL. to ſhew us the whole Compaſs of his Learning upon this Subject, further informed us, that there were ſtill ſeveral Nations in the World ſo very barbarous as not to have any Looking-Glaſſes among them ; and that he had lately read a Voyage to the South-Sea, in which it is ſaid, that the Ladies of Chili always dreſs their Heads over a Baſon of Water.

I am the more particular in my Account of WILL's laſt Night's Lecture on theſe natural Mirrors, as it ſeems to bear ſome Relation to the following Letter, which I received the Day before.

SIR,

'I Have read your laſt Saturday's Obſervations, on the fourth Book of Milton with great Satisfaction, and am particularly pleaſed with the hidden Moral, which you have taken notice of in ſeveral Parts of the Poem. The Deſign of this Letter is to deſire your Thoughts, whether there may not alſo be ſome Moral couched under that Place in the ſame Book where the Poet lets us know, that the firſt Woman immediately after her Creation, ran to a Looking-glaſs, and became ſo enamoured of her own Face, that ſhe had never removed to view any of the other Works of Nature, had not ſhe been led off to a Man. If you think fit to ſet down the whole Paſſage from Milton, your Readers will be able to judge for themſelves, and the Quotation will not a little contribute to the filling up of your Paper.

Your Humble Servant,

R. T.

The

The laſt Conſideration urged by my Queriſt, is ſo ſtrong, that I cannot forbear cloſing with it. The Paſſage he alludes to is Part of *Eve's* Speech to *Adam*, and one of the moſt Beautiful Paſſages in the whole Poem.

That day I oft remember, when from ſleep
I firſt awak'd, and found my ſelf repos'd
Under a ſhade of flours, much wondering where
And what I was, whence thither brought, and how.
Not diſtant far from thence a murmuring ſound
Of waters iſſu'd from a Cave and ſpread
Into a liquid Plain, then ſtood unmov'd
Pure as th' expanſe of Heav'n; I thither went
With unexperienc'd thought, and laid me down
On the green bank, to look into the clear
Smooth Lake, that to me ſeem'd another Skie.
As I bent down to look, juſt oppoſite,
A ſhape within the watry gleam appear'd
Bending to look on me, I ſtarted back,
It ſtarted back, but pleas'd I ſoon return'd,
Pleas'd it return'd as ſoon with anſwering looks
Of ſympathy and love; there I had fixt
Mine eyes till now, and pin'd with vain deſire,
Had not a voice thus warn'd me, What thou ſeeſt,
What there thou ſeeſt fair Creature is thy ſelf,
With thee it came and goes: but follow me,
And I will bring thee where no ſhadow ſtays
¹ *Thy coming, and thy ſoft imbraces he*
Whoſe image thou art, him thou ſhalt enjoy
Inſeperably thine, to him ſhalt bear
Multitudes like thy ſelf, and thence be call'd
Mother of human Race: What could I doe,
But follow ſtreight, inviſibly thus led;
Till I eſpy'd thee, fair indeed and tall,
Under a Platan, yet methought leſs fair,
Leſs winning ſoft, leſs amiably mild,
Than that ſmooth watry image; back I turn'd,
Thou following cry'dſt aloud, Return fair Eve,
Whom fly'ſt thou; whom thou fly'ſt, of him thou art,
His fleſh, his bone; to give thee being I lent
Out of my ſide to thee, neareſt my heart
Subſtantial Life, to have thee by my ſide
Henceforth an individual ſolace dear;
Part of my Soul I ſeek thee, and thee claim
My other half: with that thy gentle hand
Seis'd mine, I yielded, and from that time ſee
How beauty is excell'd by manly grace
And wiſdom, which alone is truly fair.
So ſpake our general Mother, ——

———————

1. imbraces: direct object of "stays" in the preceding line; would be followed by a semicolon in modern punctuation.

No. 327. 15 March 1712 (Addison)

If Ariel's presence in Belinda's dream can be taken as parallel to Satan's presence in Eve's, we again have a situation in which Adam rescues Eve (if only temporarily), whereas Belinda has no rescuer. Like Eve's, Belinda's dream is full of "high Conceits engendring Pride."

---

1. foregoing Book: Book 4.
2. two Passages: The Song of Solomon, 2:10-13, 7:11-12.
3. Turtle: turtledove.
4. *Paradise Lost*, 9:442-43.
5. *Paradise Lost*, 4:809.

The SPECTATOR.

—*major rerum mihi nascitur ordo.*   Virg.

Saturday, March 15. 1712.

WE were told in the foregoing Book how the Evil Spirit practised upon *Eve* as she lay asleep, in order to inspire her with Thoughts of Vanity, Pride and Ambition. The Author, who shews a wonderful Art throughout his whole Poem, in preparing the Reader for the several Occurrences that arise in it, founds upon the above-mentioned Circumstance the first part of the Fifth Book. *Adam* upon his awaking finds *Eve* still asleep with an unusual Discomposure in her Looks. The Posture in which he regards her, is described with a Tenderness not to be expressed, as the Whisper with which he awakens her, is the softest that ever was conveyed to a Lover's Ear.

> *His wonder was to find unwaken'd Eve*
> *With Tresses discompos'd, and glowing cheek*
> *As through unquiet rest: he on his side*
> *Leaning half rais'd, with looks of cordial love*
> *Hung over her enamour'd, and beheld*
> *Beauty, which whether waking or asleep,*
> *Shot forth peculiar Graces; then with voice*
> *Mild, as when Zephyrus or Flora breathes,*
> *Her hand soft touching, whisper'd thus. Awake*
> *My fairest, my espous'd, my latest found,*
> *Heav'n's last best gift, my ever new delight,*
> *Awake, the morning shines, and the fresh field*
> *Calls us, we lose the prime, to mark how spring*
> *Our tended plants, how blows the Citron Grove,*
> *What drops the Myrrhe, and what the balmie Reed,*
> *How Nature paints her colours, how the Bee*
> *Sits on the bloom, extracting liquid sweet.*
> *Such Whispring wak'd her, but with startled Eye*
> *On Adam, whom embracing, thus she spake.*
> *O Sole in whom my thoughts find all repose,*
> *My Glory, my perfection, glad I see*
> *Thy face, and morn return'd* ——

I cannot but take notice that *Milton*, in his Conferences between *Adam* and *Eve*, had his Eye very frequently upon the Book of *Canticles*, in which there is a noble Spirit of Eastern Poetry, and very often not unlike what we meet with in *Homer*, who is generally placed near the Age of *Solomon*. I think there is no question but the Poet in the preceding Speech remembred those two Passages which are spoken on the like occasion, and fill'd with the same pleasing Images of Nature.

My beloved spake, and said unto me, Rise up, my love, my fair one, and come away; For lo, the winter is past, the rain is over and gone; the Flowers appear on the earth; the time of the singing of birds is come, and the Voice of the Turtle is heard in our Land. The Fig-tree putteth forth her green figs, and the Vines with the tender grape give a good smell. Arise, my love, my fair one, and come away.

Come, my beloved, let us go forth into the Field; let us get up early to the Vineyards; let us see if the Vine flourish, whether the tender Grape appear, and the Pomegranates bud forth.

His preferring the Garden of *Eden* to that

> —— *Where the Sapient King*
> *Held dalliance with his fair Egyptian Spouse,*

shews that the Poet had this delightful Scene in his mind.

Eve's Dream is full of those high Conceits engendering Pride, which we are told the Devil endeavoured to instil into her. Of this kind is that part of it where the fancies her self awaken'd by *Adam* in the following beautiful Lines.

> *Why sleep'st thou Eve? now is the pleasant time,*
> *The cool, the silent, save where silence yields*
> *To the night-warbling bird, that now awake*
> *Tunes sweetest his Love-labour'd song; now reigns*
> *Full orb'd the moon, and with more pleasant light*
> *Shadowy sets off the face of things; in vain*
> *If none regard; Heav'n wakes with all his eyes*
> *Whom to behold but thee, Natures desire,*
> *In whose sight all things joy, with ravishment*
> *Attracted by thy beauty still to gaze.*

An injudicious Poet would have made *Adam* talk through the whole Work, in such Sentiments as this. But Flattery and Falshood are not the Courtship of *Milton's Adam*, and cou'd not be heard by *Eve* in her State of Innocence, excepting only in a Dream produced on purpose to taint her Imagination. Other vain Sentiments of the same kind in this relation of her Dream, will be obvious to every Reader. Tho' the great Catastrophe of the Poem is finely presaged on this occasion, the Particulars of it are so artfully shadow'd, that they do not anticipate the Story which follows in the Ninth Book. I shall only add, that tho' the Vision it self is founded upon Truth, the Circumstances of it are full of that Wildness and Inconsistency which are natural to a Dream. *Adam*, conformable to his superior Character for Wisdom, instructs and comforts *Eve* upon this occasion.

> *So chear'd he his fair Spouse, and she was chear'd,*
> *But silently a gentle tear let fall*
> *From either eye, and wiped them with her hair;*

No. 377. 13 May 1712 (Addison)

This rather heavy-handed disquisition on the excesses of amorous metaphor may lie behind the battle in canto 5, in which one combatant died in metaphor and another in song. Addison's text combines with Pope's to emphasize the affectation and unreality of the way the beaux and belles view human relationships.

1. Oroondates: a character in Mlle de Scudery's famous and high-flown romance, *Artamène ou le Grand Cyrus.*
2. Basilisks: legendary reptiles whose breath or even look was fatal.
3. fond: foolish.
4. Ring: See note to *The Dispensary*, 6:245, p. 181.
5. Tail: the train of her skirt.

The SPECTATOR.

Quid quifque, vitæ nunquam homini fatis
Cantum eft in horas —————— Hor.

Tuefday, May 13. 1712.

LOVE was the Mother of Poetry, and ftill produces, among the moft ignorant and barbarous, a thoufand imaginary Diftreffes and Poetical Complaints. It makes a Footman talk like *Oroondates*, and converts a Brutal Ruftick into a gentle Swain. The moft ordinary Plebeian or Mechanick in Love, bleeds and pines away with a certain Elegance and Tenderness of Sentiments which this Paffion naturally infpires.

Thefe inward Languifhings of a Mind infected with this Softnefs, have given Birth to a Phrafe which is made ufe of by all the melting Tribe, from the higheft to the loweft, I mean that of *dying for Love*.

Romances, which owe their very Being to this Paffion, are full of thefe metaphorical Deaths. Heroes and Heroines, Knights, Squires and Damfels are all of them in a dying Condition. There is the fame kind of Mortality in our Modern Tragedies, where every one gafps, faints, bleeds and dies. Many of the Poets, to defcribe the Execution which is done by this Paffion, reprefent the fair Sex as *Bafilisks* that deftroy with their Eyes; but I think Mr. *Cowley* has with greater Juftnefs of Thought compared a beautiful Woman to a *Porcupine*, that fends an Arrow from every part.

I have often thought that there is no way fo effectual for the Cure of this general Infirmity, as a Man's reflecting upon the Motives that produce it. When the Paffion proceeds from the Senfe of any Virtue or Perfection in the Perfon beloved, I would by no means difcourage it; but if a Man confiders that all his heavy Complaints of Wounds and Deaths rife from fome little Affectations of Coquettry, which are improved into Charms by his own fond Imagination, the very laying before himfelf the Caufe of his Diftemper, may be fufficient to effect the Cure of it.

It is in this view that I have looked over the feveral Bundles of Letters which I have received from Dying People, and compofed out of them the following Bill

of Mortality, which I fhall lay before my Reader without any further Preface, as hoping that it may be ufeful to him in difcovering thofe feveral Places where there is moft Danger, and thofe fatal Arts which are made ufe of to deftroy the Heedlefs and Unwary.

Lyfander, flain at a Puppet-Show on the 3d of *September*.

Thyrfis, fhot from a Cafement in *Pickadilly*.

T. S. wounded by *Zelinda*'s Scarlet Stocking, as fhe was ftepping out of a Coach.

Will. Simple, fmitten at the Opera by the Glance of an Eye that was aimed at one who ftood by him.

Tho. Vainlove loft his Life at a Ball.

Tim. Tattle, killed by the tap of a Fan on his Left Shoulder by *Coquetilla*, as he was talking carelefsly with her in a Bow-window.

Sir *Simon Softly*, murder'd at the Play-houfe in *Drury lane* by a Frown.

Philander, mortally wounded by *Cleora*, as fhe was a 'jufting her Tucker.

Ralph Gapely, Efq; hit by a Random Shot at the Ri...

E. ... caught his Death upon the Water, *April* the 31ft.

W. W. killed by an unknown Hand, that was playing with the Glove off, upon the fide of the fide Box in *Drury-lane*.

Sir Criftopher Crazy, Bar. hurt by the brufh of a ... ne Petticoat.

..., fhot through the Sticks of a Fan at St. *James's* Church.

Damon, ftruck through the Heart by a Diamond Necklace.

Thomas Trufty, Francis Goofequill, William Meanwell, Edward Callow Efqrs; ftanding in a Row, fell all Four at the fame time by an Ogle of the Widow *Trapland*.

Tom Rattle chancing to tread upon a Lady's Tail, as he came out of the Play-Houfe, fhe turned full upon him, and laid him dead upon the Spot.

No. 403. 12 June 1712 (Addison)

The pseudoinspirational powers of coffee were a commonplace of political satire in Pope's day, and the Baron's schemes have the same origin (*The Rape of the Lock*, 3:117-18).

---

1. City: The financial and commercial section of London, as opposed to the fashionable Court.

The SPECTATOR.

Qui mores hominum multorum vidit——   Hor.

Thursday, June 12.   1712.

WHEN I consider this great City in its several Quarters and Divisions, I look upon it as an Aggregate of various Nations distinguished from each other by their respective Customs, Manners and Interests. The Courts of two Countries do not so much differ from one another, as the Court and City in their peculiar ways of Life and Conversation. In short, the Inhabitants of St. *James's*, notwithstanding they live under the same Laws, and speak the same Language, are a distinct People from those of *Cheapside*, who are likewise removed from those of the *Temple* on the one side, and those of *Smithfield* on the other, by several Climates and Degrees in their ways of Thinking and Converting together.

For this Reason, when any Publick Affair is upon the Anvil, I love to hear the Reflections that arise upon it in the several Districts and Parishes of *London* and *Westminster*, and to ramble up and down a whole Day together, in order to make my self acquainted with the Opinions of my Ingenious Countrymen. By this means I know the Faces of all the principal Politicians within the Bills of Mortality; and as every Coffee-house has some particular Statesman belonging to it, who is the Mouth of the Street where he lives, I always take care to place my self near him, in order to know his Judgment on the present Posture of Affairs. The last Progress that I made with this Intention, was about three Months ago, when we had a Current Report of the King of *France's* Death. As I foresaw this would produce a new Face of things in *Europe*, and many curious Speculations in our *British* Coffee-houses, I was very desirous to learn the Thoughts of our most eminent Politicians on that Occasion.

That I might begin as near the Fountain-head as possible, I first of all called in at St. *James's*, where I found the whole outward Room in a Buzz of Politics. The Speculations were but very indifferent towards the Door, but grew finer as you advanced to the upper end of the Room, and were so very much improved by a Knot of Theorists, who sat in the inner Room within the Steams of the Coffee Pot, that I there heard the whole *Spanish* Monar-

chy disposed of, and all the Line of *Bourbon* provided for in less than a Quarter of an Hour.

~~~

No. 515. 21 October 1712 (Steele)

The coquette's motivation and life-style have seldom been exposed and analyzed as explicitly as here. What distinguishes Gatty from Belinda is her self-awareness and perhaps a certain self-dramatization, whereas Belinda's artfulness is quite innocent and unreflective. Jenny, of course, speaks with the accents of Clarissa.

---

1. Coupee: a dance involving a bowing motion.

The SPECTATOR.

Pudet me & miseret qui harum mores cantabat mihi Monuisse frustra---- Ter.

Tuesday, October 21. 1712.

Mr. SPECTATOR,

'I Am obliged to you for printing the Account I lately sent you of a Coquet who disturbed a sober Congregation in the City of London. That Intelligence ended at her taking Coach, and bidding the Driver go where he knew. I could not leave her so, but dogged her, as hard as she drove, to Paul's Church-yard, where there was a Stop of Coaches attending Company coming out of the Cathedral. This gave me Opportunity to hold up a Crown to her Coachman, who gave me the Signal, and that he would hurry on, and make no Haste, as you know the Way is when they favour a Chase. By his many kind Blunders, driving against other Coaches, and slipping off some of his Tackle, I could keep up with him, and lodged my fine Lady in the Parish of St. James's. As I guessed when I first saw her at Church, her Business is to win Hearts and throw 'em away, regarding nothing but the Triumph. I have had the Happiness, by tracing her through all with whom I heard she was acquainted, to find one who was intimate with a Friend of mine, and to be introduced to her Notice. I have made so good use of my Time, as to procure from that Intimate of hers one of her Letters, which she writ to her when in the Country. This Epistle of her own may serve to alarm the World against her in ordinary Life, as mine, I hope, did those who shall behold her at Church. The Letter was written last Winter to the Lady who gave it me; and I doubt not but you will find it the Soul of an happy self-loving Dame, that takes all the Admiration she can meet with, and returns none of it in love to her Admirers.

Dear Jenny,

'' I Am glad to find you are likely to be disposed of in Marriage so much to your Approbation as you tell me. You say you are afraid only of me, for I shall laugh at your Spouse's Airs. I beg of you not to fear it, for I am too nice a Discerner to laugh at any, but whom most other People think fine Fellows; so that your Dear may bring you hither as soon as his Horses are in Case enough to appear in Town, and you be very safe against any Raillery you may apprehend from me; for I am surrounded with Coxcombs of my own making, who are all ridiculous in a manner: Your Good-man, I presume, can't exert himself. As Men who cannot raise their Fortunes, and are uneasy under the Incapacity of shining in Courts, rail at Ambition, so do awkard and insipid Women, who cannot warm the Hearts and charm the Eyes of Men, rail at Affectation: But she that has the Joy of seeing a Man's Heart leap into his Eyes at beholding her, is in no Pain for want of Esteem among a Crew of that Part of

(Price Two-pence.)

'' her own Sex who have no Spirit but that of Envy, and no Language but that of Malice. I do not in this, I hope, express my self insensible of the Merit of Leodacia, who lowers her Beauty to all but her Husband, and never spreads her Charms but to gladden him who has a Right in them: I say, I do Honour to those who can be Coquets, and are not such; but I despise all who would be so, and in Despair of arriving at it themselves, hate and villify all those who can. But, be that as it will, in Answer to your Desire of knowing my History: One of my chief present Pleasures is in Country Dances; and, in Obedience to me, as well as the Pleasure of coming up to me with a good Grace, shewing themselves in their Address to others in my Presence, and the like Opportunities, they are all Proficients that Way: And I had the Happiness of being the other Night where we made six Couple, and every Woman's Partner a profess'd Lover of mine. The wildest Imagination cannot form to it self, on any Occasion, higher Delight than I acknowledge my self to have been in all that Evening. I chose out of my Admirers a Set of Men who most love me, and gave them Partners of such of my own Sex who most envy'd me.

'' My Way is, when any Man who is my Admirer pretends to give himself Airs of Merit, as at this Time a certain Gentleman you know did, to mortify him by favouring in his Presence the most insignificant Creature I can find. At this Ball I was led into the Company by pretty Mr. Fanfly, who, you know, is the most obsequious well-shap'd well-bred Woman's Man in Town. I at first Entrance declared him my Partner if I danced at all; which put the whole Assembly into a Grin, as forming no Terrours from such a Rival. But we had not been long in the Room, before I over-heard the meritorious Gentleman above-mentioned say with an Oath, There is no Raillery in the thing, she certainly loves the Puppy. My Gentleman, when we were dancing, took an Occasion to be very soft in his Oglings upon a Lady he danced with, and whom he knew of all Women I love most to outshine. The Contest began who should plague the other most. I, who do not care a Farthing for him, had no hard Task to out-vex him. I made Fanfly, with a very little Encouragement, cut Capers Coupee, and then sink with all the Air and Tenderness imaginable. When he performed this, I observed the Gentleman you know of fall into the same Way, and imitate as well as he could the despised Fanfly. I cannot well give you, who are so grave a Country Lady, the Idea of the Joy we have when we see a stubborn Heart breaking, or a Man of Sense turning Fool for our Sakes; but this happened to our Friend, and

''   1

''   Jen

" I expect his Attendance whenever I go to
" Church, to Court, to the Play, or the Park.
" This is a Sacrifice due to us Women of Genius,
" who have the Eloquence of Beauty, an easy
" Mein. I mean by an easy Mein, one which can be
" on Occasion easily affected : For I must tell you,
" dear *Jenny*, I hold one Maxim, which is an un-
" common one, to wit, That our greatest Charms
" are owing to Affectation. 'Tis to That that our
" Arms can lodge so quietly just over our Hips,
" and the Fan can play without any Force or Mo-
" tion but just of the Writt. 'Tis to Affectation
" we owe the pensive Attention of *Deidamia* at a
" Tragedy, the scornful Approbation of *Dulciamu-*
" *ra* at a Comedy, and the lowly Aspect of *Lan-*
" *quicelsa* at a Sermon.

" To tell you the plain Truth, I know no Plea-
" sure but in being admired, and have yet never
" failed of attaining the Approbation of the Man
" whose Regard I had a Mind to. You see all the
" Men who make a Figure in the World (as wise
" a Look as they are pleased to put upon the Mat-
" ter) are moved by the same Vanity as I am.
" What is there in Ambition, but to make other
" People's Wills depend upon yours ? This in-
" deed is not to be aim'd at by one who has a
" a Genius no higher than to think of being a
" very good Housewife in a Country Gentleman's
" Family. The Care of Poultrey and Piggs are
" great Enemies to the Countenance : The va-
" cant Look of a fine Lady is not to be preserved,
" if she admits any thing to take up her Thoughts
" but her own dear Person. But I interrupt you
" too long from your Cares, and my self from my
" Conquests.

I am, Madam,
Your most humble Servant.

' Give me Leave, Mr. S. ECTATOR, to add her
' Friend's Answer to this Epistle, who is a very
' discreet ingenious Woman.

Dear Gatty,

" I Take your Raillery in very good part, and
" am obliged to you for the free Air with
" which you speak of your own Gayeties. But
" this is but a barren superficial Pleasure ; for in-
" deed, *Gatty*, we are made for Man, and in seri-
" ous Sadness I must tell you, whether you your
' self know it or no, all these Gallantries tend to
" no other End but to be a Wife and Mother as fast
" as you kan.

I am, Madam,
Your most obedient Servant.

The Guardian, no. 106. 13 July 1713.

Pope himself was possibly the author of this letter to the editor, which appeared while he was working on the second version of *The Rape of the Lock*. If he did write it, we can see him using in prose images like the moving toyshop of the heart that were soon to appear in the poem. Unlike this voyeur, poor Ariel never reappeared in Belinda's heart (3:142-44). Whoever wrote the prose, it is instructive to note how the images appear in the poem in a much more concentrated form.

The GUARDIAN.

Quod latet in tacitâ non Enarrabile fibrâ. Perf.

Monday, July 13. 1713.

AS I was making up my *Monday*'s Provision for the Publick, I received the following Letter, which being a better Entertainment than any I can furnish out my self, I shall set it before the Reader, and desire him to fall on without further Ceremony.

SIR,

1 ' YOUR two Kinsmen and Predecessors of Immortal Memory, were very famous for
' their Dreams and Visions, and contrary to all
' other Authors never pleased their Readers more
' than when they were Nodding. Now it is observed, that the *Second-sight* generally runs in the
' Blood; and, Sir, we are in hopes that you your-
' self, like the rest of your Family, may at length
' prove a Dreamer of Dreams, and a Seer of Visions.
' In the mean while I beg leave to make you a
' Present of a Dream, which may serve to lull your
' Readers till such time as you your self shall think
' fit to gratifie the Publick with any of your Noctur-
' nal Discoveries.

' You must understand, Sir, I had Yesterday
' been reading and ruminating upon that Passage
' where *Momus* is said to have found Fault with
' the Make of a Man, because he had not a Win-
' dow in his Breast. The Moral of this Story is

' very obvious, and means no more than that the
' Heart of Man is so full of Wiles and Artifices,
' Treachery and Deceit, that there is no guessing
' at what he is from his Speeches and outward Ap-
' pearance. I was immediately reflecting how
' happy each of the Sexes would be, if there was a
' Window in the Breast of every one that makes
' or receives Love. What Protestations and Per-
' juries would be saved on the one Side, what
' Hypocrisie and Dissimulation on the other ? I am
' my self very far gone in this Passion for *Aurelia*,
' a Woman of an unsearchable Heart. I would
' give the World to know the Secrets of it,
' and particularly whether I am really in her
' good Graces, or if not, who is the happy Per-
' son.

' I fell asleep in this agreeable Reverie, when on
' a sudden methought *Aurelia* lay by my Side. I
' was placed by her in the Posture of *Milton's Adam*,
' and *with Looks of Cordial Love hung over her ena-
' mour'd*. As I cast my Eye upon her Bosom, it
' appeared to be all of Chrystal, and so wonderfully
' transparent, that I saw every Thought in her
' Heart. The first Images I discovered in it were
' Fans, Silks, Ribbonds, Laces, and many other
' Gewgaws, which lay so thick together, that the
' whole Heart was nothing else but a Toy-shop.
' Thele

(Price Two Pence.)

---

1. Kinsmen: Mr. Tatler and Mr. Spectator.

Thefe all faded away and vanifhed, when immediately I difcerned a long Train of Coaches and fix, Equipages and Liveries that ran through the Heart one after another in a very great hurry for above half an Hour together. After this, looking very attentively, I obferved the whole fpace to be filled with a Hand of Cards, in which I could
2 fee diftinctly three Mattadors. There then followed a quick Succeffion of different Scenes. A Play-houfe, a Church, a Court, a Poppet-fhow, rofe up one after another, till at laft they all of them gave Place to a Pair of new Shoes, which kept footing in the Heart for a whole Hour. Thefe were driven off at laft by a Lap-dog, who was fucceeded by a *Guiney* Pig, a Squirril and a Monky. I my felf, to my no fmall Joy, brought up the Rear of thefe worthy Favourites. I was ravifhed at being fo happily pofted and in full Poffeffion of the Heart : But as I faw the little Figure of my felf Simpering, and mightily pleafed with its Situation, on a fudden the Heart methought gave a Sigh, in which, as I found afterwards, my little Reprefentative vanifhed ; for upon applying my Eye I found my Place taken up by an ill-bred, awkward Puppy with a Mony-bag under each Arm. This Gentleman, however, did not keep his Station long before he yeilded it up to a Wight as difagreeable as him-
3 felf, with a white Stick in his Hand. Thefe three laft Figures reprefented to me in a lively manner the Conflicts in *Aurelia's* Heart between Love, Avarice and Ambition. For we juftled one another out by Turns, and difputed the Poft for a great while. But at laft, to my unfpeakable Satisfaction, I faw my felf entirely fettled in it. I was fo tranfported with my Succefs, that I could not forbear hugging my dear Piece of Chryftal, when to my unfpeakable Mortification I awaked, and found my Miftrefs metamorphofed into a Pillow.

This is not the firft time I have been thus difappointed.

O Venerable NESTOR, if you have any Skill in Dreams, let me know whether I have the fame Place in the real Heart, that I had in the Vifionary one : To tell you truly, I am perplexed to Death between Hope and Fear. I was very Sanguine till 11 a-Clock this Morning, when I over-heard an unlucky old Woman telling her Neighbour that Dreams always went by Contraries. I did not indeed before, much like the Chryftal Heart, remembring that confounded Simile in *Valentinian*

of a Maid *as cold as Chryftal never to be Thaw'd.* Befides I verily believe if I had flept a little longer that awkward Whelp with his Mony Bags would certainly have made his fecond Entrance. If you can tell the fair one's Mind, it will be no fmall proof of your Art, for I dare fay it is more than fhe her felf can do. Every Sentence fhe fpeaks is a Riddle, all that I can be certain of is, that I am her and,

Your humble Servant,

Peter Puzzle.

---

2. Mattadors: The three highest cards in the game of Ombre. See *The Rape of the Lock*, 3:27ff.

3. white Stick: A white staff was the symbol of certain political offices, especially that of the lord high treasurer.

PART VII

Key

KEY

Contexts	Pope's Text
104	4:93
385-88	5:147-50
23:753-862	3:25-104
Aeneid	
1:1-10	1:1-4
11-16	1:7-10
17-18	1:11-12
34-43	Am'rous causes
4:1-2	4:1-2
75-90	2:35-46
636-52	5:5-6
637	5:2
1001, 1009	3:153-54
6:336-890	4:1-88
344-45	4:39-40
384	3:92
385-97	4:25-38
398-99	4:47-48
400-403	4:41-54
889-90	1:55-56
Paradise Lost	
1:1-33	Epic invocation
24	1:5
27-33	1:7-10
322-29	2:125-36
356-507	Cf. *Spectator* 73

CONTEXTS	POPE'S TEXT
421-31	1:69-70
435-36	5:98
624	1:109; 2:141
640-41	3:57-58, 71-72
646-47	2:32, 103
3:442-96	5:113-22
5:1-94	1:21-114
1-5	1:16
10	1:24
35-37	1:25-26
44-49	1:27-28, 35-36, 45-46
77-81	1:35-36
275-86	2:55-68
592	2:64
594-99	2:138
600-603	2:73
6:320-31	3:151-52; 5.44
344-53	3:152; 1:69-70
9:502	4:43
538-48	1:27-28, 35-36, 41, 45; 2:6
1059-63	hair and virtue
1084-90	4:147-60
1091-98	4:157, 176
1119	2:118
1122-25	4:81-86

PART II *The Mock-Epic Tradition*

Le Lutrin	
1:1-14	1:1-3
15-20	1:7-12
21-24	1:3-6
91-135	1:13-120
5:33-73	4:17-54
74-100	4:57-78
221-55	5:79-86

The Dispensary

1:1-6	1:7-12
7-14	3:1-4
9-10	3:21-22
26-30	1:49-50
32-33	1:144; 3:155; 5:76
74-87	1:19-20; 4:21-24
90-93	1:146-47
94-95	1:122
107	1:17
2:5-6	4:17
9-38	4:18-38
3:9-10	4:1-2
51-56	3:19-24
58	1:17
75	4:19
77-116	2:35-46; 4:57-78
117-20	3:1-4
255-56	4:105-106; 1:78
4:5-6	3:5-8
17-32	3:9-18
178-79	1:101-102
193-96	4:39-42
241-47	3:19-22
245, 248-49	4:17-18
250-69	5:123-32
5:212-19	5:37-42
226-31	5:45-52
236-38	3:85-86
244-45	3:79-80
6:242	4:90
245	1:44
260-61	1:75-76
265	4:108
266-67	1:78; 4:105-106
270-71	4:105-106

PART III   *Le Comte de Gabalis*

187	1:35-40
188	1:45-46
189	1:67-68
190-92	1:41-66
193-94	1:67-68
194	Pope's note to 1:145
195	1:67-68
197	Another version of Eve
200	2:116
201-2	1:42, 2:56

Part IV   *Miscellaneous*

The Bible

Genesis	Pope's note to 1:145
Psalm 91	1:71-78, 41-44, 5:146
Matthew	2:14; 1:37-38
Luke	1:33

The Lock of Berenice

1-118	5:129-30
1-9	5:137-38
8-9	5:150
50-56	3:169-78
61-62	4:171-72
66	5:135
72	5:142
77-78	5:147-48

The History of Rome	5:125-26

Metamorphoses

Echo and Narcissus	1:125-26, 139-44
The Pythagorean Philosophy	1:47-66, 99-102, 135-36, etc.
308-61	5:9-34

Satire 6

627-44	1:121-48
850-53	3:158

Orlando Furioso	5:113-22
74.2	5:117
77.6	5:119
79.4	5:117
80.5-6	5:114
83.5-8	5:115-16
86.3-4	5:115

Romeo and Juliet	English fairy tradition

The Flower and the Leaf

482-83	1:47-50
490-91	2:81-82
496-97	1:71-72, 77-78
502	1:67
508-13	1:67-68

PART VI *Periodical Essays*

Tatler

113	General ambience; petticoats
121	Husbands and lapdogs

Spectator

8	1:71-72
10	Women as readers, as objects of satire.
69	1:130
73	1:121-48; 2:11; 5:9-34; cf. *Paradise Lost* 1:356-446
79	1:137-38
89	5:9-34
127	2:117-22; 5:137-40
325	1:125-26, 139-44
327	1:20-114
377	5:59-64
403	3:117-18
515	5:9-34

Guardian

106	1:99-103; 3:142-44